Bibl
Investigations

Andrew Perry

*and they shall spring up as among the grass,
as willows by the watercourse*

WILLOW PUBLICATIONS
13 St. Georges terrace
East Boldon
Tyne and Wear
NE36 0LU. U.K.
andrew.perry@christadelphian-ejbi.org

ISBN 978-0-9563841-3-3

Printed by www.lulu.com and available from:

www.lulu.com/willowpublications

Fellowship Matters
Beginnings and Endings
Head-Coverings and Creation
Before He Was Born
Demons, Magic and Medicine
Demons and Politics
Job
Isaiah 40-48
Joel

Also available from Willow:

Christadelphian EJournal of Biblical Interpretation (ISSN 1755-9227)

www.christadelphian-ejbi.org

For
Simon of London

Table of Contents

PREFACE

This book brings together essays and articles that have been written and published over the years, mostly in magazines, but except one essay (Noah's Flood), we have excluded those that have been published in the *Christadelphian EJournal of Biblical Interpretation*. Furthermore, the articles collected here from various sources, (except for two essays—Old Earth Creationism and Noah's Flood), do not include any that have eventually become part of my other books. This collection also includes new essays that have not appeared in print elsewhere and would otherwise languish on my hard disk and die the death. The previously published essays have been updated in small ways.

The title of the book, *Biblical Investigations*, indicates the scope of the essays—they are the kind of writing that a hobbyist writer collects over the years on the hard disk of his or her computer. They are, in one way or another, about **trust in the Bible**. This is probably an issue when you are young but less so for the old. The criticism of the Bible is made from every angle but it is not difficult to combat and there are plenty of apologetics books that serve this purpose.

The first essay on "Bible Study" is an introductory chapter about the process of Bible study. The second essay on "Evaluating the King James Bible" is about the value of this version and it argues that it should be one of the versions we use for Bible study. The third essay, "The Unvarnished New Testament", is a review of a translation of the New Testament that has now fallen by the wayside. The value of the review lies in the discussion of the principles of translation and it extends the scope of the second essay.

The fourth essay on "The Dead Sea Scrolls and Bible Translation" is about the processes that lie behind translation—the evaluation of alternative textual traditions. It argues that we can have confidence in the traditional Hebrew text, even as we allow the possibility that it has errors due to transmission. The fifth essay on "Inspiration" is a philosophical essay on this doctrine. It argues for plenary verbal inspiration of the Bible based on the implications inherent in the view that God has said what has been said by the writers of the Bible. The sixth essay exegetes the main inspiration passages of the New Testament.

The seventh essay is a worked example of how it can be shown that NT books are an inspired part of Scripture. If we accept the testimony of Jesus and the apostles about the inspiration of the Hebrew Scriptures, the question remains to be answered as to why a person should accept the NT writings as inspired Scripture; this essay answers that question for Luke-Acts. Since the bestowal of the Spirit in NT times is an important part of this answer, the eighth essay is a further study of that bestowal.

Essays nine through thirteen are about difficulties in believing the OT. Individuals have difficulty believing the accounts of creation and the flood; they also find the genealogies of Genesis to be unrealistic; they are not sure if the history of Israel is true and accurate or full of ideological bias; essays nine through thirteen tackle these issues.

In essay fourteen we switch attention to the NT and consider whether we can have confidence in the gospel accounts of the life of Jesus. The collection is concluded in essay fifteen with a consideration of how we find God.

May 2011

Abbreviations
Unless otherwise noted below, we utilise *The SBL Handbook of Style* (ed. P. H. Alexander, *et. al.*; Peabody: Hendrickson, 1999) for abbreviations and the general purpose style of transliteration.

CHAPTER ONE
Bible Study

1. Introduction[1]

Bible study is not rocket science, but it is greatly neglected today because of the desires involved in living life. It requires time and a concordance, prayer and like-minded company. There are also those who leave a Christian faith-community, or who reject such a basis for life, because they cannot accept that the Bible is completely the Word of God. This chapter on "Bible Study" is about trusting in the Bible and going about studying the Bible.

2. Bible Study

Attitudes to the Bible vary from the fundamentalist to the scathing sceptic. What you do with the Bible will depend on your attitude. You may study the Bible purely out of academic interest; you may be looking for faith; or you may have faith and be seeking to grow that faith through Bible study; maybe you have faith but you also have doubts about the Bible.

The approach to the study of the Bible will vary. This chapter is not about exegetical methods that a student would follow; it's about Bible study within a faith-community and how someone with faith approaches doubt about the Bible. It should also be relevant to those investigating the faith expressed in the Bible.

Faith does not come through Bible study *per se* but it is engendered through Bible reading and prayer. A person can come to faith through repeated reading, but it is possible that they will encounter obstacles to faith in the form of doubts about the Bible. These may arise after they have committed to faith or they may prevent such commitment.

Doubts come from those who critique the Bible from one point of view or another; they come as baggage with a person in the form of their background knowledge—the prejudices and presuppositions that they have when looking for the first time into what the Bible has to say.

---

[1] This is an "opinion" piece written for this volume.

A person may read widely about the Bible along with their actual reading. When they do this they are really engaged in *studying* rather than just reading the Bible. If you consult other books about the Bible, use tools for analysing the Bible, then you are engaged in study.

The only recommendations for starting the studying of the Bible are to take the time, have patience, use a concordance and lexicon, and have a conservative "introduction" to the whole Bible. Many half-truths, mistakes, misrepresentations and false ideas will come along and be entertained, but the process of studying is a process of refinement. If you are putting the time in, knowledge will expand and a lot of the early mistakes in learning will fall by the wayside. It is no different than learning in any other subject.

3. Bible Scholarship
A lot of Bible scholarship is sterile because it doesn't increase your faith. Admittedly, this is a generalization, but it is as well to state it up-front. The reasons for this state of affairs are many and varied.

A fundamental problem with scholarship is the lack of reverence for the Bible as the Word of God; scholars are the impartial masters of the text and they slice and dice it according to their theories and suppositions. Very often, the witness and evidence that the Bible text offers is de-valued when compared with competing witness and evidence in archaeology and Near Eastern texts.

However, one of the productive aspects of the current state in Bible scholarship is its creative variety; there are liberal critics and conservative critics putting forward competing views of the Bible. Working out what is true and false in this panoply of scholarship is not easy but it does mean that scholarship has not overturned the Bible's claim to be the Word of God. For every critical reading of the text, there is a conservative one; and it is entirely reasonable to accept the conservative case. This is because the differences of view and opinion are generated by interpretation that is under-determined by the hard data.

Nevertheless, it is because all branches of scholarship do produce insightful work that obscurantism is not a sensible stance; a Bible student should be critically aware and selective in his/her reading of scholars and re-configure and transfer the good material to the intellectual place in the mind where faith can grow in knowledge.

The correct balance in Bible study is to prioritize the text and the concordance/lexicon. An 80/20 rule can be followed whereby 80% of the time given to study is with the text and concordance/lexicon. This is the best method of protection against making mistakes in interpretation, even though these are inevitable. The problem with this 80/20 rule though is the inability of the intellect to be imaginative and think both vertically and horizontally in response to the text—i.e. to have ideas to check out, follow-up, reject or accept. Human nature seems to have a pull towards conformity and consensus with other human beings and this pull makes individuals give up thinking for themselves and accept what they are being told by established religious authorities.

The other 20% of the time in Bible study is background reading of secondary material related to the Bible. There is a great deal of material "out there" and it is impossible to say here what is good and what should be avoided in terms of particular authors and books. The plain fact of the matter is that there is a lot of subtle writing that is on the wrong path; in Bible interpretation it is easy to be completely wrong. Mistakes in detail are inevitable and not so much of a worry, but the capacity for human beings to be completely wrong in spiritual matters is frightening.

However, there are some guidelines for study that can be followed:

- Have conservative "introductions" to the various areas of Biblical scholarship (one of each), but progress quickly beyond their scope. It is a common failing to never progress beyond the "introductory".

- Focus on monographs for reading secondary material on various topics, both critical and conservative. Thinking about why the critic is wrong can be as productive as accepting what a fellow-thinker says on some question.

- Avoid material that is doctrinal-theological and read the more factual studies relating to background history and archaeology. The best course of action is to work out doctrine and theology with the text using your own resources and thinking.

- Rely on collections of essays for synopses of ideas; this saves a lot of time in reading full-length monographs.

- Look out for and collect authors who are imaginative, creative and think "out of the box". There are many authors who are conventional and consensus writers; one person reproducing the consensus is enough for a bookshelf.

- Remember that commentaries are largely repeating one another and there is no need to have more than one *technical* commentary on each book of the Bible; technical commentaries give you the necessary information about the language (lexica, grammar).

- The most fruitful field of Bible Criticism is literary study and so (Anglo-American) material from the last thirty years or so will be more valuable than the somewhat sterile (German inspired) higher-critical material of older generations.

- The original languages of the Bible should be learnt, starting with Hebrew/Aramaic as it will yield more value than Greek. Work with a minimum of three Bible versions from your first language, all of which should be literal rather than dynamic in their approach.

In a lay community without a tradition of Bible scholarship, there are dangers in reading scholarly material. It isn't necessary to do so for the purposes of growing your faith. There are gains but the choice is a personal one. If you find yourself just repeating what scholars have said on a topic, then this is a sign that you have not been sufficiently critical and discriminating in evaluating their ideas. The good Bible student is the one who is coming up with their own ideas and using these along with the best that others have offered.

4. Bible Criticism

There are many standard introductory textbooks on Bible Criticism. The history of scholarship recognizes and labels various types of "criticism". The terminology here refers to assumptions that define a method of approach to the Bible text. Thus, scholars define methods such as "source criticism", "form criticism", "redaction criticism" and "literary criticism" of the Bible.

There is a sequence in the history of scholarship that goes from the "source criticism" of the 19c. to the "literary criticism" of the late 20c. The methods of "source criticism", "form criticism" and "redaction criticism" were inspired and dominated by German "higher-critical"

14

scholars. They represent older methods and are largely sterile in their results and concerns about the Bible.

The sterility of this kind of scholarship is due to the *hypothetical* nature of the methods. While there are known sources for the Synoptic Gospels, this is not the case for other parts of the Bible. When scholars hypothesize about sources in, say, the Pentateuch, the exercise is inherently unstable. Hence, there has not been consensus over such sources—their extent, authorship and dating.

Form Criticism offers hypotheses about the catalysts that gave rise to the various literary forms in the Bible. The method is more successful with books like the Psalms, where individual compositions can be aligned with situations in life to do with the monarchy or the temple. It is less valuable and more speculative with the History books or with the Prophets. The method engages in comparative analysis of Israelite and Near Eastern literature in order to support its hypotheses about the purpose of the forms of literature in the Bible. As a method it has some value and is the least sterile of the historico-critical approaches.

Redaction Criticism proposes various editorial layers in the books based on its characterization of differences in the text forming a pattern which is then assigned to an editor. As a method it is highly hypothetical and there is little agreement amongst scholars in the analysis of particular books. It also puts to one side the evidential witness of the prophetic superscriptions for authorship of the Prophets, as well as the evidential witness of Second Temple Judaism on the authorship of the Hebrew Scriptures. Along with Source Criticism it is of relatively little value for the Bible student.

Pre-critical interpretation of the Biblical text is more productive of insights into the complexity of meaning in the Bible. Scholars contrast historical-critical and pre-critical scholarship in ways unfavourable to pre-critical commentators. B. S. Childs observes that "modern research has brought a new philological, historical, and literary precision to bear which was unknown in the pre-critical period".[1] Nevertheless, he recognizes that "it belongs to the nature of the enterprise that one critical theory is replaced by another" and that scholarship has produced no "clear-cut

---

[1] B. S. Childs, *Introduction to the Old Testament as Scripture* (Philadelphia: Fortress Press, 1979), 324.

15

resolutions".[1] He notes that "critical exegesis now rests upon a very hypothetical and tentative basis of historical reconstructions".[2] Childs' observations are from 1979 and have not become dated. The thrust of Childs' remarks embeds a hope or an expectation that critical methodology should have produced results and an awareness that this has not happened. Childs' comment raises the question of what would be a "post-critical" methodology.

Pre-critical interpretation takes a holistic approach to the books of the Bible and the Bible itself; it takes a harmonic view based on a doctrine of the inspiration of Scripture. It is inter-textual in that it uses Scripture to interpret Scripture and it accepts the relevance of later Scripture in the interpretation of earlier Scripture. It accepts the philological results of modern scholarship but it is sceptical of the idea of multiple editors for books where there is a note of authorship, late post-exilic dates for OT books, pseudonymous authorship of NT books, and theories that de-value the historical basis of the narrative story.

Pre-critical interpreters cannot ignore critical scholarship; otherwise they will fall foul of obscurantism. Pre-critical commentary engages critical scholarship but it challenges its hypothetical results. It offers a different and conservative critical alternative. For Bible study that is either seeking faith, or part of faith, pre-critical studies on the Bible are more valuable than historico-critical research. In fact, the term "pre-critical" is a misnomer as conservative scholarship is "post-critical" in offering a critique of critical scholarship comparable to the Enlightenment critique of medieval church scholarship. However, it is important to distinguish such studies from the devotional and sentimental type of writing around today that will not give the sort of insights into the text that is sought by the Bible student.

5. The Bible and Doubt

The Bible contains plenty of material that pleads with Israel to have faith; a person with doubts should come to the Bible in an open and honest way with those doubts and investigate the arguments for and against the faith of the Bible. The exercise should investigate the claims made in the Bible as well as the presuppositions and ideas that comprise the doubts. For example, a common point of view today is a naturalism that denies the possibility of miracles. A person doubting miracles cannot fairly appraise

---

[1] Childs, *Introduction to the Old Testament as Scripture*, 323.
[2] Childs, *Introduction to the Old Testament as Scripture*, 324.

the evidential witness to miracles in the Bible without also being willing to question their naturalist presuppositions.

However, *quid pro quo*, the Bible is not a closed book; it comprises writings that came about in historical contexts. Accordingly, a person investigating the Bible will need to engage with the historical questions raised by the Bible; extra-Biblical texts and realia are relevant to Bible understanding. A person with doubt is not required to accept the authority of the Bible as a holy book; they are free to investigate and examine the facts of a matter and adopt a liberal critical view of the Bible. If the conservative and traditional reading is going to be believed, then this should be from conviction, after appraisal of the arguments on both sides of the debate.

6. Conclusion

A Bible based faith comes by *hearing* the Word of God (Rom 10:17). We are invited therefore to read the Bible, if we are to have any faith in its message. A natural objection to this invitation is to say that *we first want a reason to read the Bible*. An objector might say that he doesn't know if the Bible is worth reading, nor does he know whether it is true or false in its message. He might say: give me reasons why I should read and trust the Bible.

The following reasons are given to those investigating a Bible based faith by Bible believers,

- the evidence of archaeology and history
- the evidence of prophecy
- the witness of Jesus Christ
- the internal consistency and harmony of the Bible
- the evidence of miracles
- the testimony of the apostles and prophets
- the witness of Israel
- the evidence of design in creation

These kinds of evidence are put forward to show that the Bible is the Word of God. Each kind of evidence is a sample or excerpt of the Bible, and the agnostic is invited to read the Bible further on the basis of a confidence that he can gain from the excerpts; the essays in this book are examples of such excerpts.

What does the Word of God do for a person? If you read the Word, a character will be formed within you and brought to birth in baptism. God will bring about circumstances that enable the Word of God to create faith. In reading the Word of God a new person is formed. This is a new individual with new values, new attitudes, new dispositions and new beliefs—all directed towards God. This means that there is substantial content to the life of the new person (Heb 11:1), and it is supplied by the Bible.

CHAPTER TWO
Evaluating the King James

1. Introduction[1]

There are many Bible versions on the market. A person approaching the Bible to study it should be careful about the version they choose. A good guide is to use versions that are not paraphrases or freer translations of the original languages. Thus, we recommend versions like the KJV, NASB, and RSV. This essay is about the KJV but it discusses many points relating to the choice of a version.

Accuracy is relative to a standard of measurement; but standards of measurement in the business of translation are many, so that the accuracy of the KJV is a complicated matter. It is easier to approach the question by thinking of the advantages and disadvantages of using the KJV and its value for a native English speaker today.

As a source text is transformed into the 'same' text, but in another language, many aspects of meaning could be translated in the process.[2] We use many descriptive words for such aspects of meaning, such as 'sense', 'reference', 'nuance', 'metaphor', 'figure', 'overtone', 'emphasis', 'stress', 'literal', 'simile', 'poetic metre', 'paragraph/sentence/clause construction', 'punctuation', 'tense', 'mood', 'passive/active', 'aspect', *and so on*. Translating some or all of the complex levels of meaning in a text is not a simple process. We cannot make simplistic judgments like "The KJV is less accurate than the NET Bible", or "The KJV is not very accurate", or even "The KJV is the most accurate version". Rather, it is best to identify the good things in the translation, and to value and use it for those reasons. Likewise, it is as well to know its weaknesses.

---

[1] This essay appeared in *The Testimony* Special Issue June 2011.

[2] For a philosophical introduction to the business of translation, see W. Haas, "The Theory of Translation" in *The Theory of Meaning* edited by (ed., G.H.R. Parkinson; Oxford: Oxford University Press, 1968), 86-108. For a recent survey of translation theory, see D. Weissbort and A. Eysteinsson, *Translation: Theory and Practice - A Historical Reader* (Oxford, University Press, 2006). The professional journal is *The Bible Translator* (1950-) which publishes technical and practical articles.

2. Judging English Versions

The KJV is *sufficiently accurate* for use by a native English speaker, and many people use it as their main version, for devotional reading and for Bible study. The argument put forward here is that the KJV offers a number of benefits to the English-speaking Bible student who has no Greek, Hebrew or Aramaic, and that it should be used alongside two other versions (for example, the Revised Standard Version (RSV, 1952) and the New American Standard Bible (NASB, 1995), so that Bible study is conducted with a working set of three versions. The inclusion of the KJV will give the student several things that are not provided by other versions. (The 1611 KJV translators also included the Apocrypha in their work, but those extra-canonical works will not be considered in this essay.)

The topic of versions can generate heated opinion. There have been books advocating the KJV as not only the best version, but also as the only providentially governed version.[1] Similarly, there have been books rebutting this view and advocating the merits of a more modern version.[2] The idea that there is a single best English version is unsustainable, and for several reasons:

- There are various levels of meaning in a given stretch of language, and different versions may be better at capturing some aspects of meaning rather than others;

- The English language is always changing, and it differs for individuals, social groups, regions and countries;

- Scholarship changes its views on matters of comparative philology, so that its understanding of the original Hebrew, Aramaic and Greek changes.

Thus, while it may be satisfying to claim that you use the best English version (whatever this is), it is a philosophical nonsense.

---

[1] E. F. Hills, *The King James Version Defended* (Des Moines, The Christian Research Press, fourth edition, 1984).

[2] J. R. White, *The King James Only Controversy* (Minneapolis, Bethany House Publishers, 1995).

3. Aspects of Accuracy

This essay does not set out to argue that the KJV is the best version or the most accurate; and the same approach would be adopted if the subject of the essay was a modern version like the NIV or the ESV. It will be enough to show that the KJV is *sufficiently accurate* for study, has a lot to offer the Bible student, and is of value for devotional reading.

Given that there are many different aspects to meaning in language, measuring accuracy is difficult and not always objective. Thus, for example, it may be possible to count the number of conjunctions in the Masoretic Text and determine how many have been rendered in the KJV. But how do you measure more subjective aspects of meaning such as the rhythm or cadence of poetry? It is possible to comment here on only a few aspects of accuracy in translation: the base text used for the translation; the use of italics and capital letters; the presence of marginal alternatives; the treatment of tense; lexical considerations; the question of dynamic equivalence; the issue of semantic fields; the approach to metaphor and idiom; the treatment of allusions, echoes and quotations; the presentation of the printed text; style and the use of archaic and modern language. Each of these will be discussed in turn.

4. The Greek Text

The choice of the underlying Greek of the KJV is often criticised. It is a mixture of the printed editions of Stephanus (1550 and 1551 editions) and of Beza (1589 and 1598 editions). The Greek manuscripts used for these editions are not fully enumerated; but they include manuscripts such as the Codex Bezae (dating from the fifth to the sixth century), and the Codex Claromontanus (c. sixth century). One of the reasons why they cannot be enumerated is that Beza used Stephanus, while Stephanus used the Complutensian Polyglot translation of 1514, which did not enumerate the underlying Greek manuscripts that it used from the apostolic library in Rome. Stephanus also used the edition of Erasmus which was based on perhaps half a dozen tenth to fourteenth century manuscripts from the library in Basel. Hence, the textual scholar B. M. Metzger says about the KJV that "its textual basis is essentially a handful of late and haphazardly collected miniscule manuscripts, and in a dozen passages its reading is supported by no known Greek witness".[1] The spin that Metzger is here placing on the KJV is somewhat negative, and in order to balance it up we

---

[1] B. M. Metzger, *The Text of the New Testament* (Oxford, Clarendon Press, second edition, 1968), 106.

21

need to consider the relative value of the textual basis of the King James version.

The KJV was not a new translation from the Greek and Hebrew/Aramaic, but rather a version *that had regard* to the Greek and Hebrew/Aramaic and the best English translations of the day, such as the Bishops' Bible. One estimate is that 39% of the KJV was translated direct from the Greek and Hebrew/Aramaic. The Greek manuscripts underlying the texts edited by Erasmus, Stephanus and Beza were predominantly Byzantine; but it is important to note that those editions were not simply a reproduction of the Byzantine text, or what is often termed the Majority Text. This is because, for example, the Codex Bezae and the Codex Claromontanus are not Byzantine texts. Thus, it can be said that the KJV New Testament is based on eclectic texts,[1] but that the number of the underlying texts is small and *mostly* Byzantine.

With regard to the question of the *accuracy* of its New Testament Greek text, the value of the KJV lies in its being a translation of a predominantly Byzantine text; modern versions are invariably translations based around the critically constructed eclectic text published by the United Bible Societies, or possibly that of Nestle-Aland, with any additional changes preferred by the translators. For the Bible student, having a translation of a Byzantine-like text is a valuable resource, as it will alert him or her to the need to investigate the underlying Greek where a modern version is substantially different from the KJV. This use of a Byzantine-like text is also advisable because there are textual scholars today who argue that the Majority Text is more true to the original than the modern eclectic text.[2] If they are right, this would make the Greek text underlying the KJV more accurate than modern versions; but the matter is beyond the scope of this essay.

5. The Hebrew Text
The Hebrew text underlying the KJV Old Testament is a Ben Asher text in the Ben Hayyim edition of 1524-1525.[3] This edition was based on late medieval manuscripts and it remained the standard edition of the Hebrew

---

[1] The *Concise Oxford Dictionary* defines 'eclectic' as "deriving ideas or style from a broad and diverse range of sources".
[2] Z. C. Hodges and A. L. Farstad, *The Greek New Testament According to the Majority Text* (Nashville: Thomas Nelson, second edition, 1985).
[3] E. Würthwein, *The Text of the Old Testament* (Oxford, Basil Blackwell, 1957).

Bible until the twentieth century. In terms of accuracy, it has been superseded by the use of the tenth-century Ben Asher Leningrad Codex in *Biblia Hebraica Stuttgartensia* (third edition onwards). While the consonantal texts of Ben Hayyim and of the *Biblia Hebraica Stuttgartensia* are substantially the same, there are changes in the pointing, in the marginal notes, and in the critical apparatus. Modern translations are based on the *Biblia Hebraica Stuttgartensia*, and take into account the Dead Sea Scrolls (DSS), the Septuagint (LXX), and the Ancient Versions in determining the original Hebrew.[1] The KJV translators followed the same policy, but obviously did not have the DSS to take into account. Thus, we can say that the Hebrew text used by modern versions is *better* than that used by the KJV translators; but because it is substantially the same, the differences have little practical effect for the native English speaker who has no Hebrew or Aramaic.

6. Italics and Capitals

In order to provide a smoother text and to compensate for 'missing' words in the source language, the KJV translators used the device of adding words in italics. This is a valuable feature for the native English speaker, since it helps them understand where the translator is more explicitly doing the work of an interpreter.[2] The absence of this device in modern versions is regrettable; and it makes the KJV more accurate in this respect. Another useful feature of the KJV is the rendering of the Divine name YHWH with the capitalised "LORD". The names and titles used for God in the Bible are many and varied, and distinguishing among them in this way serves to add to the accuracy of the KJV.

7. Marginal Alternatives

Consulting any lexicon will reveal that Greek and Hebrew/Aramaic words have a range of meaning, and the lexicon will cite several verses that illustrate the various uses of a word. While translators are usually certain of their translation, this is not always the case; and the KJV translators

---

[1] A new critical edition of the Hebrew text is being produced - *Biblia Hebraica Quinta* - which is continuing the tradition of reproducing the Leningrad Codex.
[2] This guideline is still good advice, since with study Bibles the consensus scholarship they include can often be a source of error. The original printed editions did not use the device of italics; these were used in later editions.

acknowledged this by placing alternative translations of words in the margin.[1]

In doing this they were being more accurate in how they represented their state of knowledge about the Greek and Hebrew/Aramaic. The absence of marginal alternatives in modern versions does not mean that their translators are now certain about everything; rather, they have made the editorial decision not to include alternatives in the margin of the Bible. For a native English Bible student without Greek or Hebrew/Aramaic, it is obviously valuable to have marginal alternatives, since this indicates those places where the translators were uncertain. The student can legitimately choose to go with the marginal alternative if their own Bible study suggests reasons why it should be chosen.

8. Tense

Hebrew has two grammatical forms that do a lot of the work of carrying tense, namely, the Perfect and the Imperfect.[2] English has more complicated structures for making a distinction between the Simple Past, the Perfect and the Pluperfect for the Past tense.[3] The difference between the relative simplicity of Hebrew and the complexity of English means that translators have to make interpretative choices about how to represent the Perfect in Hebrew: should they choose the Simple Past, the Perfect, or the Pluperfect? The use of three versions in Bible study (as suggested earlier) serves to alert the reader to the choices that the translators are making at this level. The KJV is a useful version to have in this regard, because it tends to be less flexible in translating the Perfect in Hebrew as something other than a past form in English. This does not mean that the KJV is necessarily right; but it signals the presence of the Perfect form in Hebrew more readily than other versions.[4] Bible students

---

[1] It was a specific guideline of King James that the translation should have no marginal notes other than strictly linguistic ones so as to avoid doctrinal troubles.

[1] C. H. J. van der Merwe, J. A. Naudé and J. H. Kroeze, *A Biblical Hebrew Reference Grammar* (Sheffield, Academic Press, 2002), 141-2.

[3] The grammatical forms used vary and it possible to further distinguish progressive forms of the past tenses. See: M. Swan, *Practical English Usage* (Cambridge, University Press, 2005), 421-5 and 455-60.

[4] The New American Standard Bible (1995) has this same characteristic, and is also useful in this regard. From the point of view of this writer, in fact, the NASB is the best version for representing Hebrew tenses.

will form their own judgment as to how accurate the KJV is in this respect.

9. Lexical Considerations

Hebrew is a simpler language than English in terms of the number of conjunctions, prepositions, relative pronouns and articles. Thus, for example, Bible translators have to make a choice from an array of English conjunctions about which one to use for the corresponding Hebrew. Moreover, since Hebrew frequently uses conjunctions, translators have to consider whether to translate them in all instances. The KJV translates Hebrew conjunctions more often than modern versions, and this contributes to a Hebraic style for its Old Testament prose.

Representing the words of the source language in the target language is a desirable goal; and the KJV is more likely than modern versions to represent the smaller words like conjunctions, articles and prepositions. This is valuable for a Bible student, as it helps them to appreciate how modern translations are smoothing the flow of the text. This is particularly important for the Greek, where a sophisticated theologian like Paul can be making very precise points using a range of prepositions. In this respect the KJV scores points over a version like the New International Version.[1]

One area in which the KJV is lexically weak is in its understanding of difficult Hebrew words. Since the days of King James, comparative philology has progressed, and there is now far greater knowledge of cognate languages. Moreover, the Dead Sea Scrolls have increased our knowledge of Hebrew. It is more likely that a modern version is correct when there is a difficult word in the Hebrew. Here, it is worth following the guideline of using more than one modern version from different translation committees and eras. This is because there are fashions in scholarship, and opinions change on whether or not this or that cognate word illuminates a difficulty in Hebrew. For instance, using the RSV (1952) and the NASB (1995) together helps the native English speaker to locate where the difficult Hebrew words are and to see how two different translation committees have used comparative philology to render the text. So, for example, the New English Bible was particularly influenced by the Dead Sea Scrolls and by North-West Semitic philology. The

---

[1] See: R. Martin, *Accuracy of Translation and the New International Version* (Edinburgh: Banner of Truth, 1989).

Revised English Bible (the 1989 successor to the NEB) has, however, made 'corrections' in this regard.

In respect of the Greek, the KJV is recognised as having made mistakes arising from the use of grammar and lexicography of Classical rather than Koine Greek. Since the seventeenth century a large number of papyri have been discovered and analysed that contribute to our understanding of Koine Greek. In this regard the KJV is less accurate than modern versions; but the Bible student can make use of lexicons to spot errors and make corrections to the King James translation where appropriate. Lexical weakness in the KJV (Hebrew or Greek) should certainly not lead Bible students to dispense with the KJV, since the number of words involved is small, and the lexicons will still be needed to check on any modern versions used. The Hebrew teaching grammars make it clear that a student needs only some 750 words to be able to read about 80% of the Hebrew Bible, and this relatively small vocabulary was as well understood in the days of King James as it is today.

10. Dynamic Equivalence

There are two philosophies of translation: *dynamic equivalence* and *formal equivalence*. Where a translator gives priority to the source language and seeks to render its words and syntactic constructions in the target language, they follow a literal approach to translation. Where a translator gives priority to the target language and seeks to convey the meaning of a source text in natural syntactic constructions of the target language, they are following the philosophy of dynamic equivalence. The KJV is a literal translation in this sense: it more closely follows the syntax of the Greek and Hebrew and, in its rendering of the Old Testament, this contributes to its 'Hebraic' style. While both philosophies have their validity, for the Bible student, the KJV is useful and fairly accurate in conveying in English something of the syntactic constructions of the Hebrew and Greek.

11. Semantic Fields

One of the deliberate policies of the King James translators was not to require uniformity of phrasing or the use of the same English words for correspondingly identical Greek, Hebrew or Aramaic. Thus, in translating the Synoptic Gospels, where the Greek was identical for a given saying or narrative detail in Matthew, Mark or Luke, the KJV translators did not use identical English. In this policy, they were favouring the target language and were confident in using synonyms; the principle also embodies the recognition that the words of a source language have semantic fields and

26

that such fields are not necessarily represented in the target language by another single word, but sometimes by several words. The KJV is therefore not a 'same-word-for-the-same-word' (literal) translation, and this can be regarded as contributing to its accuracy.[1]

12. Metaphor and Idiom
A standard choice that translators make is whether to favour the source language or the target language in translating metaphor and idiom. This is because the metaphor or idiom in a source language may have no counterpart in the target language. The KJV translators rendered some metaphors and idioms literally; but others they converted to plain language. It is difficult to say whether this makes the translation more or less accurate, though sometimes the idiom or metaphor is given in the margin alongside a plain rendering in the main text.

13. Allusions, Echoes and Quotations
The Bible has a dense intertextual weave and this is recognised by Bible students.[2] The quality of a version can be assessed on how much of this intertextuality the translators embed in the translation (either in the text or by means of marginal cross-references). Critically, this aspect of their work does not depend so much on expertise in ancient languages, but rather it is a function of the translators' knowledge of the Bible which they have gathered as Bible students. The KJV is a good version in this regard, and it is advisable for Bible students themselves to use only one main version for reading and study, since this will help them to pick up gradually on the intertextuality of the Bible. A literal version like the KJV or the NASB is better for this purpose.

14. Presentation
The KJV is rightly praised for its poetic phrasing in the Old Testament, albeit as a literary work of Shakespeare's day. Elements of poetry such as rhythm and cadence are aspects of meaning to which a translator must pay attention. In this regard, the KJV can be regarded as a work of high quality. It is not possible, however, to draw any comparison with modern

---

[1] In fairness, however, a case could be made for the use of the same English for the parallel Greek of the Synoptic Gospels.
[2] The 'intertextuality' of the Bible refers to the multiple (and sometimes very subtle) ways in which parts of the Bible text can only be properly understood by reference to other parts, owing to the presence and use of quotations, allusions or echoes.

translations, simply because the literary quality of the KJV belongs to its period.[1]

Nevertheless, the KJV did not lay poetry out in verse form in the printed edition, and it chose to retain the verse and chapter divisions of the Bishops' Bible. This constraint introduced inaccuracy into the translation both for poetry and prose because the larger divisions in the text (such as the stanza, paragraph or discourse) are not represented in a natural way.[2] Nevertheless, readers soon become aware of artificial verse and chapter divisions and compensate for this inaccuracy.

15. Style

Under this category of assessment we should include notions such as the balance of language, elegance, and tone. We should also consider the reading qualities of the translation, which was a particular concern of the King James translators. While Hebrew/Aramaic and Greek have their own reading qualities for a native English speaker, the writings of the Bible would have originally been *heard* by most people rather than *read*. Thus, while it is the mark of a good translation if it is 'good on the ear', the style and tone of the KJV is probably too literary and too elevated compared with the common language of the market-place and the ordinary letters that we have in the Bible.

16. Archaic and Modern Language

Finally, we should consider the question of 'out-of-date' language. From a modern point of view, it is certainly true that the KJV uses archaic language. Some of its English words are obscure; other words have changed their meaning since the days of King James; the phrasing of the KJV is old and not current.[3] Nevertheless, the archaic phrasing of the KJV is closely modelled on the Hebrew; and the same can be said about the Greek, in which the extended punctuation of the KJV reflects the punctuation of the miniscules. A reader without Greek and Hebrew/Aramaic therefore gets at least some access to this aspect of the original languages with the KJV.

---

[1] L. Long, *Translating the Bible* (Aldershot, Ashgate, 2001), 188.
[2] The KJV did use a symbol (¶) for marking paragraphs in the Old Testament, but not for the whole of the New Testament (it is speculated that the printer ran out of type).
[3] For a full discussion of the archaic nature of the KJV, see: A. C. Partridge, *English Biblical Translation* (London, André Deutsch, 1973), chapter 7.

28

Whether a person wants this in their study is a personal choice. A native English-speaking Bible student could decide to put the KJV to one side for reasons of archaism; but the difficulties of reading involved are no greater than those for the learning of Shakespeare, which is regularly taught in schools. There are advantages in learning the style of the KJV, even though familiarity will require time and effort. If a more modern version of the King James is needed, the New King James Version (NKJV) and the Revised Authorised Version (RAV) are available. Modern versions come and go with the changing face of English; to have an enduring version of the Bible in English is of some value for the student.

17. Conclusion

This essay has argued that the KJV is a valuable version for the native English-speaking Bible student. It is sufficiently accurate; it translates mainly from the Byzantine (Majority) text and a standard Hebrew consonantal text; and it has useful features such as its italics and marginal notes. The KJV is obviously not a version for use with speakers and readers for whom English is a second language.[1] Within the English-speaking world, it is not the best version for preaching because its language is not current and it requires a fairly sophisticated level of English. Of course, the KJV is still widely used in churches, and so it is sometimes the best version to use with those from other churches. These limitations in the practical use of the KJV do not arise from it being inaccurate or less accurate as a translation, but rather because the English is old and not of a suitable grade[2] for preaching. Even after all this time, it remains a useful version for study and should be considered for the default version in a set of three such as the KJV, NASB and RSV.

---

[1] For an overview of the typical difficulties that speakers of other languages have with English see M. Swan and B. Smith, *Learner English* (2nd ed.; Cambridge: Cambridge University Press, 2001).
[2] The notion of 'grading' here is simply about using language appropriate to the audience.

CHAPTER THREE
The Unvarnished New Testament

1. Introduction[1]

"The Unvarnished New Testament" is a new translation by A. Gaus.[2] The purpose behind this translation, as stated in the publisher's blurb on the back cover, is to present the NT, "as it would have appeared to someone reading the original, unvarnished Greek—as though 2,000 years of Christian history had not occurred". The claim is made that most translations of the NT are made by committees who interpret the original text through theological doctrines and dogmas which arose centuries after the books were written. Hence, it is argued that there is a need for a translation to present the NT simply as it appears in the original Greek. Such a premise is entirely reasonable, and likely to find a sympathetic audience amongst Christadelphians.

2. Grading the English

Getting rid of theological jargon is not a sufficient justification for a new translation, even if we were to judge that the translator had succeeded in his enterprise. This is because the NT is not just made up of theological buzz-words set in theological passages—it is also made up of ordinary writing of various kinds: historical biography (Synoptics), historical reporting (Acts), the letters, and an apocalypse.

We cannot just evaluate this translation with the measure: does the translator succeed in getting rid of 2000 years of Christian history? We have to consider: is the translator faithful to the ordinary original Greek? On this count, the publisher's blurb further claims that the translation is "fresh", "simple" and "direct", "portraying an ageless beauty which no earlier translation has captured". Such claims may appear to be somewhat subjective; however, 'simplicity' and 'directness' can be measured. The translation would be 'simple' if Gaus has used a restricted vocabulary, keeping as close as possible to Basic English. As far as I can tell, he has done this. The translation would be 'direct' if a statistical sample of

---

[1] This review essay was published in *The Testimony* (date unknown).
[2] A. Gaus *The Unvarnished New Testament* (London: Phanes Press, 1991).

readers experienced few misunderstandings and few re-readings of sentences in order to get their sense. We cannot carry out this test, but it seems direct only in the non-theological passages of the New Testament. I still found myself having to read and re-read the theological passages of Paul in order to understand his rather complex thought. As for the claim of 'freshness', reading a new translation can be a refreshing experience, and this example is no exception, and for this reason it is a useful addition to a student library.

3. Dynamic Equivalence
The translation is a "dynamic" one rather than a "literal" one. The two types of translation are summed up in these words:

> Literal equivalence in translation favours the source language, preserving its linguistic structure, and demands that the receptor language change and grow to accommodate a new range of usage, figures and metaphors...Dynamic equivalence favours the receptor language, and demands that the pattern of usage o terms in the source language should be changed, in order to bring it into line with the pre-existing pattern of usage in the receptor language.[1]

Gaus' translation may want to represent the simplicity and directness of the original Greek, but he chooses to do so by ensuring the English is simple and direct—he does not represent the simplicity and directness that is actually in the Greek. Simplicity and directness in one language is not necessarily simple and direct if it is literally represented in another language, and so Gaus has had to be dynamic in his approach to the Greek. The merits and demerits of both approaches are discussed at length by N. Mullen from which the above quotation is taken.

Meaning is multi-faceted or multi-levelled, and it is impossible for any one translation to capture all the levels of meaning that exist in an original. For example, the 'force' that a text or passage has may be lost in some literal translations, but carried across in a dynamic translation. Or again, the workman-like character of a text may not come across in a literal translation. On the other hand, dynamic translations are likely to drop pronouns, prepositions, conjunctions, change the sentence structure, and

---

[1] N. Mullen "Beyond Babel" in *Which Translation?* (ed. T. Benson; Norwich: The Testimony, 2000), 27-36 (30).

31

be freer with noun-phrases and predicates. In following a dynamic approach, a translation may capture aspects of meaning like: readability, a reporting 'style', 'intimacy' in communication, *and so on*, but it will do this by making the receptor language the controlling medium. We do not learn what it was for a letter to be intimate in the original language, but we do experience the intimacy of the letter in the English.

The translation is presented as an ordinary book, without columns, verses, marginal references, and with hardly any footnotes. It is presented in paragraphs, and we are invited to read the book as we would read other books—normally; this is a valuable approach.

4. Translating the Original Languages

We are not told what text of the NT is being used, so we can only assume that it is using the standard 3rd edition of the United Bible Societies Greek text, or possibly the more recent 4th edition, depending on when the translation was undertaken. The translation doesn't signal when particular variations in the text are followed, although it does note that there is a shorter and a longer ending to the Gospel of Mark.

Furthermore, the translation doesn't justify its translational choices in any detail. There is a short glossary of 'technical' words and phrases appended to the translation, in which the author justifies his translational choices for words like 'baptism', 'gospel' or 'parable'. Most of the forty three examples are from the Gospels, and this indicates, I think, the translator's bias: his anti-theological treatment has a strong case in the Gospels. However, the lack of any justification for the translational choices he makes hinders any assessment. All we really have from the author is the end-result of his thinking.

The only other introductory material in the book is a short overview of the dating and authorship of the various books, in which a fairly conventional position is presented—the sort of consensus among Anglo-Saxon Biblical Scholarship that one can find in under-graduate "Introductions" to the New Testament. These short overviews are of relatively little value.

As a way of appreciating these issues, we will take a couple of examples from Gaus' treatment of Mark. The Synoptics lend themselves to a dynamic approach in translation, whereas the epistles impose more constraints on the translator.

In Mark, Gaus has avoided using certain words that have come to have a more technical theological meaning, words like 'spirit' and 'baptise' are eschewed in favour of 'breath' and 'bathe':

> And all the country of Judea was coming out to see him, and all the people of Jerusalem too, and were being bathed by him in the Jordan River, admitting their mistakes. And he was proclaiming, 'After me comes someone so much stronger than me, I am not great enough to bend over and untie the things of his sandals. I bathed you in water, but he will bathe you in holy breath'.

We might ask: Is it correct to avoid the word 'baptise'? We might agree that it is a theological word, and that it is helpful to have a translation avoid the word and substitute the sense that it is a bathing in water—there is no possibility of unconsciously reading the act as an act of christening!

The change of preposition from 'with' to 'in' (bathed you in water) reflects the Greek and also helps avoid the idea of christening. Nevertheless, we might still have misgivings about dropping the word 'baptise'. The issue for a translator (and us) is whether the original term is a theological word. If the original is such a word, it might be best to keep it, even if it is misused by orthodox churches.

Similar misgivings arise over the translation of 'holy breath' for the Greek here of πνεύματι ἁγίῳ, normally translated 'Holy Spirit'. This title is also the normal rendering for the related Greek, τὸ πνεῦμα τὸ ἅγιον. Gaus generally prefers 'sacred breath' as a translation of this latter Greek expression (e.g. in Mark 3:29; 13:11), but in Mark 12:36 he prefers 'Holy Spirit': "David himself said in the holy spirit". It's not clear why he should change his preferences for these closely related Greek phrases, especially as the Greek is the same in Mark 3:29 and 13:11.

The translation doesn't explain such choices. But this is not my criticism. My point is that Gaus has made choices, and these look theological. As his readers, we can't avoid asking what these terms mean, and this question requires a theological answer.

5. Conclusion
Our conclusion therefore is that this new translation is useful for a Bible student interested in the principle and practise of translation. It is useful

for Bible readers and other students if it is used with care and not as a substitute for a more formal translations.

CHAPTER FOUR
The Dead Sea Scrolls and Bible Translation

1. Introduction[1]

The aim of OT textual scholarship is to present, on the balance of probabilities, from all available evidence, what it takes to be the original Hebrew (and in parts of Daniel and Ezra - the original Aramaic) OT text. In achieving this end, scholars principally compare the traditional Hebrew text (Masoretic Text - MT), the Dead Sea Scrolls (DSS), the Samaritan Pentateuch,[2] early translations of the OT such as the Septuagint (LXX), and ancient Jewish and Christian commentaries.

The Dead Sea Scrolls are scrolls and manuscript fragments (mss.) found at three principal sites around the Dead Sea. The most famous site is the Qumran settlement on the northern shore of the Dead Sea, but scholars also include smaller finds in the vicinity under the rubric 'Dead Sea Scrolls', such as those at the Herodian fortress of Masada and a cave at Wadi Murabba'at.

Prior to the discovery of the DSS, the earliest manuscripts of the Hebrew OT dated from the Middle Ages (the earliest is put at 895 A.D.). There are three main medieval manuscripts, known as the 'Ben Asher manuscripts', so-called after the Jewish Masoretic family responsible for the text. It is the text in these manuscripts which represents the 'received' Hebrew text of the OT - the Masoretic text - and which is printed in the standard critical edition of the Hebrew OT—*Biblica Hebraica*.

---

[1] This essay appeared in *The Testimony* and then was collected together in the follow-up Testimony publication, *Which Translation?*

[2] The Samaritan Pentateuch is the 'Bible' of the Samaritan community mentioned in the NT, and our manuscripts date from the late Middles Ages. It is a popularised text derived from the original, and changed at key points to reinforce Samaritan doctrine.

The fact that we have few manuscripts from the Middles Ages,[1] and the fact that earlier manuscripts no longer exist, stems from the practise of the Jews to destroy their old and worn out scrolls. Synagogues kept their old and imperfect scrolls in Genizas (the equivalent of a modern day attic), and periodically disposed of the accumulation (the equivalent of clearing out of the loft). Nevertheless, by chance, one Geniza at Cairo was walled up and forgotten. It was discovered in the 19c., and has yielded many thousands of manuscript fragments. These manuscript fragments have supplied scholars with material that allows them to sketch the development of the MT during the early Middle Ages.[2]

Prior to the discovery of the scrolls, scholars followed the MT when translating the Bible into English, but there were some who argued that the LXX (with mss. dating from the 4c. and 5c.) preserved the original text in several places. There are many differences between the MT and the LXX, and the main issue for scholars was whether the LXX preserved a more reliable Hebrew text, or whether its differences were due to the processes of translation and interpretation. The same question also applied in respect of the relationship between the MT and the Samaritan Pentateuch. The chief problem for scholars was the fact that they did not have Hebrew manuscript evidence from around the time when the LXX translation was produced (probably during the third century BCE over several decades by a number of translators).

The DSS have changed this situation because they have supplied corroborative evidence for the MT, the LXX and the Samaritan Pentateuch. Scholars now have much more data to use in their determination of the OT text, and recent English versions have likewise incorporated readings based on the DSS material. The RSV (1952) was the first version to utilize the scrolls in this way, and since then every

---

[1] There are 31 extant Masoretic manuscripts dating from the 9c. to the 11c., and three thousand thereafter – see B. M. Metzger, ed., *The Oxford Companion to the Bible* (Oxford: Oxford University Press, 1993), 501.

[2] In addition to these manuscripts, there is also the Nash Papyrus, which contains the Ten Commandments (in a form which partly follows Exodus 20 and partly Deuteronomy 5) and the Priestly Blessing of Deuteronomy 6. This means that it is not a *Biblical* text, but a text used for liturgical or educational purposes. Its date is disputed, but scholars assign dates from the Maccabean period to the 2c. BCE. On this and the other Hebrew manuscripts see, Würthwein, *The Text of the Old Testament*, 24-27.

major translation has taken into account the evidence of the scrolls, either in footnotes or in the main body of the text.

There has been a great deal of popular interest in the DSS in recent years. Since 1992, a flurry of new texts has been published, and photographs of all the scrolls have now been released. Given that the scrolls were discovered in the late forties and early fifties, their delay in publication had caused some to speculate about a "Dead Sea Scrolls Deception"[1] in which there was a conspiracy to prevent the wider academic community from acquiring evidence for a damaging re-appraisal of the origins of Christianity. Such a journalistic claim hasn't gained much support, and the slow publication of the scrolls appears more to have been the result of bad organization and human nature.[2]

Actually, 'scrolls' is a bit of a misnomer, since very few entire scrolls have been recovered.[3] The texts are mainly fragments that scholars have to piece together. You can get a mental picture of the fragments 'belonging' to a scroll, if you imagine trying to do a 250 piece jigsaw without a picture to guide you, without any straight edges to form the border of the picture, and with only two colours—faded ink and a yellowy background. So what do these fragments have to say about the Old Testament text?

2. The Old Testament Text
In order to appreciate the impact of the DSS on the text of the OT, it is necessary to have an overview of how the Hebrew OT was transmitted after the Word of God was received by the prophets.

Scholars discuss the transmission of the OT text in terms of 'stages' in its history, in terms of different 'text types',[4] and in terms of the 'geographical or sociological origins' of such texts. A fourfold approach is

---

[1] M. Baigent and R. Leigh, *The Dead Sea Scrolls Deception* (London: Jonathan Cape, 1991).
[2] On this, see G. Vermes, *The Dead Sea Scrolls (Qumran in Perspective)* (London: SCM, 1994), chap. 1.
[3] H. Shanks observes that depending on what one means by 'intact', only as many as 12 scrolls were recovered, see his "Of Caves and Scholars, An Overview" in *Understanding the Dead Sea Scrolls* (ed. H. Shanks; London: SPCK, 1992), xvi.
[4] A 'text type' is a term of art in textual criticism referring to shared characteristics among several manuscripts—hence, manuscripts are grouped into families.

common amongst scholars,[1] although they differ in the way they classify the stages. The following would be a 'consensus' way of looking at the history of the OT text:

Stage 1: The writing of the original text.
Stage 2: The production of variations alongside the original.
Stage 3: The establishment of a 'received consonantal text'.
Stage 4: The vocalization of the text.

The first stage is self-evident (even if oral traditions lie behind the writing of the text).[2] The prophets certainly claimed to be speaking the word of God, and therefore we can expect that both they and their disciples accurately preserved their words for future generations. That the Law of Moses was passed on by those in authority over Israel is evident in the OT, not only when they entered the land, but also after the Babylonian Exile.[3] As for the other books of the OT, there is good literary evidence that as the years passed and prophets came and went, later prophets used earlier prophetic writing. This is seen, not only in their explicit mention of early Scriptures,[4] but more generally in the knowledge they show of earlier books.[5] The use of the OT in the NT is part of this prophetic practise.[6] We have therefore good evidence for the gradual build-up of the OT canon.

By the time we come to the NT era, there is good evidence that the Jews had a sense of Scripture that emphasized the importance of detail and accuracy across all of what we know as the Old Testament. The

---

[1] See H. Scanlin, *The Dead Sea Scrolls and Modern Translations of the Old Testament* (Cambridge: Tyndale Press, 1993), 36-37.
[2] For example, the 'books/historical accounts/generations' that make up Genesis and used by Moses (Gen 2:4; 5:1; 6:9; 10:1, 32; 11:10, 27; 25:12, 13, 19; 36:1, 9; 37:2).
[3] See for example, Josh. 1:1, 8; 23:6; Ezra 7:6, 11; Neh 8:1, 8.
[4] See for example, the cross-referencing between Kings and Chronicles (e.g. 1 Kgs 14:19), or the use made of Jeremiah by Daniel (Dan 9:2).
[5] A principle example of how the later OT books use the earlier works can be seen in the many patterns and types of Scripture. There are an abundant number of textual patterns in later writings that fall into line with similar patterns in earlier works. While we may see this as the product of inspiration, at the human level, the correspondences also illustrate deep knowledge of early Scripture by later prophets.
[6] See, for example, Luke 11:51; 24:44; and John 10:35.

contemporary Jewish historian, Josephus, comments in *Contra Apion* (circa. 90 CE), "and how firmly we have given credit to those books of our own nation is evident by what we do; for during so many ages as have already passed, no one has been so bold as either to add anything to them or take anything from them, or to make any change in them".[1] Josephus divides these books into three groups of 5 books (the Law), 13 books (History and Prophets) and 4 books (the Writings, including the Psalms).

However, the preservation of the original Scriptures was accompanied by the emergence of various differing texts. The DSS illustrate this second stage in the transmission of the OT text. We may think of this stage with an analogy: there are many different English versions of the Bible today, from literal 'word for word' versions to quite free paraphrases like the Good News Version. The purpose of a literal version is self-evidently different from the aim of paraphrase, yet each purport to be the 'Bible'. It is likely that differences in OT texts arose for similar reasons.

We might ask: How can a text be produced in the same language that differs from that written by a prophet, for instance, the book of Jeremiah? The possible answers to such a question are limited only by our imagination. A text can be popularised in various ways. It may incorporate received synagogue readings along with an official text; it may use more up to date Hebrew spellings and grammatical forms; and it may 'fill out' the text with parallel detail; it may be a colloquial or regional text. The manuscript pieces that we have today may illustrate any one of these factors. Moreover, we cannot assume that the DSS we have are 'published' texts. Some may represent scrolls or incomplete scrolls that were rejected for reasons of inaccuracy; some may represent 'private' writings that were not part of an official synagogue collection; some may represent 'training material'. These are possibilities allowed by the circumstances of the day.

In the 1c. environment, where we know that there were various 'versions' of the OT, we naturally ask today, 'Was there at that time an authoritative text?'. By the time we get to the Middle Ages, there is such a 'received text' and variations have fallen by the wayside—so how do we account for this 'falling away' and consequent agreement? Scholars describe the establishment of a 'received' text as the third stage in the development of the OT text.

---

[1] *Josephus*, (trans. W. Whiston; Grand Rapids: Kregel, 1980), 609.

We can discern from the DSS that the various OT texts did not compete on an equal footing in the first century. The main type of text by far is the same text as the MT, i.e. the DSS represent manuscript fragments that share the same characteristics as the later MT of the Middle Ages. E. Tov, an editor-in-chief of the DSS, has offered the following analysis:[1]

Texts aligned with Masoretic Text	60%
Texts aligned with Samaritan Pentateuch	5%
Texts aligned with Septuagint Text	5%
Non-Aligned texts	20%
Texts written in Qumran practice	10%

These figures show that the textual tradition in which the MT stands is early and not an invention of the Masoretes. If there was an authoritative text in the 1c., then the MT tradition is the only real candidate. (It is interesting to note that the MT is the only type of text found at Masada and the Wadi Murabba'at).[2]

The canon of the Jewish Scriptures was most probably established at a synod, which was convened at Jamnia near Jaffa, between 90 and 100 CE. Here, certain disputed questions were settled about some of the writings, for instance, Esther and Ecclesiastes. Did the synod establish a type of MT as the authoritative text? The MT is not an eclectic text constructed

---

[1] This table is supplied in E. M. Cook, *Solving the Mysteries of the Dead Sea Scrolls* (Carlisle: Paternoster Press, 1994), 185. Cook actually thinks that the percentage figure for texts aligned with the MT is higher than Tov allows. He says Tov includes texts like the large Isaiah scroll in the 20% of texts written in Qumran practice because of *grammatical* disagreement, whereas such scrolls actually agree *textually* with the MT. J. C. VanderKam quotes new percentages supplied by Tov reducing the MT aligned texts to 40%, and increasing the number of texts that are not aligned to 25% and the Qumran practice texts to 25%, with Samaritan and LXX aligned texts remaining at 5% each; see his *The Dead Sea Scrolls Today* (London: SPCK, 1994), 134.

[2] If we were to guess in advance where the MT comes from, we would probably suggest the Southern tribes rather than the Northern ones. In this connection, it is interesting to note that the language of the Lachish letters (c. 600 BCE) is the same classical Hebrew as the Masoretic Text. On this, see D. W. Thomas, "The Textual Criticism of the Old Testament" in *The Old Testament and Modern Study* (ed. H. H. Rowley; Oxford: Oxford University Press, 1951).

from readings selected from various manuscripts, so that if the Jamnia synod established a text, they did not do so by picking and choosing from various sources. Rabbinical tradition says that the text was chosen from three model scrolls, and the Jamnia synod is often proposed as the council that made this decision. Subsequent to the council, translations like the Vulgate and old Greek translations by Aquila, Symmachus and Theodotion indicate that they used the same Hebrew consonantal text as the MT, and scholars call this the 'proto-Masoretic' text.[1]

The Hebrew textual critics, (known firstly as the Sopherim and then the Masoretes), responsible for the transmission of the text since the first century, show a concern about the text itself and preserving its smallest details, as against a concern for giving a contemporary rendering appropriate to their own times. They counted verses, words, and letters, as a control on the manuscripts. Such a concern was obviously a great bulwark against corruption of the text, and it accounts for the similarity amongst the manuscripts. The 'need' for a contemporary 'text' was supplied by marginal readings rather than by changes in the actual text.[2]

Vocalization was an oral tradition, and only partly indicated in the text itself through the use of certain weak consonants as vowel-letters. The Masoretes, anxious to fix its vocalization for posterity, incorporated its pronunciation into the text from about the fifth century onwards through a system of points above and below the consonants. This vocalization was not settled straightaway, but took a number of centuries to become fixed. Scholars identify a pointing system developed by the Babylonian Masoretes and another used by the Masoretes in Palestine—it was this system that prevailed. The final stage therefore of the OT text is this vocalization of the text.

---

[1] On this see, Vermes, *The Dead Sea Scrolls, (Qumran in Perspective)*, 176-177, 187-188; Vermes presents the standard view of Jamnia.
[2] There were various kinds of marginal readings: Würthwein, *The Text of the Old Testament*, 13-14, 21-22, notes four kinds: i) Some letters or words had dots over them indicating textual queries (15 cases); ii) an inverted letter (Nun) occurs occasionally indicating transposition of verses (9 times); iii) there are several hundred examples (Würthwein mentions 350 cases) of marginal readings where scribes placed the word they expected in the margin over against the word that occurs in the text; and iv) there came to be over 1300 passages where scribes placed guidance on how the text was to be read in the margin.

All languages evolve until they become dead, and the writing of the Hebrew OT spans many centuries.[1] During the life of a language, books can be 'adapted' to the needs of the people. We see this today in modern adaptation of earlier English literature. When the people cease to speak the original language in which a book was written, adaptation is no longer required, but rather translation into the new language of the day is needed. The effective death of Hebrew after 70 CE has meant that we have preserved for us the OT with which the apostles would have been familiar. The discoveries of the Dead Sea have yielded variations of the Hebrew Bible, but these have not affected the dominant position of the MT, and they have not substantially affected English translations.

3. The Dead Sea Manuscripts

The Bible is a best-seller out of copyright, and new versions in English appear each decade. These may be revisions of existing versions, or they may be new versions altogether. One of the ways in which new versions distinguish themselves is in the 'original' text that they purport to translate.

The translation committees of the various post-war English versions of the Bible have had available, not only the traditional Hebrew text, but also the Dead Sea Scrolls, early translations, and quotations from early Jewish and Christian writers. Their versions illustrate different approaches to this OT textual material.

While the MT is the baseline text for each version, translators have generally not hesitated to depart from the MT in cases where they believe the MT is corrupt, or where they believe other witnesses to the original Hebrew are 'more likely' to report the original. Where they depart from the MT in favour of other witnesses, they produce in effect an eclectic text - i.e. a composite text made up from different source traditions. Some translation committees, however, have not relied on producing an eclectic text, but rather they have sought to translate the MT, for instance, the New Jerusalem Version.

In this section, we want to look at some specific examples where the DSS have influenced modern English versions. Our objective is to gain some

---

[1] Differences in the style of the language can be observed between the early books (the Pentateuch) and the later works (like Ezra), and this is one argument for the early date for the books of Moses.

understanding of the process of textual criticism—of how we get our English Bible.

Of the DSS, one scholar observes, "most people will be surprised to learn that there are relatively few passages in modern English translations of the OT that have been affected by this manuscript evidence".[1] The reasons for this are, first, the manuscripts are quite fragmentary, and secondly, most of the manuscripts reflect the MT and give no occasion for change. All the Biblical books are to be found in the manuscripts, except Esther, but they are not equally represented. The Pentateuch (70 mss.), Isaiah (18 mss.) and the Psalms (27 mss.) dominate out of a total cache of 175+ manuscripts.[2] Besides these three sections of the Bible, Samuel, Jeremiah and Habakkuk manuscripts have proved influential with scholars in their 'determination' of the OT text. Other parts of the Bible have largely been unaffected.

The DSS testify to a variety of OT versions, however, there is no conclusive evidence concerning how the versions originated. Scholars speculate about there being three centres of production for texts - Babylonia Palestine and Egypt. As a consequence of the Babylonian Captivity, centres of Jewish scholarship existed in these three areas. The LXX was translated in Alexandria from Hebrew texts during the third century before Christ, and this establishes Egypt as a major centre of text production. However, the Jewish priestly establishment were exiled to Babylon, and no doubt took official the copies of the Scriptures with them, and after the exile these were brought back (Deut 31:25-26; Ezra 7:12-14).[3] Scholars make Babylonia the place where Jewish scribes preserved the text that became what we know as the 'Masoretic Text', and they call it the 'proto-Masoretic' text. In this way they associate the Jewish establishment with this textual tradition, and thereby account for the dominance of this textual tradition among the DSS. In addition to these two centres of text production, the Jews left behind in Palestine would

---

[1] Scanlin, *The Dead Sea Scrolls and Modern Translations of the Old Testament*, 107.

[2] Vermes, *The Dead Sea Scrolls (Qumran in Perspective)*, 178.

[3] We have little evidence of how the Jewish canon was officially expanded to include the Major and Minor Prophets. While the disciples of the prophets and, more generally, those *of the truth*, recognised their words, the establishment of the day were often opposed. It was perhaps the exile that brought official recognition of the prophets for, deprived of their land; it confirmed to the children of the exile the folly of their fathers.

have maintained their own copies of the Scriptures and new versions may have come about as a result. The Samaritan version of the Pentateuch is one such example that originates from the inter-testamental period, and the DSS constitute evidence for yet other contemporary versions.[1]

Generally, English translations have been inclined to follow a DSS reading when it has confirmed the LXX. The LXX represents an alternative textual tradition to the MT, and we now know (as a result of the DSS) that a number of its variations reflect contemporary Hebrew versions. The discovery of the scrolls has given scholars more confidence to choose LXX readings. The DSS have also lent weight to particular variations among the MT manuscripts, the Samaritan Pentateuch, as well as supplying unique readings that have found favour with modern scholars.

Translation committees have varied widely in the number of times they depart from the MT. For example, in the case of 1 Samuel, a book where there is a fair amount of diversity between the MT, the LXX and the DSS, the NIV departs from the MT in 15 instances, whereas the NAB differs on 230 occasions.[2] With such diversity, it is hard to resist the conclusion that there is a fair amount of subjectivity in involved in making such textual choices.[3]

Old Testament textual criticism is an academic discipline. Scholars do not only consider textual questions when deciding on a reading, i.e. they don't

---

[1] The many synagogues of the land would have had their own copies of the Law and the Prophets (in Hebrew), since their common order of worship required a passage to be read from both these parts of Scripture with an accompanying translation into Aramaic—the common language of the day. It is impossible to tell whether they all used one official copy, appointed, as it were (like the King James), to be read in the Synagogues. Synagogues may have used different versions for different reasons, much like modern day ecclesias.

[2] Scanlin, *The Dead Sea Scrolls and Modern Translations of the Old Testament*, 26. Scanlin includes the following statistics for variations from the MT in 1 Samuel: TEV (51), RSV (about 60), NRSV (110) and NEB (160).

[3] For example, the NEB committee took the view that the MT was 'full of errors' whereas the committee for the REB comments, "Despite the care used in the copying of the Masoretic Text, it contains errors". (Cited Scanlin, *The Dead Sea Scrolls and Modern Translations of the Old Testament*, 31).

just consider manuscripts and the data[1] they offer for determining the original text. They also bring to the process their historical views on the underlying sources for books, the authors and editors of books, the time of writing, and any supposed 'revisions' to the book. Literary considerations are also brought to bear on the process, and comparisons with comparative Semitic texts.[2] A conservative scholar is likely to take a different view to a liberal critic. We can only make a judgement on a particular choice on the part of a translator if we know his assumptions and reasoning.

4. Variations in the English Old Testament

We have set out in Table One some representative examples of variations. How do we handle such differences? Do we follow the Masoretic tradition, based as it is upon a text which we can identify as dominant in the 1c.? Or do we take a piecemeal approach, and construct an eclectic text, making changes to the MT as and when we consider it to be corrupt or inferior to other texts? We will now consider three specific examples.

4.1 The Number of Jacob's Descendants

Is the number of Jacob's descendants seventy or seventy-five (Exod 1:5)?[3] Translators following the MT read 'seventy', but a Qumran text (4QExod[b]) and the LXX has 'seventy-five', and the NIV and NEB footnote this alternative number. Stephen mentions 'seventy-five' in his speech (Acts 7:14), so does this indicate that he or Luke used the LXX or a different Hebrew OT, rather than the text that underlies the MT?

---

[1] As we noted above, the MT mss. are rich in marginal annotations about the text, and this is the kind of data which I principally refer to as *textual*. Other kinds of textual consideration include the division of the consonantal text (where word breaks occur), and the pointing of the text (a different choice of vowels can mean a different word), as well as obvious errors in transmission.

[2] This is important when doubt exists over the Hebrew construction—scholars will use a wider group of texts in related languages to establish the identity of a word.

[3] For a discussion of this case, see VanderKam, *The Dead Sea Scrolls Today*, 127. In his treatment, the manuscript is given as '4QExod[a]', but this is probably a typographical error. See also R. Hendel, "When the Sons of God cavorted with the Daughters of Men" in *Understanding the Dead Sea Scrolls*, (ed. H. Shanks; London: SPCK, 1992), 167-177.

Text	MT and KJV	DSS[1]	Modern Versions
Gen 1:9	unto one place	4QGen^h	into one basin (NAB)
Exod 1:5	seventy	4QExod^b	seventy-five (NEB and NIV footnotes)
Deut 32:8	children of Israel	4QDeut^j	sons of God (NEB)
Deut 32:43	Rejoice, O ye nations, with his people	4QDeut^q	Rejoice with him, you heavens, bow down, all you Gods (NEB)
1 Sam 10:27-11:1	No text	4QSam^a	Extra paragraph about Nahash the Ammonite (NRSV)
Isa 49:12	Sinim	1QIsa^a	Syene (NAB, NIV, RSV)
Isa 49:24	the captivity of the just	1QIsa^a	the captives of a tyrant (NIV, RSV/NRSV, NEB)
Hab. 1:17	empty their net	1QpHab	unsheathe the sword (NEB)

Table I

The basis for the two numbers lies in Genesis 46 and the list of Jacob's descendants. The LXX adds three grandsons and two great-grandsons to Joseph's children in Gen 46:20 making an extra five for the total mentioned in Gen 46:27. Does the LXX reflect the original Hebrew?

The table of nations has seventy names, and these nations were separated (Heb: *prd*) in the time of Peleg (Gen 10:5, 25). This separation is referred to in Deut 32:8, where it is recorded that the sons of Adam were 'separated' (Heb: *prd*) according to the number of the 'sons of Israel'. It would seem then that the correct number is 'seventy'. Such a

---

[1] Dead Sea Scrolls are denoted in the following way: Qumran mss. are designated 'Q' with their cave of origin given, e.g. '4Q'; biblical mss. are indicated by an abbreviation of the book's name, e.g. '4QIsa', and if several mss. of, say, Isaiah were found in a cave, they are further identified by a superscript letter, e.g. '4QIsa^a'. Qumran commentaries or *pesher* have a further letter 'p' inserted into the mss. designation, e.g. '4QpHab'.

correspondence fits in with the role of Israel to be the ruling nation[1] of priests to the earth (Exod 19:5-6).

The witness of the Qumran manuscript, and the matching testimony of the LXX, illustrates an historical expansion of the text, but one which introduces a disharmony in its teaching concerning Israel. The expansion is not historically inaccurate, and the speech of Stephen reflects this common knowledge. Stephen's enumeration is about Joseph's 'kindred' (cf. Acts 7:13), which properly includes his grand-children, whereas the genealogy in Genesis 46 is Jacob's. We should conclude in this case that Qumran and the LXX do not reflect the original text of Genesis 46.

However, there is a complication for this conclusion. It might be argued that the evidence of Stephen's speech in Acts tips the balance in favour of Qumran and the LXX as witnesses to the original Hebrew. Stephen says,

> And Joseph sent word and invited Jacob his father and all his relatives to come to him, <u>seventy-five persons</u> in all. Acts 7:14 (NASB)

Genesis 46:26 records that 66 "went down" into Egypt with Jacob, giving 67 in total, and these were therefore the number "called into" Egypt according to Acts 7:14. In Genesis, this enumeration of 66 with Jacob excludes Joseph and his two sons. We need to distinguish the number of those "called into" Egypt from the number which "came into" Egypt (Gen 46:27). This last number (70) includes those who "came into" Egypt by other means than Joseph's invitation; the LXX makes this number 75.

When we consider Stephen's speech, we have to ask what his figure of 75 means. The figure of 75 does not tally with Jacob and the 66 who were "called" into Egypt. We could assume that Stephen's figure of 75 comprehends unnamed children of Jacob that were called into Egypt with their father, but the MT and the LXX clearly preserve an ancient tradition that any extra children belong to Joseph and indigenous to Egypt. We should therefore maintain the distinction between those called into Egypt (67) and those that "came into" Egypt (70, MT; 75, LXX, Qumran, Acts).

---

[1] The symbology of 'seventy' and rulership is further seen in the appointment of seventy elders to help Moses (Exod 24:1), and in the appointment of seventy to disciples to exercise dominion over demons (Luke 10:1, 17).

It would appear from Acts 7:14 that Stephen knows of only one type of number - viz. the number of those 'called into' Egypt. If this is the case, Stephen quotes neither the MT nor the LXX tradition which agree on the number Jacob and 66. But this observation overlooks the dynamics of speech, and the way in which Stephen could assume shared traditions with his audience. If one of the received numbers for those who ended up in Egypt was 75, Stephen could tag this number onto the end of his sentence and expect his audience to understand the distinction between those 'called into' Egypt and those who 'ended up' in Egypt, without using further description. A shared pool of knowledge allows many such shortcuts in dialogue.

The LXX tradition, which was contemporary knowledge in Stephen's day (e.g. Philo knows of this number), is too significant to discount as an explanation of Stephen's number. However, it is not the number of those called into Egypt. Accordingly, it is more likely that the MT preserves the original count of 70 because it is easier to explain LXX/Qumran as an expansion used by Stephen; it is difficult to explain why the MT would cut out extra names. Stephen's use of the same knowledge as that embodied in LXX/Qumran doesn't prove that the LXX reflects the original Hebrew. There are other points to take into account.

4.2 Sons of God or Children of Israel
Deuteronomy 32:8 is another example of variation, with a tiny Qumran fragment (4QDeut^j) having 'sons of God' instead of 'sons of Israel' in '...according to the number of the children of Israel' (KJV). The NEB has chosen to follow 'sons of God', and the NIV includes this as a footnote. The LXX differs from the Qumran manuscripts in having 'angels of God' instead of 'sons of God'. If the LXX and the Qumran manuscripts preserve the original 'seventy-five' in Exod 1:5, then there is no reason to link the 'seventy' in the table of nations with the sons of Israel who came into Egypt. Hence, Qumran and the LXX is consistent in opposing the MT, for it would hardly do to retain a reference to the seventy 'sons of Israel' in Deut 32:8, and keep the figure of 'seventy-five' in Exod 1:5., as this would introduce a discrepancy.

With such a small fragment, it is not possible to identify its status. It may not be part of an 'official' copy of Scripture; it may have been part of a free rendering of the Song of Moses. The reading would indicate an angelology whereby the nations were apportioned to the rule of seventy angels. Is such an angelology likely to have been part of the ancient Song of Moses? Elaborate angelologies are a feature of the inter-testamental period, including the DSS,[1] and we might reasonably suppose that it was more likely that the Song of Moses was adapted in later times.

This argument puts forward a theological consideration for identifying the original text, and this kind of argument is not uncommon in the literature. For example, VanderKam puts forward this consideration on Deut 32:8,

> Here the reading in the Masoretic Text ("the sons of Israel") may represent a theologically motivated change from an earlier phase: the reading "sons of God" refers in this context to divine beings, whom the uninformed reader might consider lesser gods - a thought precariously close to polytheism. As recent translators have recognized, the reading of the Septuagint, now supported by a Qumran copy of Deuteronomy, is more likely to be original, since it is easier to explain why someone might change "sons of God" (a theologically suspect phrase) to "sons of Israel" than it would be to account for the reverse.[2]

What textual critics regard as 'easy to explain' depends on many factors, not least of which will be their working assumptions. We have argued that "the sons of Israel" is more likely to be original because this fits in with the Mosaic doctrine that Israel was to be a kingdom of priests to the nations. It is more likely that the expression 'sons of God' reflects a later adaptation of the Song, perhaps during the exile, with Israel out of their land, in order to maintain the text's mention of the rule of God over the nations—but through angels.[3] The book of Daniel shows that angels are assigned to direct the affairs of nations, so the change is not un-biblical.

4.3 The Worship of Angels
Another Qumran manuscript (4QDeut[q]) illustrates possible adaptation of the Song of Moses, this time in Deut 32:43. The NEB and NRSV follow this evidence in making several changes to the text:

---

[1] See G. Vermes, *The Dead Sea Scrolls in English* (4th ed.; London: Penguin, 1995), 254-263. Vermes includes a selection of liturgies which describe angelic orders and their worship of God.

[2] VanderKam, *The Dead Sea Scrolls Today*, 128.

[3] The Qumran manuscripts may not intend angelic beings, since 'sons of God' can be used of men (Gen 6:2-4; Job 38:7), but the LXX evidence does indicate such an interpretation.

49

Rejoice with him, you heavens, bow down, all you gods, before him; for he will avenge the blood of his sons and take vengeance on his adversaries; he will punish those who hate him and make expiation for his people's land. Deut. 32:43 (NEB)

Rejoice, O ye nations, [with] his people: for he will avenge the blood of his servants, and will render vengeance to his adversaries, and will be merciful unto his land, [and] to his people. Deut 32:43 (KJV and MT)

The NEB has put 'heavens' for 'nations', 'sons' for 'servants' and added the extra clause 'bow down, all you gods'. We can see how the NEB closely follows the Qumran manuscript:

Rejoice, O ye heavens, with him and all ye gods worship him; for he will avenge the blood of his sons and will render vengeance to his adversaries, and will reward them that hate him; and will make expiation for the land of his people. (Qumran)[1]

The LXX is different from the Qumran manuscript in having additional clauses, and in including a reference to 'angels' rather than 'gods' in 'worship him, all angels of God':

Rejoice, ye heavens, with him, and let all the angels of God worship him; rejoice ye Gentiles, with his people, and let all the sons of God strengthen themselves in him; for he will avenge the blood of his sons, and he will render vengeance, and recompense justice to his enemies, and will reward them that hate him; and the Lord shall purge the land of his people. Deut 32:43 (LXX)[2]

Interestingly, this larger text includes the clause 'rejoice ye Gentiles, with his people' as in the MT, which the NEB has chosen to drop in favour of the Qumran text. We can see that the LXX expands on the MT tradition

---

[1] This translation is taken from J. Allegro, *The Dead Sea Scrolls (A Reappraisal)* (London: Penguin, 1964), 75.
[2] This quote is from Bagster's edition of the LXX, which is essentially the Vaticanus Codex.

with an extra clause, "and let all the sons of God strengthen themselves in him", to balance the poetry of "Rejoice, ye heavens, with him, and let all the angels of God worship him". This mention of 'heavens and earth' at the end of the Song complements the mention of 'heavens and earth at the beginning of the Song (v. 1).

The Qumran manuscript is not part of a copy of Deuteronomy, because it ends with the last verse of the Song of Moses, and it has a wide outer margin indicating that it was not attached to another manuscript panel. The Song is also arranged in hemistichs, which further indicates that the manuscript is not part of a copy of the Law. It is possible that the Qumran manuscript represents an adaptation of the Song incorporating lines from the Psalms (Ps 96:11; 97:7). The LXX may likewise reflect an expansion of the original along the same lines, since it enlarges upon the Qumran text with an exhortation not only to the 'heavens' but also the 'earth' (cf. 1 Chron 16:31).

How do we decide between these kinds of variation? Without further evidence, it is not possible to be certain, but the MT reading is the more difficult of the three readings of Deut 32:43 and less easy to explain as a development of either of the other two possibilities. It is with a consideration such as this, that textual critics would prefer the MT in this case.[1]

5. Conclusion

The DSS have affected the Old Testament text in three ways: i) they have confirmed the reliability of the MT, supplying mss. a 1000 years older than our previous oldest mss.; ii) they have supplied evidence of Hebrew texts underlying the LXX; and iii) they supply evidence for there being more 'versions' of OT books current in the days of Christ. The variations that exist in the DSS affect no first principle, rather they impinge on historical details, either adding or taking away detail.

---

[1] On this principle and others that textual critics use, see Würthwein, *The Text of the Old Testament*, chap. 4.

CHAPTER FIVE
Inspiration

1. Introduction[1]

What sort of book do we have in the Bible? An answer to this question would obviously involve historical investigations into the origins of the Bible. However, we are not interested in literary-historical questions. Rather, I am concerned to discuss how the Bible can legitimately be described as "communication" from God. Historical matters such as the date, authorship and content of the Bible are important, but of far greater significance is the question of *how God can be described as having said what we find in the Bible.* This is the important issue and it constitutes the defining question of a Theory of Inspiration.

If it is not possible for God to communicate with man, then it is silly to investigate the Bible for divine utterance (divine saying). But if it is possible, we want to know how this has happened. How do we go about settling this issue? Since inspiration is a matter to do with how God can be described as having said what we find in the Bible, an understanding of language and the use of language are going to be crucial. It is plausible to suggest therefore that we need to think about inspiration in terms used by those disciplines that examine language.

There are many perspectives on language and universities offer a wide range of degree courses in the study of language. There is Logic, Philosophy of Language, and Linguistics. Within Linguistics there is the discipline of Pragmatics, which studies the contextual use of language. Since our question is—how can the Bible contain what has been said by God?—it will be obvious that the disciplines that examine the *act of saying* are the ones that are going to be most relevant to our concerns.

Our interest has to do with the persons directly involved in having said what we read in the Bible. We are interested in the following questions:

- What would it be for men to speak to God?

---

[1] This is an essay largely written in 1985 in response to a person who came to adopt a liberal view of inspiration and who left the fellowship of Christadelphians for the Church of England.

- What would it be for God to speak to men?

- What would it be for men to say things on behalf of God?

- What would it be for God to say what men have said?

To answer these questions we need to appreciate the nature of *what it is to say something* from a philosophical point of view. How are the various parameters of conversation between God and men established? How can God delegate his speaking to another individual? What are the conditions that need to be satisfied for an individual to represent God's words to an audience?

2. Popular Views of Inspiration

Politics provides a useful analogy for understanding theories about inspiration. We can contrast a liberal view of inspiration with a conservative or traditional view of inspiration. But to understand how this contrast works out in practice, we need to appreciate something of the general character of theories of inspiration. Broadly speaking, theories of inspiration address two phenomena:

- They attempt to describe the relationship that God has to the prophets and authors of the Biblical writings

- They aim to specify the relationship that God has to the writing itself

Conservative theories subscribe to what is known as a "plenary verbal" view of inspiration (*every* word is God's word), whereas liberal theories reject this view.

2.1 God's Relationship to the Writing

Can God truly be described as "saying" the words of a particular prophetic writing? Can each word, as used by the prophet/writer, truly be described as a word used also by God? If so, such an understanding would be in line with traditional Christian thinking on inspiration. On the other hand, would it be more accurate to look at the prophetic writings as *containing* the message of God in and amongst a human product? Would it be better to sever the link between God and (either all or some of) the actual words used by the prophet? Ought we to talk of inspiration only at the more abstract level of ideas, concepts, and messages, or perhaps just feelings? If we consider these strategies to be the way forward in

53

understanding the Bible, we will be adopting a liberal position of some kind. Liberal and Conservative views of inspiration differ on how they see God's relationship to the Scriptural writings.

2.2 God's Relationship to the Writer

How do theories of inspiration describe God's relationship to the prophet or writer of the text? Often the answer to this question involves talk about the *mind*. Some scholars treat inspiration as the activity of God's Spirit upon the mind of the writer of the particular Biblical book in view, guiding the thoughts and controlling words being used by the prophet to express those thoughts. A scholar might describe the inspirational processes as a heightening of a prophet's religious perceptions and faculties, so that he was empowered to write what God intended. Inspiration might be described in terms of having a dream, or an ecstatic experience, or a vision, *and so on*.

Talk about the mind of a prophet doesn't tell us whether or how God can be said to be the author of the Bible. A liberal scholar might claim that whilst the Spirit worked in such a way as to control the very thoughts of the writer, nevertheless in the writing down of those thoughts there was freedom of expression. A conservative scholar might offer some sort of 'dictation' or 'amanuensis' view of inspiration. God, through an angel dictated the words of the message to the prophet or apostle, who later wrote it down.

Over against this approach is the suggestion that God relates to the prophet just by guiding his life and experience. This might be called a 'providential' view of inspiration. This says that God has carefully guided events so that the Biblical writers have written exactly what he desired. He has been at work since the writer's birth, and even before that, preparing the way for his work. His birth into a given family, his exposure to particular cultural influences; these were no accident. The hand of God directed all his education, occupation and experiences. Thus, his ways of thinking, and even his vocabulary and style of writing, were the outcome of divine providence. By the time he came to write his particular portion of the Bible, the very words he used were precisely the ones that God willed him to use, although there might be no clear consciousness that this was the case on the part of the writer.

Yet another theory might be called the 'institutional' theory of inspiration, and may be succinctly summarised as claiming that insofar as there existed institutions - religious institutions - prophets, chroniclers, lawgivers, judges, wise men and poets would speak and write within the umbrella of such institutions, and their work would carry the authority of God.

It is important initially to be open to the wide range of ideas on inspiration. However, if any sort of progress is going to be made in this area, it will be necessary to be careful and clear in what we say. We have said enough on kinds of inspiration theory to get a flavour of what theologians have thought it important to stress in giving an account of inspiration. Our sketches are crude and simplistic, but some of the reasons why scholars disagree on this issue should now be plain. As we proceed, we shall explain much of what we have only briefly touched upon here, and we shall find that a satisfactory account of inspiration needs to be centred on an explanation of how God can be described as having said what has been said in the Bible.

3. Models of Saying

The key notion that we will use to develop a theory of inspiration will be that of **saying something**. If we are to determine whether the Bible is the Word of God, we need to know first whether it is possible for God to communicate with man, and if so whether and how he has so communicated. In addressing ourselves to this problem, we will have to consider general principles concerning *what it is to say something*, dipping our toes into popular folk linguistics as we go, before we are able to show how the Bible is the Word of God.[1]

The problem of communication here has three parties rather than two,

$$\text{God} \text{———} \text{Man} \text{———} \text{Man}$$

Traditional theories of inspiration focus on the first relationship when describing inspiration—how does God inspire a man (prophet); however, equally we should focus on the second relationship: how is what man says to man the sayings of God? An adequate theory of inspiration needs to describe both relationships.

3.1 Agents

Let us map out some of the variety of ways in which something can be said for someone by an agent.

---

[1] For the philosophy see N. Wolterstorff, *Divine Discourse* (Cambridge: Cambridge University Press, 1995), chap. 2.

(A) There are those situations where an agent is **acting autonomously** in the saying of something. So for example,

1. There is the oral speech situation, which might be either a monologue or some sort of dialogue, where the agent is active himself in the use of a spoken language. Because this is the most prevalent way of saying something, it is often taken as the paradigm of what it is to say something, but there are also aspects where non-verbal behaviour is used to say something, e.g. mime, facial expressions, and one's general comportment; again certain conventions underlie such behaviour.

2. Or, there are other situations where some non-aural system is used to say something, for example a written language, sign-language or semaphore. The agent says something, as it were, on paper—a headline, a poster, or in a book, *and so on.*

In (1) and (2) the agent doing the saying is acting independently for someone; saying something without the involvement of the one on whose behalf they are acting.

(B) And there are those circumstances where there is **some element of delegation or direction in the situation**. The one on whose behalf the saying is being done is involved.

1. Again, there are many examples of oral representative speaking. Press reporting is one example, where, for instance, in a government press conference, it is understood that it is the government that is saying something, and not the particular spokesman presenting the information. Another case is the legal profession where counsel speaks on behalf of clients, having been instructed by them.

2. Amanuenses are often used by authors, and secretaries are very prevalent in business. These kinds of people are generally involved in the transcription of what others want to say. Or again, ghost writers are used who may receive acknowledgement as a co-writer, but do not have the status of having said what is being said in a celebrity autobiography

3. An interesting set of cases that involve an element of indirection concern the use of electro-mechanical devices such as computers, telephones and communication equipment, to convey what people are saying.

While this distinction between the two broad means of achieving the saying of something (A) and (B) is rough and ready, it nevertheless points to important and crucial characteristics in the phenomenology of human behaviour. If it is going to be possible for a God to communicate with man through a medium such as the written word, then unless God writes down what he wants to say himself, it is going to be necessary for God to work in situations that involve indirectedness and delegation. If we are to understand how God might have worked to accomplish the writing of the Bible books, then it seems that we are going to have to look at how humans communicate with one another. In detailing our model, it will be important not to constrict the variety of ways that the achieving of having said something can come about through the involvement of other people and other things.

Here are some brief sketches of the kinds of situation that I have in mind when I talk of there being indirect means involved in the saying of something.

a) An author or a company director could dictate something to a secretary, who might then go away and write down the content of the dictation. Alternatively, the secretary or amanuensis could directly transcribe the dictation as it is given into a presentable form. In either case, the secretary would normally carry out some operations with the acquired material. Often this will be to pass on information to a relevant party, perhaps a critic or business partner. In this case, although the secretary has been instrumental in delivering the letter or the report, the content of these items is understood to be attributable to the director.

Or it might be that the secretary duplicates a written document and circulates this around various office departments or publishers. At any rate, it is easy to think of a myriad number of things that the secretary might do with the dictated material; the point being made is that this is nevertheless understood to emanate from the director.

b) One variation (among many) upon the above situation might be this: directions could be given by the director, say, or these could be laid down on record, and these instructions might significantly affect the content of the final material.

For example, a secretary might be directed to use filed formulations, or include some already existing material, perhaps a set of cross-references. In these kinds of situation there is a delegated authorisation to augment the given material in some way. This might be explicit in the form of some stated directions, or in some situations it may be understood that certain material is augmented in standard ways, say, with standard paragraph headings, or introductory modes of address.

c) A third kind of situation expands upon this latest thought. The use of the knowledge of another in the saying of something can be quite extensive. But if this is the case, the key factors in determining who is saying what lie in the various relationships of the socio-linguistic situation. For example, in group research situations, assistants may work under the control and direction of a team leader. It may be the case that the results are published as *his* results, and any new theories may very well be ascribed to him. This is possible because of the ongoing control and authorisation of the progress of the research.

Notice in these three examples we have expanded the situation envisaged in small steps. However, a number of characteristics remain constant in them. There is the feature of the publically recognised institutional relationship existing between the *sayer* and the vehicle of the saying. Another feature of the examples is a transactional use of language between sayer and vehicle of speech which is relevant to the sayer achieving what he wants to say through the vehicle of speech. And finally, a third feature of these scenarios is that the sayer has control over what is said through the vehicle of speech. If we were going to restrict our attention to just these limited situations, our preliminary hypothesis would be this: a delegated saying event is achieved if there is some institutional relationship between sayer and vehicle of speech, if there is some element of control over what is said, and if there is some transactional use of language between sayer and vehicle relevant to what is going to be said. Such a hypothesis is not all-embracing, and important things have been left only hinted at, but it allows us to gain a foothold in this area.

3.2 Autonomy

We have been describing models of saying that do not require the involvement of the vehicle of speech (an agent) in the processes where the main bulk of what is said is determined and decided. The relationship between amanuensis and author, or the director and secretary is often formal and any involvement in the process of creating what is to be said on the part of the agent is usually minimal. Since it is apparent that the Biblical writers are often very involved in their messages, we need to consider if there are other models of delegated saying that will cater for this greater involvement. The model that suggests itself is that of the "personal assistant" (PA).

Let us outline some characteristics of the PA's functional relationship:

1. The relationship that the PA has with a director is formal, institutional and publically recognised.

2. The director has authority over all matters in his domain and any authority the PA has in that domain is purely derivative. The director remains very much in control of affairs.

3. All information, skills and judgment necessary to the affairs to be handled lie in the control of the director, and will accordingly be impressed upon the PA. Nevertheless, the PA will bring his/her own skills and knowledge to the role at the behest of the director, and indeed the director may have chosen the PA for such skills. More significantly, the PA may have been trained by the director.

4. There is a close working relationship of superior and subordinate which is cultivated over the years, and is a key reason as to why the delegated saying situations involving the PA works successfully. These situations go beyond those that involve a secretary, amanuensis, junior reporter, *and so on*, in that the PA is more involved in the saying situation, and this involvement goes back to the genesis of what is said.

5. The PA then can stand as the director in the delegated situation, for example, in the issuing of instructions, counselling, training and teaching. S/he is understood to express the will of the director.

6. As a specialized example of this relationship, we can consider a director of research and his/her team of researchers. The UK tradition is that the results of the team are published under the name of the director. Their role has been one of guidance/directing matters to bring together the published results of the team; in practical terms, overseeing the compilation and presentation of the written results. S/he may have had no direct involvement in the writing of parts of the work, but is responsible for the work because of the relationship s/he has with the team.

There is, perhaps, an obvious analogy with the PA (1)-(6) and the office of the prophet. There is a formal institutional and publically recognized relationship between the prophet and God. As a result of this, the prophet has a derived authority. For example, in Paul's letters there is the voice of authority on every page; for instance, "And so I ordain in all the churches" (1 Cor 7:17). Paul claims to be speaking the Word of God (1 Thess 2:13), standing as God to the Christians (1 Thess 4:8; cf. Acts 5:1-9 as well as his benedictions).

The Spirit of God was upon men of God, directing and controlling affairs; witness the record of Acts, where we read of the Spirit instructing the apostles. It was also present as a deposit of knowledge (1 Cor 2:7; Gal 1:12, 16-17; Eph 3:5-8; 2 Cor 13:3). Further, though there was this special revelation, the Spirit of God was providentially operative in the lives of the prophets up to the time of their calling equipping them for the work of God. Thus, we can see how Paul can be understood to be saying things on behalf of God as a man of God, since his position is similar to the position of a PA today speaking on behalf of the director of a company.

There is a "hands-on/hands-off spectrum here: the inspiration of Scripture might have been as close as a voice, a vision or dream; it may have been as distant as the confidence and foreknowledge that God has of what his prophet will say to the people.

3.3 Transactions

A providential theory of inspiration—the theory that states that inspiration is just a matter of guiding the life of the prophet—is inadequate. It is not enough to say that the writer's ways of thinking were the outcome of providence in his life. Large-scale aspects of a man's life have no causal connection with the particular words transcribed on a page. Providence, no doubt, lies in the background, but a theory of inspiration needs to account for how what is said in the Bible has been said by God.

A delegated saying relationship, like that of God-to-prophet, justifies the identity claim that the Bible is the word of God. However, as in the analogies of delegated saying situations in human society, there needs to be a transactional use of language whereby what is to be said is given or delegated. The calling or appointment of a prophet is one transaction; ongoing revelation (voices, dreams, visions) are other transactions. We should note though that the transaction that establishes the relationship of God-to-prophet is sufficient for the prophet to speak on behalf of God.

3.4 Samesaying

The relationship that the prophet has with God places both into the position of a **samesayer**. When we quote, allude to or echo what has been said by others in our own writing, we become samesayers with them; we take over an aspect of what they have said and say it in our own writing. The relationship that the prophet has to God involves the prophet saying what God has said and in this sense he is a samesayer.

However, the relationship also works the other way. God will also say some of what the prophet says in his capacity as a prophet of God. He does this because he has foreknowledge of what the prophet will say and he has a close working relationship with the prophet. Conventionally, a theory of inspiration is developed in one-way terms—how does the prophet speak on behalf of God. However, the relationship between God and the prophet is such that Scripture also records God saying what the prophet has said—being a samesayer with the prophet. This is most obviously seen in the personal aspects of the letters of Paul. It makes no sense to say God said these first and Paul then said them for God; rather, God's relationship with Paul is such that he says what Paul says in these aspects of the letter. In this way, the status of all that is written is the Word of God.

The phenomenon of samesaying can be seen in human concourse when two minds are in sync and each says what the other is thinking. The one in command in a delegated saying situation may adopt what is said by the representative because they know their spokesperson and have confidence in them. When we factor in God's foreknowledge, it is evident that he could same-say what a prophet or an apostle writes.

There should be no qualms about the personal dimension in Scripture. It is often said that this personal dimension is purely human and not part of inspiration. Although clearly the heart and mind of men are involved in, say, the Psalms, this does not mean we can separate off a human element in Scripture from a divine element. The relationship of God-to-prophet is close and God is a samesayer with the prophet just as the prophet speaks on behalf of God.

4. Human Element

Is there an *exclusively* human element in the Bible? This is often argued and to affirm this is a marker of a liberal theory of inspiration. Several aspects of the text could be said to be the human dimension (its human conditioning): style, a choice of words or phraseology, perhaps a figure of speech; content attributable to the writer's own knowledge, for example, historical facts, emotional remarks, or observations; errors of fact are usually attributed to the human dimension, *and so on*.

Unless the Biblical writers were automatons, there is a human dimension to the writing, but this is not an *exclusive* dimension. If Scripture is inspired then what has been said is attributable to both God and the prophet through whom he has spoken. Where there is a relationship between God and an individual such that the person represents God to the people, then given God's superintendence, that person speaks on behalf of God and declares his Word. The writing that results from this situation cannot have an exclusive human dimension.

In order to say something it is necessary for a person to *intend* to say something and use a language or conventional system to say that thing. Parrots do not say things, because they do not use a language nor intend to say anything, though of course they make noises. Speakers of English as a second language may intend to say one thing and say another, but provided they have used English, they have said something. If God can be described as saying what is said in the Bible, he can be described as *using that language*. This is a fundamental point that blocks a theorist identifying an exclusively human element in that language. Whatever the language contains in its use is attributable to God as well as the human writer. A key feature of delegated saying frameworks is that the delegator has control over the mode of the language use—in this case, the prophet.

For example, style is a pattern observed in the meaning of language, and as such it is a function of language use, as much as other aspects of meaning like sense or reference. If God can be said to have used the language in the Bible, the style we observe in that usage is necessarily attributable to God. To make room for an exclusively human element of style in Biblical language, it is necessary to mark it off from God's usage. This is impossible if God has said what there is in the Bible. The investment that a person has in their use of the language is an all or nothing affair. For this reason, we cannot slice apart language usage for the person or persons who have ownership of that language. It is futile to ascribe to the human writer, say, a stylistic preference for intensive action verbs and to God the use of the subject nouns and less intensive verbs. (This argument applies *mutatis mutandis* to any aspect of meaning a theorist tries to attribute exclusively to the human writer.)

The God-prophet relationship is about the use of language and the saying of something. Since there are many aspects of meaning encoded in the use of Biblical language, we would require a discriminating principle to separate off aspects that were not part of what God wanted from his representative. Later prophets commenting on or using earlier prophets do not demonstrate such a discriminating principle. Earlier material is used holistically with its inherent authority as Scripture. We don't have a principle given in the Bible that lets us pick and choose what is the Word of God.

It might be counter-argued that we do discriminate between the spokesperson and the one on behalf of whom s/he is speaking. We readily garner what is said from how it is said and we pick out aspects that are due to the spokesperson and discard them while retaining what is said. Journalists at a press conference do this for their reports. The basic observation here is that the spokesman is free and may well exercise this freedom in performing his role. The question therefore is: has God allowed prophetic spokesman freedom?

The answer to this question is that however prophecy comes about, it does not do so by the will of man (2 Pet 1:20-21), in which case the counter-argument above fails in its basic requirement for freedom of expression. What is said by the prophet therefore is what is said by God without redundancy. This does not mean that human beings did not have freedom in their expression because God superintends that freedom. He knows the possibilities of the prophet's expression; he has taught the prophet, revealed his message to the prophet, has confidence in the prophet, and from this the expression (and its writing) flows.

Let us take a worked example. Suppose someone argues that the dialogue of the three friends in Job is the expression of human thinking and not divinely inspired. Elihu spoke on God's behalf (Job 32:8, 18; 36:2-3) rather than three friends; so his criticism of the friends (Job 32:3) shows that they were not speaking on behalf of God.

This argument does not work. What is being said by God in the book of Job is set on a larger scale. The book has been crafted to represent a dialogue on the suffering of Job (and Hezekiah) and all points of view are relevant to the book as a work of art. There is nothing to be said against the view that God would be a samesayer with the author on this subject in order to bring out the lessons that are illustrated. There is plenty of false and faith-denying speech in the Bible; it has its place as God's Word. It is *part* of what God has said but not what God has said: it is, in effect, quoted by God. If what we read is inconsistent with the character of God, then necessarily it is not what he himself is saying.

5. Verbal Inspiration

What does the phrase "verbal inspiration" mean? What is a theory of verbal inspiration? Obviously, it is not just about verbs, but rather words. Is it realistic to advocate such a view? The alternative is to affirm something abstract like ideas or thoughts are the locus of inspiration and not words. The problem with this proposal is that it is logically incoherent.

What, for example, do scholars mean when they use such words as 'concept', 'idea', or 'thought', as the locus of inspiration? More often than not, views on inspiration are stated that lack any consideration of such questions. As a result, false claims are made that fly in the face of received theories in logic and linguistics.

To take an example, is it coherent to separate language and thought? Many views on inspiration suppose that language is but the clothing of thought and as such of no great importance. Thus it is held that whilst God has inspired certain thoughts (ideas) in the Prophets, he has not restricted the way in which they expressed these thoughts. Such a view as this is inconsistent with certain logical principles.

Frege claimed that a thought was the sense of sentence;[1] M. A. E. Dummett comments on this that, "A sentence is a linguistic unit: it is the smallest bit of language which one can use to say anything...A word, regarded from a different viewpoint, is another kind of linguistic unit: it is the smallest bit of language to which one can attribute a sense".[2] In short we say what we think! Taking this claim with another doctrine of Frege's, namely, that the sense of a word consists in the contribution it makes to a sentence, it follows that if the Bible is what God has said, the words are an integral part to this saying. Any doctrine of inspiration, which trades on the notion of saying, must therefore be a 'verbal' view of inspiration—that God used the vary words of Scripture to say what he wanted to say.

---

[1] G. Frege, "The Thought: A Logical Enquiry" in *Philosophical Logic* (ed. P. F. Strawson; Oxford: Oxford University Press, 1967), 17-38. This is the classic statement.
[2] M. A. E. Dummett, *Frege: Philosophy of Language* (London: Duckworth, 1973), 34.

Inspiration is often defined as the mechanism through which God authored the Scriptures; the mechanism that gave the Scriptures their divine quality. It is often defined in relation to the mind of the prophet or Biblical writer. We have seen that this is too narrow a view. The Scriptures are God-breathed (2 Tim 3:16), but this is a metaphor to describe how they are what God has said, as it were, with his mouth.

Inspiration pertains to Scripture but "revelation" is a broader concept. God reveals himself in and through acts, one of which includes inspiration. Given that God is omniscient and omnipotent, it follows that if Scripture is what God has said, it is inerrant. We could avoid this conclusion if we identified in the Scriptures elements of meaning that were purely human and fallible.

It is important to define inerrancy. If Rabshakeh asserts that "God is like the gods of the nations" and this is recorded in Kings, God is not saying this; he is saying "Rabshakeh asserts that God is like the gods of the nations". Rabshakeh is in error, but the report and what God has said through his prophet is true as a matter of history. Saying is an intentional action and in reading Scripture we need to identify *what* God has said in its use of language before we cast around an accusation like the Bible is full of myth, folktale, legend and error. Bible writings show God engaging such things and so they are presented in the Bible.

Inerrancy is about what is said in sentences, since sentences are the smallest unit with something can be said. Truth and falsity, as predicates, attach to used sentences. Words contribute to the sense of sentences, and so verbal inspiration is part of what makes for inerrant Scripture. The inerrant nature of Scripture follows from the proposition that Scripture is what God has *said* and God is omniscient, omnipotent and good.

The critical notion for inspiration is that of *saying*. It can be used in a criterion of identity for the Bible: For all x, x is Biblical, if and only if x is what the God of Israel has said. Inspiration is about describing how God can be a samesayer with humans in the writing that we have in the Bible. Ideas of "verbal" inspiration and "inerrancy" are logically implicit in the notion that God has said things with and through delegated representatives. Conceptually, the theory of inspiration is not difficult.

6. Biblical Books
Having set down some preliminary ideas about what it is to say something and in particular what it is to say something through another, we need to

65

examine the Biblical material. The theory of inspiration is obviously a linguistic hypothesis insofar as we are modelling divine use of language, and subject to confirmation and disconfirmation in the Bible. What I will need to do is take representative books of the Bible and describe how these can be the words of God.

6.1 Evidence

Is the data (the Bible) consistent with an attribution of divine inspiration? One line of evidence, traditionally defended, is about the quality of the writing: it is free from contradiction, factual error; it is intricate and subtle in its literary design; and it is spiritually satisfying. For reasons such as these, it is said that the Bible requires the explanation that it was divinely inspired. This line of argument is not our focus in this essay.

A second line of argument is the authority of Jesus. He said that the Scripture could not be "broken" (John 10:35) and the compass of Scripture for him was from Abel to Zacharias (Matt 23:35), which is the Hebrew order of books from Genesis to Chronicles. If we accept the authority of Jesus, then the OT as we have it was divinely inspired. This is a conclusive argument for Christians and it needs only to be stated in this summary fashion.

To support this second line of evidence with regard to the NT, it is further argued that the bestowal of the Spirit in the church ensured that any of their writings (e.g. apostolic ones) could be regarded in the same light as the Old Testament. That some writings were so regarded is shown by the way that they came to be preserved in the early church. We could reject this witness, but it dates to the early second century.

If we do not accept the witness of the early church for a canon of NT writings, we can accept writings on internal grounds. They have a quality that requires the explanation that they are inspired. It is evident that the historical writings in the NT (Gospels, Acts) continue the story of Israel in the OT and continue it is such a way as to be regarded as a Scriptural record. (We will examine this argument further in a separate essay in this book.)

Similarly, with the letters of Paul or Revelation, we could accept them as inspired on the basis of their quality. They have a dense intertextual weave with the OT writings in terms of their quotations, allusions and echoes.

6.2 The Prophets

Much prophecy is direct communication from God to and through the prophet. Take Jeremiah as a representative example: God commissions him as a prophet; commands him to speak for him; and puts words in his mouth (Jer 1:9; cf. Ezek 2:2, 8-10; 3:1; Isa 6:8-9). Thus throughout Jeremiah we have phrases such as "Hear ye...for the Lord hath spoken (Jer 13:4), which introduce oracles of God. Throughout all the Prophets such phrases re-occur, and when they are absent, we have the witness of the form of speech itself which is an oracle. This phraseology and the oracles themselves reflect the reality that the prophet is representing God to the people and speaking on his behalf. God is achieving the saying of something to king and people in virtue of the relationship he has with his prophet. Crucially this relationship is a matter of public knowledge. The written superscription of the prophetic book confirms the identity of the prophet and his status.

The Spirit has authorised and commissioned the prophet; the prophet has been providentially brought to the people; the prophet is in a publically recognized relationship with God; consequently, both he and God are samesayers in presenting the will of God. Visions or dreams may have engendered the message; the prophet's own reflections on earlier prophetic writings (or the Law) may be the source of his teaching; his message may arise out of his observation of the king and his people. In any of these cases, the relationship that he has with God and the confidence placed in him as a spokesman ensures that what he says is divinely inspired—his life is carried along by the Spirit (2 Pet 1:20-21).

Much of the prophetic material is not oracle or vision. There are dialogues between God and man, prayers of the prophets, intercessions, praise, lamentations, interlocutory remarks, and expressions of feeling. We have changes of speaker, records of what others have said; sometimes God speaks in the first person for himself; sometimes the prophet speaks in the first person. What we have is material that reflects the reality of the prophet's situation. Sometimes the word is directly attributed to the Lord; many other times the prophet is speaking on his authority. In this latter case, God is a samesayer with the prophet; in the first case, the prophet is a samesayer with God—presenting his very words.

6.3 The History Books

The authorship of the history books is unknown; they lack the familiar superscriptions of the Prophets. The history books could have been compiled over time by prophets and/or scribes and editors. They begin with Joshua (grouping Genesis-Exodus with the Law). Some notes of authorship are given: Joshua is the author of the book that bears his name (Josh 24:26). The book was added to the "book of the Law of God", which suggests the existence and use of the Law of Moses. In Kings and Chronicles there are notes of prophetic authorship such as Samuel the Seer, Nathan the prophet or Gad the seer (1 Chron 29:29; cf. Iddo and Ahijah—2 Chron 9:29). The history that these men wrote varied in size, but Nathan, for instance, begins his ministry in 1 Samuel 7 and continues until Solomon, so his history could have been substantial. Another example would be Isaiah who wrote part of Kings; hence, 2 Chron 32:32 ascribes to him a record of the acts of Hezekiah. It would seem then that prophets were partly responsible for the history books, even if they are unnamed (cf. 1 Kgs 12:22; 1 Chron 17:3).

Anonymous scribes and editors are often inferred to be behind the Scriptural text. For example, in the report of Moses' death or the last chapter of Joshua; or perhaps in giving explanatory notes to do with geography. The history books are said to include source material of varying age and provenance; this is evident in Genesis. In the case of hypothetical scribes and editors, or in the case of Moses as a compiler of Genesis traditions (or the scribes working with him), inspiration is not a matter of an activity of the Spirit upon the mind, but of the framework in which the authoritative text is produced: it is a matter of the prophet supervising the work and the adoption of the work as Scripture. The work of the Spirit here has more to do with the circumstances and life of those who are involved later in the process (as in the analogy of the director of research). In logical terms, God is saying what *has been* produced—he has become a *samesayer* with the original author of the material.

For example, if we ask how it is that God could be understood as saying what we have in Genesis, then it is sufficient to postulate that Moses was directed to collect and compile records, and/or alter scribes edited Genesis under the direction of a prophet or within a framework of preserving the authority of what was written.

6.3.1 The Pentateuch
While scholars do not think that the Pentateuch is the work of Moses, the consistent witness of Second Temple Judaism and the NT is that Moses is behind the first five books as a collection. There are indications of writing in the books. In Exod 17:14 there is a command of God to write up the Amalekite victory; in fact, there are a number of references to 'war' books (e.g. Num 21:14). In Exod 24:3-7 we have a record of Moses writing

down the covenant; in Lev 24:46 we have a note to the effect that the Lord made statutes, judgments and laws between himself and Israel *by the hand* of Moses; and Leviticus has an end title which gives author, date and content of writing (Lev 27:34). The book of Numbers has a similar end title specifying the hand of Moses (Num 36:13). Further, Deuteronomy picks up on this ending and places Moses in the plains of Moab and reciting the Law to the people. Ending this oral delivery, Deut 27:1 records Moses exhorting the people to keep the commandments he has recited (Deut 29:1), the substance of which was written down (Deut 31:9, 24).

There is then internal evidence for the authorship of the Pentateuch by Moses; he was a prophet (Deut 18:15; Num 11:24-25), commissioned by God to speak on his behalf (Exod 4:10; cf. v. 30), and this he did orally and through writing. The inspiration of the first five books is relatively straightforward to understand. On many occasions God spoke directly to Moses through angelic mediation, the Angel of the Presence (Isa 63:9). The conversational records are given in the oft-repeated phrase "The Lord spake unto Moses, saying". As a prophet God may have been a samesayer with Moses in some of what was said and written, particularly the history. With Deuteronomy being a long oration, it could be that the Spirit was at work with Moses' faculties on this occasion. However, over-riding anything we might want to say regarding the work of the Spirit, Moses was a man of God and this recognition means that God was working with him in a relationship of samesaying.

6.3.2 Genesis
Genesis is punctuated by the lines translated in the KJV "These are the generations of", but in other versions along the lines of "history-origins" (Gen 2:4; 5:1; 6:9; 10:1, 32; 11:10, 27; 25:12, 13, 19; 36:1, 9; 37:2). These lines are not always attached to genealogies, but rather historical accounts. Hence, the lines are thought to be indicative of records, whether genealogical or historical.

In Genesis we have a number of historical records that have been brought together; for instance, the records of Adam are called a "book" (Gen 5:1). The records are connected with the chief figures in the narrative in hand, figures like Noah, Shem, Terah, Ishmael, Isaac, Esau and Jacob. Paul remarks that the middle chapters of Genesis were written for Abraham's sake, perhaps as the text indicates, by his sons Ishmael and Issac (Rom 4:23). Such a collection of records was brought together by Moses as the prolegomena to his own history and the Law. The work of editorial compilation is seen in such editorial notes relating to changed place names (e.g. Gen 14:2). With regard to the question of the inspiration of Genesis, we could say that the original records (the tablets) were inspired as each family patriarch had it written; on the other hand, equally, their authority as the Word of God may stem from Moses' collection and validation. On this latter supposition, God is a retrospective samesayer through Moses of the Genesis records.

6.3.3 The Gospel of Luke
Another example of editorial historical work is the Gospel of Luke, but for Luke the work seems to have been with the spirit-activated remembrances of the Christian prophets (John 14:26).

> Forasmuch as many have taken in hand to set forth in order a declaration of those things which are most surely believed among us, Even as they delivered them unto us, which from the beginning were eyewitnesses, and ministers of the word; It seemed good to me also, having had perfect understanding of all things from the very first, to write unto thee in order, most excellent Theophilus, That thou mightest know the certainty of those things, wherein thou hast been instructed. Luke 1:1-4 (KJV)

This statement (a classic historical prologue) gives some idea of the scope of superintendence involved in the inspiration of the Gospel of Luke. It involves historical research on the part of Luke, interviewing witnesses, gathering sources and writing up the order of the narrative.

6.4 The Writings
The personal involvement of the writer in what is being written is seen in the third division of the Hebrew Canon—the Writings. Psalms and the book of Job illustrate writing that comes from the depths of the human psyche. Is such writing inspired? What is the model of inspiration?

The personal writing that we have in the Bible is "spiritual". In the case of the Psalms of David, he attributed his writing to the Spirit (1 Chron 25:1; 2 Sam 23:1-2), so possession of the Spirit is not incompatible with spiritual writing that comes from human experience. Here again, the critical factor is the relationship that God has with the psalmist or with the author of Job. Whether the Spirit engenders thoughts, ideas or words in the life and thinking of the man of God, the words that he writes can

70

be equally said by God if he chooses them for an authoritative record of spiritual thinking. It is not necessary therefore to exclude the imprecatory psalms from those writings that are said to be inspired, provided it is understood that there have been selected in the providence of God for his Word to teach spiritual truths about imprecation.

7. Proof
Can the inspiration of the Bible be proved? Can the self-testimony of the Bible function in a proof of inspiration? The problem here is that some would argue that, "The Bible would say that it's inspired about itself wouldn't it—we need an external proof".

The request here is for something compelling outside of the Bible. The quality of the Bible in itself is not enough for the person who puts forward these questions; they are in a state of doubt. One external witness would be the resurrection of Jesus since Jesus' attitude to Jewish Scripture was that it could not be broken. Similarly, his miracles are an external witness to the inspiration of the Old Testament.

Extraordinary happenings in history are a kind of external witness to the Bible. Another line of argument is the fulfilment of prophecy: if Scripture contains prophecy and what is prophesied comes to pass, then this is an external validation of the inspiration of the text. The premise here is that prophecy is not humanly possible. The Bible contains both short range prophecy (up to forty years for fulfilment) and long range prophecy (hundreds of years) that has been fulfilled as a matter of historical record.

Of course, a sceptic might say that such "prophecy" was written after the event and is suitably vague as to admit any interpretation that fits the facts. However, this is not a relevant objection to whether there can be external proof of the Bible: the proof of the Bible is the external witness of history if that witness exists. Schematically, the proof has three premises:

> P1: Prophecy is not humanly possible
> P2: Prophetic statement
> P3: Historical witness

> Conclusion: The writing containing P2 is inspired

71

Any proof is challenged in its premises through rejection, and so a sceptic can reject P2 on the grounds of vagueness or because it is not prophetic. However, if P2 meets these objections, the proof works.

There is a transfer of credibility from the prophetic proof to the non-prophetic writings of a prophet. Thus, the fulfilled prophecy in the book of Revelation validates the credentials of the apostle John as a prophet for his other writings (gospel and letters). Again, the point here is not that a Bible critic will not challenge whether John is the author of all these texts; rather, it is a statement of one reason why we can accept the inspiration of all "his" writings when prophecy is only part of them.

The transfer of credibility from the prophetic to the non-prophetic is why we can accept all of the Prophets as inspired. The fulfilment of their prophecies makes the whole of their writings inspired. So, for example, the fulfilment of Moses' prophecies about Israel, imparts credibility to his writings as those of an inspired prophet.

Jesus' miracles, his resurrection or prophecy are examples of external witness to those who are acting as agents for God and this validates their words. Miracles in the OT record perform the same validating role for the prophet or servant of God.

More broadly, the historical witness to the Jewish Scriptures (P3) is Israel. They are declared to be witnesses to their God (Isa 43:10), and they function as witnesses to their Scriptures because they have been dispersed throughout the world and brought back to their homeland. This history is the subject of prophecies as early as Moses, and as late as those of Jesus (gospels) and John (Revelation).

8. Conclusion

We have argued that the Bible is the verbally inspired and inerrant Word of God. We have used the notion of samesaying to explain how the Bible can be language used by God when written by human beings. We explained that the most important feature that makes inspiration work is a relationship of delegation between God and those who are his prophets and writers. Over and above this there are various ways that God has brought about his Word through his agents. We can accept the human dimension of the Scriptures, but there is no *exclusive* human dimension, because God has said what has been said in the Bible.

72

CHAPTER SIX
Exegetical Considerations relating to Inspiration

1. Introduction[1]

There are three main NT texts that relate to the topic of "inspiration". This means that there is relatively little to work with in developing a doctrine of inspiration. Instead, the inspiration of Scripture should also be seen as a logical consequence of the bestowal of the Spirit in Biblical times. Hence, we should also include those texts that give information about God speaking through prophets and his commands to write down what he has communicated in setting out this doctrine. In this essay, we consider the three main NT texts.

2. 2 Timothy 3:16

> All scripture is given by inspiration of God, and is profitable for doctrine, for reproof, for correction, for instruction in righteousness: 2 Tim 3:16 (KJV)

The concept of inspiration is a **literary concept** insofar as it is 'Scripture' or 'the Writings' (γραφὴ) that are said to be inspired or God-spirited (2 Tim 3:16). Being God-spirited is a property of what Paul terms 'the writings'. Furthermore, it is *all* the writings that are said to be God-spirited. A translation of the Greek which suggests that all the writings might not be inspired is generally thought to be implausible. The Greek clause and the two renderings in question are these:

πᾶσα γραφὴ θεόπνευστος καὶ ὠφέλιμος

All scripture (is) God-spirited and profitable...

Every inspired scripture (is) also profitable... (RSV mg.)

The regular way of construing this construction would be to treat it as a noun/complement structure with two adjectives in the predicative

---

[1] This is an essay has the same provenance as the previous one.

position conjoined by καὶ (and). The alternative way of understanding this construction makes the first adjective's use attributive and takes the noun/complement structure to exist between γραφη so qualified, and ὠφέλιμος. However, this interpretation requires taking καὶ to mean 'also', and this is a comparatively rare usage. Moreover, where this usage is intended, it is quite evidently required by the context of its occurrence. Consequently, it can be stated with a fair degree of certainty that, as there are no contextual factors requiring construing καὶ as 'also', such a use is not intended.

All scripture then is God-spirited, or idiomatically, the whole of scripture is inspired. What does this mean? Any answer to this question labours under the difficulty that there is a lack of information surrounding the nature of inspiration. However, this constraint only requires that we be careful in formulating what we have to say. First, it is necessary to identify what Paul would have taken to be the Scriptures. In making this identification, we may proceed along a number of routes.

1. Paul was a Jew and a student of the Jewish sacred writings. He had undergone the usual academic theological training of his day, and there is evidence that he was a zealot for Judaism. It is reasonable to suppose therefore that he took the Scriptures to be those authoritative Jewish writings regarded as having been written by the prophets. For example, in Rom 16:26 Paul refers to the 'holy' Scriptures of the prophets, a phrase which Matthew also uses (Matt 26:56). Indeed, it seems clear that 'the Prophets' constituted an authoritative body of writings in the early church (cf. Luke 24:27).

2. We can identify what Paul took to be the Scriptures by examining the use he makes of quotations. Thus, we find that he quotes from Deuteronomy (1 Tim 5:18), Genesis (Gal 4:30; Rom 4:3), Isaiah (Rom 11:2) and Exodus (Rom 9:17). This procedure doesn't give us all the writings of the OT; however, it does direct our attention to a certain corpus of writings—those writings held as authoritative among the Jews.

3. We need to employ a further line of argument to identify what Paul took to be the Scriptures. In Rom 15:4, Paul states that "whatsoever things were written aforetime were written for our learning, that we, through patience and comfort of the Scriptures might have hope". Such things that were so written are then what Paul takes to be the Scriptures, or the Writings. To identify what Paul takes to be this corpus, we need only examine his use of the familiar locution: 'It is written', and similar

derivatives. Such an enquiry reveals a large portion of the writings of the Old Testament.

4. A further line of argument to establish what Paul took to be the Scriptures can be developed from an enumeration of Paul's use of written material. This is overwhelmingly the OT, as might be expected, but the important point is that this usage manifests a desire to expound and teach certain religious doctrines about Jesus Christ from the Old Testament. Further, such usage illustrates the inculcation of moral principles in disciplinary contexts. These features of Paul's use of this written material are precisely those which he extols in relation to Scripture in 2 Tim 3:16.

In the light of (1)-(4), the question arises that whilst Paul took the Scriptures to be the OT, what did he understand by the **concept** of Scripture? Remember that 2 Timothy is not a theological treatise, but a pastoral letter. Related to this issue there is the problem of whether Paul would have regarded the NT as Scripture. Certainly, Peter viewed Paul's letters as Scripture (2 Pet 3:16); and Paul himself quotes Luke as Scripture (1 Tim 5:18). But what can we point to apart from these explicit remarks in solving this question?

An important preliminary issue is this: Someone might claim that 2 Tim 3:16 only encompasses the OT at most, since these were the only recognised Scriptures of the day. Such an argument would be premature; the logical construction of Paul's statement in 2 Timothy allows for the NT writings to satisfy the quantifier 'all'. Logically, the statement means that 'for all x, if x is Scripture, then x is inspired', and the variable ranges over all objects. Thus, if the NT writings are Scripture, they will be inspired. Observe here that there is no temporal restriction upon the range of the quantifier. Paul does not use the past tense; he does not say that all Scripture *was* inspired. The construction is assumed to be in the present tense. Accordingly, part of the book of Luke is inspired Scripture and, for Peter, all of Paul's letters are inspired Scripture.

Would Paul have regarded the NT letters and Gospels as Scripture? To answer this question, let us look at the phenomenon of **being inspired**. Here, I have no suggestion to make except that this implies that such writings as are inspired are thereby said to have come out of God. The connection is made in the Old Testament.

75

> By the word of the Lord were the heavens made; and all
> the host of them by the breath of his mouth...he spake
> and it was done. (Ps 33:6, 9; cf. Heb 11:2)

This text establishes a connection between God saying something and the spirit of God's mouth—his breath. This connection has its parallel in mankind in that men and women use breath (among other things) to speak and be sayers. The text supposes the situation to be the same with God as it is with men (we can place the issue of anthropomorphism to one side). In the light of this text, the claim that there is something that has been said, and that moreover that this is 'God-breathed' is the claim it has been said *by God.*

By way of contrast, if we posited that a mountain was God-breathed, we would not be saying that the mountain was something said by God. "God spoke and it was done" is a causal hypothesis about the origin of the mountain, but the mountain is not a sayable entity. However, it is because Scripture is by its very nature *something said* that to claim it is God-breathed is to claim it is said by God.

The point being made here is that while the concept of the Spirit of God is multi-faceted, an important strand is being picked up in 2 Timothy. This thread which Paul focuses upon is that feature of the Spirit of God which is identified with the breath of God's mouth and what he says with this breath. It is as if Paul is homing in on this aspect of the Spirit of God because he wants to make a point about something (written material) that has been said, connecting this written material to God. Seeing how what God has said is explicitly connected to his breath or spirit, Paul goes onto make this same connection in respect of Scripture. Paul is not saying that **men** were inspired to write down what God uttered to them or delivered to them in dreams. He isn't offering a suggestion on the mechanism of inspiration in relation to men. He is merely playing on the use of breath to say things in order to connect God and Scripture.

3. Hebrews 1:1-2b

> God who at sundry times and in divers manners <u>spake</u> in
> time past unto the fathers by the prophets hath in these
> last days spoken unto us by a son... Heb 1:1-2b

The first thing to observe about this statement is the claim that God can speak. The Greek verb (λαλέω) used here is the ordinary Greek verb

76

denoting a speech act. Here, it is important to distinguish saying something and speaking. We might employ any number of means to say something, but speaking is only one of these means, even if it is the most prevalent means employed. In what way can we understand God as speaking? With Moses it is said that God spoke face to face and not in dreams and visions as with other prophets (Num 12:6-8). One way in which God spoke was through angelic mediators (Acts7:38, 44). Their voices were understood as the voice of God. Note that it says that God spoke in different ways *to* the fathers. It does not say he spoke in different ways to *the prophets*, it says he spoke *by* the prophets.

This implies that for God it is possible to speak to others even though this involves an intermediary. Men and women say things in a variety of ways through other people, and it is not the intermediaries that are understood to be 'speaking'. We say that, for example, a presidential spokesman speaks for the President, and we look upon him *as if* the President is speaking. We can maintain a distinction between the spokesman and the one who stands behind him. Consequently, we tend to talk of what the President has said through his spokesman. With God and the prophets, this distinction collapses: God is the one who speaks when a prophet speaks:

> ...God hath spoken by the mouth of all his holy prophets since the world began. Acts 3:21

> ...well spake the Holy Spirit by Isaiah the prophet unto our fathers. Acts 28:25

> Take, my brethren, the prophets, who have spoken in the name of the Lord..." Jms 5:10; cf. Luke 1:55; Acts 4:29; 7:6)

God spoke to the fathers in a variety of ways by the prophets. What could this variety referred to by Paul indicate? There is a contrast in the verse between the employment of prophets and the fact that God had spoken in those last days by a Son. But we cannot be more specific in identifying what this variety might indicate, other than by saying that it points to a variety in the **context and import** of the speech act in which the prophet is involved.

We can describe speech acts from different perspectives, and see different kinds of variety in such phenomena. Accordingly, we could classify speech acts as acts of promising, describing, commanding, telling, stating, cajoling, *and so on*. Such a variety of acts exist in the OT records, and we can describe God as using such a variety in the communication of what he has to say to the leaders of Israel. However, we can also gather that visions, dreams, the placing of words on the lips of men, angelic contact, and unseen voices are ways in which God communicated with the prophets. These men of God then went on to communicate what they had received to the leaders of the nation and the people themselves. They uttered oracles, judgements, communicated promises and warnings, *and so on*. It would be premature to exclude any of these kinds of variety from the picture been drawn by Heb 1:1-2. God spoke in a variety of ways to the fathers, as he saw fit. Sometimes it was warning, sometimes it was encouragement, sometimes a dream was involved, and sometimes words were given to the prophet *as he spoke*.

A lot of the Bible is plain narrative, but much of the Prophets consists of records of speech. The whole character of the writing is such that it appears as dialogue and conversation. As an example, take Isaiah 2-4. With this passage it is easy to see a picture of Isaiah delivering the oracle in a market place. It is a fact that the prophets were commissioned to take the prophetic message to the people. Amos is an example of a market place prophet. (Amos 7:14-15; cf. Isaiah 6).

A prophet would have had disciples (e.g. Isaiah). It is not hard to see that these disciples may very well have helped in the delivery of the message. Indeed, the conversational structure of much of the book of Isaiah suggests this possibility. When we look at the Prophets it is not hard to see that there is often a constant shifting around of a restricted number of themes. Moreover, there is a flux in the manner of presenting these themes, so that in one instance, it might be the prophet addressing the people with warning, in another instance with a plea, in another instance with a story, *and so on*. Furthermore, these shifts are often accompanied by changes in pronouns, so that it appears that either God, or the Prophet, or a spokesman for the people, or a narrator, or a disciple appear to be speaking. It is not difficult to appreciate therefore that these changes reflect a conversational context of origin, so that what we have in parts of the Prophets are records of dialogues delivered by the prophet and others to the people under the superintendence of the Spirit.

Ostensibly, Heb 1:1-2b has nothing to do with the topic of inspiration and the writings known as the Hebrew Scriptures. However, the result of inspiration is that something *has been said in writing*, and the context in

78

which this comes about is what interests us in the topic of inspiration. This context is often one where there is spoken communication between God and the leaders of Israel. If we can understand how it is possible for God to speak to the fathers, we will be making some progress towards seeing how the 'Scriptures' could be words of God. We will find that we can go some way towards describing inspiration to that extent to which we understand *what it is to say something*. But it is essential to bear in mind that, as with men and women, there are a variety of ways in which they say things, so too with God there might also be a corresponding variety with his speech acts. The implication of this point is that the Bible will be understood to have been written from a variety of speech acts. Our description of these will constitute our account of inspiration.

4. 2 Peter 1:20-21

> Knowing this first, that no prophecy of the scripture is of any private interpretation. For the prophecy came (φέρω) not in old time by the will of man: but holy men of God spake as they were <u>moved</u> (φέρω) by the Holy Spirit. 2 Pet 1:20 (KJV)

This passage is interesting, and I want to note two points:

1. It is prophecies that are said not to come by the will of men. Such prophecies 'come' by holy men speaking as they were 'moved' (KJV, φέρω) by the Holy Spirit. The contrast in this verse is between the will of man—by which prophecy is not brought (φέρω); it does not 'come' by man's will—but prophecy comes or is brought by the Holy Spirit.

The Greek participle of φέρω (φερόμενοι) translated 'move' in the KJV is a fairly ordinary word occurring several times in the context of 2 Peter 1 and elsewhere in the New Testament. The overwhelming use of the word conveys the sense of the **bringing of something** and therefore the **carrying of something** to someone (Acts 4:34, 37; 5:2; 2 Tim 4:13; 2 John v. 10; Rev 21:24, 26). It is easy to see how such a use can also be associated with the idea of "bearing" a load (Heb 12:20), and also the sense of something coming to individuals (Acts 2:2). Accordingly, in earlier verses of this passage, Peter describes a voice as being "brought" to Christ "by the magnificent glory" (v. 17), "carried" to him from heaven (v. 18). In this context Peter goes onto contrast the more sure word of prophecy. This is not "brought" by the will of men; it is spoken from God by men—"brought" by the Holy Spirit. The point being made by

79

Peter here is probably that presupposed by Stephen in his defence when he says,

> ...ye do always resist the Holy Spirit...Which of the prophets have not your fathers persecuted... Acts 7:51 (KJV)

This passage raises the question as to whether all Scripture is to be understood as "prophecy", and also what it means to say that Holy men of old were **carried** or **brought** by the Holy Spirit. Is Peter referring to the Prophets strictly understood, or does he mean to refer to the Law and the Writings as well? Should we understand the word "carried/brought" as indicating a direct operation of the Holy Spirit upon the mind of the prophet—a state of ecstasy, or an impulse and drive in the prophet; or do we take "carried/brought" in the sense of being "carried/brought to" by the Spirit?

The contrast of the verse is between the will of man and the will of the Spirit. Whilst it is conventional to interpret the verse as referring to a direct operation of the Spirit upon the mind of the prophet, in fact the verb "to carry/to bring" allows a broader view of the prophet being carried/brought to the people by the Spirit in its work among the people.

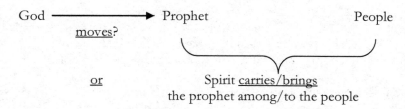

Inspiration is traditionally seen as the activity of God's Spirit upon the mind of the prophet (or writer), guiding the thoughts and controlling the words being used by the prophet. The text in 2 Peter is the principal supporting passage, but its verb "to carry/bring" is broader than this traditional reading. Without excluding the operation of the Spirit directly upon the mind of the prophet or in engendering his experience, as and when, we should also see the Spirit carrying/bringing the prophet to the people.

5. Conclusion

Inspiration pertains to the writing that is the Bible. A doctrine of inspiration is about how we relate God to what is written. We can do this with the notion of **saying**: the Bible is the Word of God or *what God has said* to people. In 2 Timothy we have the apostolic view that Scripture is spoken or God-breathed, and a publically recognized framework of delegated speaking in which a prophet speaks on behalf of God achieves this outcome. In Hebrews, there is again an emphasis upon God speaking through prophets; in 2 Peter, the Spirit is involved in the description of their speaking telling us that prophets were carried/brought to the people by the Spirit.

CHAPTER SEVEN
Luke as Scripture

1. Introduction[1]

This essay is a single argument towards establishing that Luke-Acts is a work of Jewish Scripture. The conclusion is that this two-volume work was intended by Luke to be a work of Scripture and that in this he was inspired to produce the two books. Rather than write a defence of the whole New Testament as Scripture, we have chosen one example as a case study.

While it is straightforward to establish the Hebrew Bible as inspired Scripture on the basis of the authority of Jesus and the apostles, it is less straightforward to show that the books of the New Testament are also Scripture. There are two parts to this exercise: first we must show that the author of a New Testament book intended his writing to be **part of Jewish Scripture**; secondly, we must show that such writing took place during a period of the bestowal of the Spirit.

This is as much as can be done in a positive manner. The conviction that any book of the New Testament is a work of Jewish Scripture is grounded in reading and appreciation of the book rather than in an intellectual exercise. However, sceptical people are not in this position and so the intellectual exercise in this essay is an honest attempt to engage with the sceptical mind.

The conclusion of the essay and its reasoning is conservative in its treatment of Luke-Acts. Furthermore, it is not a full-length discussion of Luke-Acts; it is a rather narrow and uncontroversial summary and presentation of the view that the genre of Luke-Acts is "Jewish Scripture". Others have made the same argument and there is no pretence to originality in any of what follows. It is designed to be a convenient summary, nothing more.

---

[1] The essay, part of a wider dissertation on Luke-Acts, not previously published, was written in 2006; thanks go to K. Rowe for his help on the research.

2. Literary Questions

The question as to what kind of writing we have in Luke-Acts is one of genre. The question presumes that it is appropriate to discuss the question of genre in respect of Luke-Acts as opposed to Luke and Acts. Scholars have argued that Luke and Acts are different genres, but of itself this does not exclude an assignment of genre to Luke-Acts as a whole when they are considered as two parts of one work.[1] Given that Luke-Acts is made up of Luke and Acts (*sic*), we can obviously discuss the genre of each, viewed separately. Nevertheless, in order to retain a narrow focus for our question, we presume the unity of Luke-Acts[2] as a two-volume work. Luke-Acts can be considered to be a *retrospective* two-volume work if it is judged that Luke did not prospectively entertain a two volume production when beginning his gospel.

A. Fowler[3] shows that genre pertains to the sociology of reading and writing and is a term for sets of conventions that govern the production and reading of texts. It is a term of intertextual classification for patterns of similarity and dissimilarity that are recognised by authors and audiences. Recognition of a genre can control the reading experience as well as the writer. R. Burridge states that genre,

> ...is widely acknowledged as one of the key conventions guiding both the composition and the interpretation of writings. Genre forms a kind of 'contract' or agreement, often unspoken or unwritten, or even unconscious, between the author and a reader, by which the author sets out to write according to a whole set of expectations and conventions, and we agree to read or to interpret the work using the same conventions, giving us an initial idea of what we might expect to find.[4]

---

[1] See I. H. Marshall, "Acts and the Former Treatise" in *The Book of Acts in its Ancient Literary Setting* (eds., B. W. Winter & A. D. Clarke; Grand Rapids: Eerdmans, 1993, 163-182 (178).

[2] Following many studies, we presume a unified author for Luke-Acts as a two-part work, for example, see R. Maddox, *The Purpose of Luke-Acts* (Edinburgh: T & T Clark, 1982), chap. 1.

[3] A. Fowler, *Kinds of Literature: An Introduction to the Theory of Genres and Modes* (Oxford: Oxford University Press, 1982), 20-24. See also J. Culler, *Literary Theory: A Very Short Introduction* (Oxford: Oxford University Press, 1997), 72-73.

[4] R. Burridge, *Four Gospels, One Jesus?* (London: SPCK, 1994), 5.

However, such is the creative process that genre need not constrain the communicative process. A text may be part of one or more genres, and it may also expand the boundaries of its genre(s). The task of analysis is to give a satisfactory account of how a text participates in any assigned genre.

The literary co-text for analysing the genre of Luke-Acts comprises the literature available to Luke. Our task is therefore to consider the affinities of Luke-Acts. The principal proposal is that Luke-Acts is a history, and the main choice is between Hellenistic and Jewish historiography. Is this two-volume production a typical Hellenistic history, or does it have particular characteristics that confine recognition of its genre to a narrower social group? Jewish historiography can be further divided into two sub-species: non-Scriptural and Scriptural. Does Luke-Acts require an audience versed in Jewish Scriptural traditions and is its genre to be related to those writings? Or is Luke-Acts comparable to Jewish Hellenistic authors like Josephus? These are not modern questions as,

> ...[a]n awareness of genre and its conventions was widespread in the ancient world through elementary schooling, particular in its use of rhetorical exercises and moralistic stories of the heroes.[1]

The three options are not necessarily competing alternatives; Luke-Acts may participate in all three genres. Indeed, Luke-Acts may participate in genres other than historical ones. A discussion of historical genre is therefore an appropriate platform from which to discuss other genre classifications. Whether Luke-Acts is judged to be multi-generic, or a species of history-writing, the real value in this exercise is that genre discussion identifies usable reading strategies.

These three options correspond to three kinds of argument in genre discussion. Assignment of genre can proceed on the basis of *literary forms*, common aspects of *content*, or the intended (or actual) *use* of a piece of writing. Scholars tend to assign a genre of "Hellenistic historiography" on the basis of Luke's literary technique; an assignment of "Jewish Hellenistic historiography" usually accepts this verdict, but argues that the content of Luke-Acts makes it a "Jewish Hellenistic History". Over against these two options, the argument for classifying Luke-Acts as a "Scriptural" writing is

---

[1] R. Burridge, *What are the Gospels?* (Cambridge: Cambridge University Press, 1992), 69.

based on the consideration that Luke's intended *use* of the work is as a continuation of Jewish Scriptural history. Our presentation of the issues follows this progression of argument and concludes that in terms of genre assignment, considerations of **use** outweigh arguments based on form or content, because usage is more closely tied to the sociology of reading. Hence, our argument is that Luke-Acts was intended to be used as an addition to Jewish Scriptural history.

3. Jewish Historiography

Is Luke-Acts a work of "Jewish Historiography"? There is an obvious difference of subject-matter, but the principal source of doubt lies in the intended function of Luke-Acts vis-à-vis Jewish Hellenistic histories.

T. Penner offers a recent discussion of the function of Jewish Hellenistic histories.[1] He notes that the older view of such histories as having a propagandistic function has been overturned in recent scholarship.[2] His work has shown that "…apologetic work edifies the Jewish audience by presenting a particular Hellenistic-Jewish fusion that situates Jewish identity in the midst of the larger value system of the Greco-Roman world".[3] Jewish history was restructured, "defining itself over against but also within the larger sociocultural environment".[4] This required a presentation of Jewish history in a praiseworthy manner, using rhetorical techniques.

Penner offers a review of praiseworthy rhetoric. He observes that such "literature encourages group-cohesion as a natural function of its value-laden underpinnings". By way of example of such rhetoric he notes such characteristic features in relation to individuals as good birth, education, worthy features of character, physical appearance, wealth, power, fortuitous circumstances, *and so on.* An apologetic purpose is served when this type of detail is used to praise an individual or a people. Penner concludes that such "discourse is thus not focused on deeds and characters for their own sake, but on the way in which deeds and characters are exemplary".[5]

---

[1] T. Penner, *In Praise of Christian Origins* (Edinburgh: T & T Clark, 2004), chap. 4. Penner's review of scholarship, (pp. 1-8) follows the same threefold division of the issues presented in this paper.
[2] Penner, *In Praise of Christian Origins*, 225.
[3] Penner, *In Praise of Christian Origins*, 228.
[4] Penner, *In Praise of Christian Origins*, 228.
[5] Penner, *In Praise of Christian Origins*, 234.

Penner illustrates the praiseworthy nature of Jewish writing mainly from the *Letter to Aristeas*, commenting that "...the overarching feature seems to be an extended narrative praising Judaism, which develops and elaborates the pivotal themes of temple and law against the foil of the commissioning of the Greek translation of the Jewish law."[1] He also shows similar praiseworthy motives in Esther, Daniel 1-6, Aristobulus, Eupolemus, and Philo's *Life of Moses*.[2] Of Josephus, Penner states, "...Josephus not only retells the story of Israel up until his own time, but he also rewrites that story so as to reflect the recognized values of the Hellenistic world, including extensive efforts to reconfigure biblical characters in order to correspond to the main categories delineated in Greek praise of individual virtue".[3] Accordingly, Penner claims that Luke-Acts is "...a premiere example of early Christian historiography written in the traditions of Jewish apologetic literature".[4]

Penner's analysis of the apologetic function of Jewish Hellenistic historiography is a consensus view. However, certain differences with Luke-Acts emerge:

1) Luke-Acts is, in one sense, about Jewish identity, but it is not about Jewish ethnic identity vis-à-vis outsiders; it does not have an apologetic purpose of presenting the Jews in a favourable light. On the contrary, Jewish authorities are cast in a bad light. While Jewish praiseworthy literature allowed contrasting blame to function as praise for a group or individual, this is not the kind of blame that cements Luke-Acts into Jewish Historiography.

2) Luke-Acts has value as an evangelistic work, but it is not explicitly structured to address outsiders. The implied reader is required to have a substantial "inside" background knowledge in relation to individuals, theological terms and Jewish traditions. Luke is not seeking to present his material to any other audience.

---

[1] Penner, *In Praise of Christian Origins*, 241.

[2] In the case of Moses, Philo casts his conquest of the land east of Jordan in terms "consonant with the Greek tradition of the origin of city-states", Penner, *In Praise of Christian Origins*, 259.

[3] Penner, *In Praise of Christian Origins*, 246.

[4] Penner, *In Praise of Christian Origins*, 260. Pinner's worked example is Stephen's speech, which shows a re-write of Jewish scriptural history, a common literary form in Jewish Hellenistic historiography.

3) Luke presents his main characters in a praiseworthy manner; Jesus and Paul are presented as innocent victims of Jewish caprice. Other minor characters are presented in an exemplary manner, for example, in the birth narratives. However, many episodes illustrate deficiencies: the disciples fail to understand Jesus' teaching, and are shown to be ambitious, John the Baptist is shown to have a crisis of faith and, within the church, there are disputes and arguments between ethnic groups, and leading figures. The picture presented appears to be less than praiseworthy.

4) Luke is critical of central aspects of the Jewish polity such as the temple and the destruction of Jerusalem is presented as a judgment of God upon Jesus' generation. Luke is not presenting a story that validates the abiding worth of the Jewish people, but rather one that has the shadow of an end cast over such a people.

In addition to these points there is a problem of method with Pinner's thesis. Luke-Acts may illustrate praiseworthy characteristics in relation to *its* people, but if these people are not "the Jews" as such, can it be grouped with Jewish Hellenistic historiographical writings? The problem of method here is one of level: for example, Pinner notes that Jewish Hellenistic historiography is concerned with reinforcing Jewish identity and he claims that Stephen's speech is "the rewriting of the biblical tradition so as to construct a particular identity within the community and to promote it without".[1] But there is a shift of level from the community of "the Jews" vis-à-vis the wider Hellenistic world to a community within "the Jews" and the definition of that community over against "the Jews". This shift of level critically affects Pinner's thesis because it seems, on the basis of his own primary texts, that Jewish Hellenistic apologetic is (*sic*) "Jewish". Sharing praiseworthy rhetorical techniques is not sufficient to outweigh this difference between Luke-Acts and Jewish Hellenistic historiography.

Accordingly, our conclusion is that Luke-Acts does not share the *Jewish apologetic function*; at best, it has as one of its functions a Christian apologetic function.

4. Jewish Scriptural History
Our argument in this essay is that Luke intends Luke-Acts to *function* alongside the Jewish Scriptures. Shared Hellenistic literary forms and a

---

[1] Penner, *In Praise of Christian Origins*, 261.

Hellenistic historical method do not outweigh this intention. We now need to sketch this case.

Scriptural writings illustrate a cyclical history presupposing a covenant relationship between Israel and God and revolving around periods of disobedience, punishment, repentance and deliverance. The Chronicles History offers an "ideal" picture of the history of Judah, Jerusalem and the Temple. In this history, the calamities that befall Judah are attributed to the sins of individuals rather than the unfaithfulness of the people. The Pentateuch contains a history of national origins, and offers a cyclical view of Israel's early history similar in structure to the History Books; this shared pattern uses creation, chaos and re-creation motifs to structure Israel's history.[1]

A number of evidential features support an identification of Luke-Acts as a species of Jewish Scriptural history, but these pertain mainly to *content* rather than *form*. Firstly, Luke continues the story elements (plot lines, events and characters) of the Jewish Scriptures; secondly, he imitates Jewish Scriptural episodes; thirdly, he uses a Septuagintal style in writing; and finally, Luke presents a theological history which continues the salvation-historical acts of God in respect of Israel.

These features present a *sufficient* case for identifying the genre of Luke-Acts as "Jewish Scriptural history", because their presence in the two works dominates its character when compared to the Hellenistic characteristics. This quantitative dominance[2] implies a Scripturally sensitive reader and invites such a reader to read Luke-Acts *alongside* the Jewish Scriptures. To require a reader to read a work *alongside* other works is a strong indication of genre. Given that genre is a concept of association, and a concept that captures the conventions governing a communicative process, the literary co-text that Luke requires of his readers is the most natural group of writings to suggest as the genre of Luke-Acts. This raises the question as to whether Luke-Acts has a Scriptural status. Our proposal is that Luke includes a point of view on

---

[1] For a summary of the cyclical pattern, see W. J. Dumbrell, *The End of the Beginning* (Eugene, Oregon: Wipf & Stock, 2001) or A. Perry, *Beginnings and Endings* (3rd ed.; Sunderland: Willow Publications, 2011).

[2] Ahead of our discussion below it is worth noting here that one measure of this quantity is the relative attention paid by scholars to Lucan intertextuality.

the Jewish Prophets which makes it certain that he did indeed view his work as having such a status.

4.1 Formal Elements

While a composition history of the Jewish Scriptural histories would offer a complex classification of literary forms, for the purposes of comparison with Luke and Acts, our question is whether Luke expects his implied reader to make a formal link with Scriptural materials in addition to any linkage that they might make because of commonality of content.

D. E. Aune offers[1] the following summary of formal characteristics of Scriptural histories: i) discourse predominates as the way to narrate and move forward the story; ii) the narrative has an episodic quality, where many short episodes resolving an action or an event are concatenated[2] as a "history" of a given individual; and iii) summaries are used for the reign of kings and to connect or conclude episodes, and are often theological in nature.

These three characteristics bear comparison with Luke-Acts, but clearly Luke-Acts has formal characteristics that reflect a different cultural milieu to that which engendered and maintained the Scriptural histories.

The principal objection to the proposal that Luke is writing Scriptural history is the presence of the literary preface to his gospel, which suggests that Luke is consciously writing a history in Hellenistic style. Moreover, this preface does not state any theological theme; theological concepts are absent, and there is no mention of his principal characters or story-line. Luke's second preface does mention Jesus and re-use theological concepts mentioned in the gospel. Furthermore, other NT writings have no parallel to Luke's prefaces, although John 20:30-31, 21:24-25 bear some comparison as statements of purpose. This observation is all the more telling because it is arguable that Matthew *is* a Scriptural history, and it starts more conventionally with a genealogy in the style of the Chronicler's history. The Hellenistic pretensions of the preface, (whether narrowly construed as historiographical or more broadly as indicative of Hellenistic conventions for a preface regardless of the genre of the ensuing work), therefore do not suggest a Scriptural writing.

---

[1] D. E. Aune, *The New Testament in its Literary Environment* (Philadelphia: The Westminster Press, 1987), 102-103.

[2] One trivial illustration of this is the paratactic style of Hebrew narrative and its implication of causality through the conjunction (ו).

This objection raises in an acute way the question of what it is to assign a genre to a piece of writing. The Jewish Scriptural materials reflect literary forms in surrounding cultures contemporaneous with their composition. Thus, oracles of doom, political prognostications, oracles of success and prosperity are evidenced in Mesopotamian texts; the precise dating of the restoration prophecies of Haggai reflects Persian influence; the prologue of Job is comparable to the Babylonian Theodicy, *and so on*. The inclusion of common forms of writing within the Jewish Scriptures did not exclude a genre assignment of "Scripture" in Luke's day. The point here is that the subsequent *use* to which writing was put **created a genre** regardless of formal similarities with texts in surrounding cultures.

Luke's use of compositional techniques from his literary context does not settle the question of genre; it is necessary to consider the intended *use* for his two volumes. Here our proposal is that the *content* of Luke and Acts shows an intended use alongside the Jewish Scriptures. To reformulate our argument: if "genre" pertains to the sociology of reading and writing and is a term for sets of conventions that govern the production of reading of texts, then a genre classification must be based on considerations of usage. Luke's preface is one indication of intended usage, but the *weight* of its contribution to a determination of reading is slight compared to the effect on the reader of the content of Luke and Acts.

4.2 The Content of Luke-Acts
Luke has consciously sought to present his narrative as a *written continuation* of Israel's history. While a continuation narrative need not necessarily participate in the same genre as the precursor literature, this is a possibility for investigation, and might be considered a reasonable presumption.

If Luke is continuing Israel's Scriptural story, a minimum requirement for such an implied claim would be the continuation of a discernible **plot line** extending from the Jewish Scriptural story into Luke-Acts. In order for a plot line to survive the death of characters, a change of centuries, a different political order, and a different social-economic climate, an author would have to code his continuities in "nationalistic" terms. This strategy is made necessary by the fact that the Scriptural story "time" "ended" with Malachi and Chronicles in the fifth century.

The constants available to Luke include (at least) the God of Israel, the "people" themselves, divine messengers, the Spirit of God and those expressions of national hope embodied in the Jewish Scriptures. Luke's own story can only "continue" the plot of the Jewish scriptures if that story has not "ended" and if expectations built up in that story are "fulfilled" in Luke-Acts. The category of prophecy and fulfilment is important to Luke. In literary terms, the use of the category of "fulfilment" ties Luke's writing to those writings that contain the prophecies. It is demonstrable that Luke has constructed his story to continue the plot of the Jewish scriptural story using these structural elements.

This literary argument is to be distinguished from the more general theological point that Luke conceives of his story in salvation-historical terms. Literary evidence for a continuation of a story should advert to textual connections with precursor writings that contain the prior instalments of the story.

4.2.1 Character
The notion of character is a critical literary construct. The two major characters of the gospel are trailed with the citation of Scriptural *prophecies*, and in this way Luke cements a continuation of story.

1) Luke includes a specific *literary* linkage with the *end* of the Prophets (Mal 3:1; 4:4-6) and the *beginning* of his story; John the Baptist is presented in terms of the Elijah prophecies of Malachi (Luke 1:17; 3:16; and 7:19-20).

2) Jesus is trailed in terms of Zacharias' programmatic pronouncements of impending fulfilment of Israel's national hopes. Zacharias extols the "God of Israel" who has "visited" his people (Luke 1:68) echoing the story of Moses; he then mentions the fulfilment of the Davidic promise (Luke 1:69) and the oath sworn to Abraham about the deliverance of Israel from Egypt (Luke 1:73; Gen 15:13-14). Similarly, Simeon pronounces about the "glory of thy people Israel" (Luke 2:32), and Anna witnesses to the "redemption" to come through Jesus (Luke 2:38). Jesus has been the subject of all the holy prophets (Luke 1:70).

3) In addition to Scriptural citation, intertextual allusion is a second method for conveying a sense of fulfilment in respect of Jewish traditions. In the case of John the Baptist, Luke paints allusive detail relating to Elijah in locating his ministry around Jordan (Luke 3:4); in the case of Jesus, Luke includes allusive detail in Stephen's speech relating to the rejection of Moses that compares to Jesus to Moses. The point in this allusive detail, noted by many scholars, is that the Jewish Scriptures had

predicted the return of Elijah (Mal 3:1, 4:4-6) and the coming of a prophet like Moses (Deut 18:15).

In summary, the central characters of Luke's story continue the Jewish scriptural story insofar as, i) they are prophets sent to the nation just like the prophets of old, and ii) they are prophets that have been predicted in the prophecies of that former story.

4.2.2 Plot

The notion of a plot is critical to narrative theory; there are several literary linkages between Luke-Acts and the plot of the Jewish Scriptures.

1) In terms of the plot-line of the gospel, Luke is careful to present the rejection of Jesus and the death of both his characters (the main plot) as predicted by Scripture. The death of Jesus is presented as the fulfilment of Scripture (Luke 24:26-27; Acts 3:18; 17:3; 26:23), and a necessary event prior to the fulfilment of any restoration for Israel (Acts 3:21). Likewise, the resurrection of Jesus is presented as a fulfilment of scripture (Acts 2:24-30; 4:11; 13:33, 37).

2) In terms of secondary plots in the gospel, Luke presents Jesus' offer of the kingdom as an offer of restoration to Israel, and he presents the message of deliverance given by John the Baptist, Jesus and the apostles in relation to Scriptural expectations about the day of the Lord (Luke 3:7; 21:23-28; Acts 2:40). If the people responded to the call of the gospel, they could participate in the restoration that was to follow the day of the Lord (Acts 1:6; 3:21). This secondary plot, of moving about the land preaching, ties together the various episodes that Luke describes in the gospel.

This plot follows the pattern in Jewish Scriptural history where the prophets are sent by God to the people before crises, bringing a message of repentance and offering a vision of hope beyond the imminent judgment from the Lord for those who respond to the call. The case of Isaiah before the crises of 734-732 and 701 BCE is Luke's model. He ends the account in Acts with a quotation from Isaiah's call (Isa 6:9-10) in such a way that it is an evident summary of the preaching of the apostles and the reaction of the Jews (Acts 28:26-27). Aune observes that "this group emphasis is largely absent from Greco-Roman historiography".[1]

---

[1] Aune, *The New Testament in its Literary Environment*, 103.

3) Furthermore, as with the delineation of characters, allusion is another way in which Luke ties his plot to Jewish prophecies. An example of this can be seen in his account of Pentecost. This account contains allusive detail to the oracles of Malachi relating to the work of the lord who is to come after the herald (Mal 3:1). Thus, Luke replicates Malachi's themes of the need for Levitical purification in his focus upon the temple and the teaching of the apostles — the "fire" of the Spirit (Mal 3:2-4). Or again, in the case of the bestowal of the Spirit and the fulfilment of Joel's prophecy, Luke includes allusive detail in his account beyond Acts 2 in his continued mention of "signs and wonders" performed by the apostles (Acts 2:43; 5:12).

4) A different kind of linkage, which doesn't trade on notions of quotation and allusion, is to re-tell an earlier story within a later story and specifically advertise continuity. Luke uses speeches in Acts to link his story to that of Israel. Stephen's speech is a clear example of a "rehearsal of Jewish history", albeit highly selective, to which there is appended the martyrdom of Stephen as continuous with the rejection by the people of all the prophets (Acts 7:52). Again, Paul's Antioch speech connects Luke's story with the Jewish story and makes the plot-line jump at the David promise (Acts 13:22-23).

5) W. S. Kurz[1] observes Luke is able to continue his story beyond Acts 28 and show how it is linked to "last days" material in the Jewish Scriptures through a description of an "end" (e.g. Luke 17, 21).[2] The presence of this material in Luke-Acts affects the reader's perception of the whole story and what is being done in the life of John the Baptist, Jesus and the apostles.

Thus, there is "wrath" to come (Luke 3:7; 21:23; cf. 2 Chron 29:8-10); there is condemnation of that "generation" (Luke 21:32; Acts 2:40; cf. Deut 32:5); there is a sequence of events in relation to Jerusalem and the land that are to happen before the return of the Son of Man (Luke 21:27; Acts 7:56; cf. Dan 7:13). With the prospect of this impending crisis, to which the return of Jesus is linked, the missionary story is one of escape and deliverance (Luke 3:7; 21:21; Acts 2:40).

---

[1] W. S. Kurz, "Luke-Acts and Historiography in the Greek Bible", *SBLSP* 19 (1980): 283-300 (284).

[2] We have excluded here Luke's genealogy as a link and the Jewish story as this does not function as a plot device.

Luke does not narrate the fulfilment of these predictions but they nevertheless condition the implied reader's perspective on his story. Jesus and the apostles are not preaching an *actual* restoration of Israel inaugurated in their actions, but offering a prospective restoration in which those who respond to the gospel can participate (Luke 1:74). This is the classic story-pattern of the Jewish prophets: they prophesy impending doom and offer a prospective salvation conditional upon repentance (Acts 3:19-21).

6) The plot-line of Acts, when this is considered independently of the gospel, supports this replication of the role of the Jewish prophet. The apostles are commissioned to preach throughout the land and to the "end of the earth" (Acts 1:8). This expression is one of Luke's Septuagintal phrases of choice; it occurs, for example, in Isa 49:6, which is a key text for Luke (Luke 2:32; Acts 13:47; 26:23; 28:28). This text gives a Jewish perspective to the perceptual geography of the phrase "end of the earth". This is an idiom for "outside the land" where the Jews have been scattered. The LXX interpretation of the MT explicitly connects the phrase to the Diaspora.

The use of "end of the earth" elsewhere in Isaiah confirms this idiomatic sense. Thus, Isa 48:20 associates the phrase with the Babylonian captives proclaiming a message of liberation to the "end of the earth". The point of the proclamation by Yahweh in Isa 45:22 is that the "end of the earth" should look unto Zion for salvation, and the same point is found in Isa 62:11. The sense of the phrase in Acts therefore is not a cipher for Rome,[1] or Spain, or a distant *location*, but rather an idiom for all countries outside the land where the Jews have been dispersed. Luke's story shows proclamation throughout the "end of the earth".[2]

This proposal changes the rhetoric of Paul's assertion in Acts 13:47,

---

[1] Thus, instead of seeing the plot of Acts as "movement to Rome", this should be treated as a sub-plot of the Diaspora plot implied by Acts 1:8 — a sub-plot initiated by Acts 19:21.
[2] Perceptual Geography is a branch of Human Geography that studies the perceptions of communities about space. For example, it studies the use of spatial expressions about the compass such as what is the "south": where does the "south" begin, and where does it end? It cannot be simply assumed that "end of the earth" in the mouth of a Galilean character signalled "Rome" as opposed to Dan or Beersheba, Babylon or Spain.

> For so the Lord has commanded us, saying, `I have set
> you to be a light for the Gentiles, that you may bring
> salvation to the uttermost parts of the earth. Acts 13:47

The usual interpretation of this assertion is that "the ends of the earth"
are "the Gentiles" and that Paul is making a contrast between those who
are of Israel and those who are "of the ends of the earth"; the gospel is
being taken to the Gentiles. However, this gives an unsupported ethnic
cast to the expression. The logic of the citation may just be that the
apostles have been appointed to be a light for the Gentiles in addition to
the Jews who live alongside Gentiles as part of the Diaspora.

7) Luke concludes his story in a manner consistent with Scriptural history.
The conventional demarcations of Ezra, Nehemiah and Chronicles do not
conclude with an obvious sense of closing a period of history. The final
verses of Chronicles open the next historical period by duplicating the
first two verses from Ezra. Both Ezra and Nehemiah close with the
handling of mixed marriages; they do not conclude with the successful
restoration of the temple and city. Kings does not close its history insofar
as Jehoiachin continues to remain in Babylon at the behest of the king
partaking continually of a daily allowance (2 Kgs 25:27-30). Had the writer
wanted to close the history, he would have done so with the destruction
of Jerusalem and offered a closing summary of the reasons for the end of
Judah; however, this theology comes in the account of account of
Manasseh's reign (2 Kgs 23:26-27). Similarly, Luke concludes with Paul
preaching "unhindered" in his own hired house for two years; there is
openness to the story.

There is no closure to the apostolic preaching, either to Jews or Gentiles.
Luke's last quotation from Isaiah 6 reaffirms "Go to this people" (Acts
28:26), which in its original context is Isaiah's commission to go to the
Jews. The negative response implied in Luke's quotation does not negate
this affirmation of a continuing mission to the Jews. The response of both
Jews and Gentiles in Acts has been one of partial acceptance,[1] and Luke's
motif of "turning to the Gentiles" in his closing scene (Acts 28:28) no
more implies the end of a Jewish mission than in earlier occurrences (Acts
13:46; 18:6). Luke cannot conclude with such a theological statement
without violating his Diaspora plot as announced in Acts 1:8 and without
negating his use of Isaiah. Paul is a light to the Gentiles so that he can

---

[1] Acceptance and rejection is one of the major devices with which Luke
moves his plot from episode to episode.

bring salvation to the Jews as far as the ends of the earth i.e. in the Diaspora. Luke presents the motif of "turning to the Gentiles" as a provocation to the Jews, and the motif is complimented by the narrative note of their "jealousy" (Acts 5:17; 7:9; 13:45; 17:5).

4.2.3 Imitation of Episodes

Imitation[1] can place a work into a genre; Luke imitates Scriptural episodes in his narrative. His method for achieving this is intertextual, and thus his episodes reverberate with Jewish Scriptural stories. This literary characteristic supplies another kind of continuity with the Jewish Scriptures. Luke ties his story to Jewish prophetic literature by citation and allusion, and through these devises he shows that his characters and his plot is a continuation of the "story" of Israel. To reinforce this "fulfilment" continuity, Luke imitates Scriptural history-writing. This kind of imitation was a standard rhetorical Hellenistic technique. Scholars have discussed many[2] examples, but to cite just three instances:

1) Luke uses strategies in the infancy narrative that would be familiar to readers familiar with the Jewish Scriptures. The purpose of these is to compare his characters (Jesus and John) to key characters of Jewish Scriptural history. Thus, he narrates an angelic announcement (Luke 1:11; Samson, Judges 13) and compares John to Samson; he includes a "barren" birth story (John), which compares to similar stories about Isaac, Joseph, and Samuel.

2) T. L. Brodie has shown how the healing of the widow of Sarepta's son by Elijah (1 Kgs 17:1-24) is the model for Jesus' healing of the widow of Nain's son (Luke 7:11-17).[3] Story elements common to both accounts include a meeting at the city gate, a widow, a dead son, the raising of the son, speaking on the part of the son, the giving of the child to the

---

[1] T. L. Brodie notes that in Greco-Roman culture the practice of imitation was widespread, and observes that "in the period from about 100 BC to 100 AD the literary world was largely concerned with reshaping the great texts of the past", see "Luke 7:11-17 as an imitation of 1 Kings 17:17-24" *NTS* (1986): 247-267 (247-249).

[2] Again, this is a quantitative measure that signals a dominant characteristic in Luke-Acts; this dominance outweighs the formal similarities with Hellenistic historiography.

[3] Brodie, "Luke 7:11-17 as an imitation of 1 Kings 17:17-24", 247-249.

mother.[1] In addition, there are more subtle correspondences: Luke states that Jesus had compassion (Luke 17:13), whereas this is implied in Elijah's cry of lament (1 Kgs 17:20); the son is laid out on a bed in the Elijah story, whereas in Luke's story the son is laid out on a bier — in both stories the movement towards the grave is halted; the response to the miracle in each case is a recognition of the presence of a prophet.

Brodie concludes that Luke's use of the Elijah story is "subtle and complex" and "requires a literary explanation",[2] rather than one accountable through aural association and oral transmission.

3) Many scholars have compared Pentecost to the giving of the Law on Sinai. Similarities with the Scriptural account include details such as the following: the people were gathered together (Exod 19:8) prior to the theophanies in the third month after leaving Egypt (Exod 19:1), and similarly, Pentecost was in the third month after the crucifixion and the disciples were gathered together;[3] the Sinai theophanies involved "sound" and "fire", which are features also mentioned at Pentecost (Exod 19:16-18; 20:18; Acts 2:2-4); and the Sinai theophanies accompanied something that was "given", viz. a law, likewise the Spirit was "given" at Pentecost. Finally, a comparison can be made between the 120 at Pentecost and the group of elders who approach God on Sinai, while the people remain "afar off" (Exod 20:18; Acts 2:39).

4.2.4 Typology

Luke's use of imitation is a typological method designed to tie his narrative to the Jewish Scriptures. In crafting episodes using Scriptural materials, Luke encodes typological correspondences at multiple points in his narrative.

A number of scholars argue that the rationale for typological exegesis in the NT is the concomitant belief that the events surrounding Jesus and the church are part of a scheme of salvation history that is moulded by

---

[1] Brodie sets out the lexical correspondence, "Luke 7:11-17 as an imitation of 1 Kings 17:17-24", 252-253.

[2] Brodie, "Luke 7:11-17 as an imitation of 1 Kings 17:17-24", 259.

[3] The word in Exod 19:8 (LXX) is used in the Majority Text of Acts 2:2, 46. This manuscript tradition may be influenced by a perceived typological correspondence.

God to "reveal and illumine His purpose".[1] Such moulding, it is argued, illustrates a selective and escalating repetition of pattern so that OT actions, events, institutions and persons bear similarities to corresponding entities in NT history. The OT elements are therefore seen to have a predicative quality that is matched to NT fulfilment. This rationale is not necessary for an explanation of Luke's use of typology. Instead of working with a pre-emptive and predictive model of revelation, Luke could be working typological links into his narrative *retrospectively*. This is a weaker thesis without the theological freight of a philosophy of history: Luke has read the Jewish Scriptures and modelled his story here using patterns[2] and themes that he has found in those writings.[3]

Luke's use of a typological method is consistent with the cyclical conception of history implicit in the History Books, and this conception is a specialised case of the recognition of analogies and repetition over the course of history in proverbial wisdom. Thucydides states of his account of the Peloponnesian War that it conveys "a clear view of both of the events which have happened and of those which will some day, in all probability, happen again in the same or a similar way".[4] The Scriptural conception extends Thucydides' observation by subordinating repetition to a providential scheme: God controls affairs in regular ways.

Luke's use of a typological method in narrating contemporary events is consistent with Jewish interpretative practise. To cite just three examples: i) Josephus evidently saw himself in the role of a latter day Jeremiah, and he has embellished his re-telling of the Jewish Scriptural story with an eye

---

[1] E. E. Ellis, *Paul's Use of the Old Testament* (Edinburgh, Oliver & Boyd, 1957), 128. Similar theory is presented by L. Goppelt, *Typos: The Typological Interpretation of the Old Testament in the New*, (trans. D. H. Madvig; Grand Rapids: Eerdmans, 1982), chap 9.

[2] R. Alter calls these patterns, "type-scenes" in *The Art of Biblical Narrative*, (New York: Basic Books, 1981), 50.

[3] Thus, a typical definition would be that of D. L. Block, who argues that Luke's use of quotation is "…'typological-prophetic' in that the pattern of God's activity is reactivated in ways that mirror and enhance his acts of old" in "Proclamation from Prophecy and Pattern" in *The Gospels and the Scriptures of Israel* (eds. C. A. Evans and W. R. Stegner; Sheffield: Sheffield Academic Press, 1994), 280-307 (282).

[4] *Thucydides*, (trans. C. F. Smith; Loeb Classical Library; London: Heinemann, 1919), Book I.22.4.

on his own life;[1] ii) The author of 1 Maccabees evokes Phinehas' killing of the malefactor in his description of Mattathias' heroism (1 Macc 2:26); and iii) Amalek, the traditional enemy of Israel is used as the type for Rome in the *Mekhilta* 17.8.

Typological analysis is a description of mimesis. D. R. Macdonald has proposed six criteria for "detecting mimesis in ancient texts".[2] The first criterion, accessibility, assesses the likely availability of the imitated text. The second criterion is based on how many authors in a literary context imitate the same text. The third criterion counts the volume or density of parallels between the imitated and imitating text. The fourth criterion looks for shared sequencing of details in the two texts; a shared sequence strengthens the claim for imitation. The fifth criterion examines distinctive traits that might cement two texts in a relationship of imitation. And finally, the sixth criterion is interpretability—an explanation of why the two texts might be related needs to be offered. It is beyond the scope of this essay to apply these criteria in our consideration of Luke's typology; however, our presentation of the shared patterns between Luke-Acts and Luke's Scriptural source materials is amenable to Macdonald's six tests.

4.2.5 Septuagintal Style
Scholars have long observed a "Septuagintal" character to Luke-Acts; this has been in terms of vocabulary, style, quotations, and allusions. W. K. L. Clarke's essay[3] is, perhaps, the classic expression of this thesis. Clarke offers certain statistics:[4] i) Luke's unique vocabulary is found in the LXX

---

[1] See D. Daube, "Typology in Josephus", *JJS* 31 (1980), p. 18-36 (26-35).
[2] D. R. Macdonald, "Introduction" in *Mimesis and Intertextuality* (ed., D. R. Macdonald; Harrisburg: Trinity Press International, 2001), 1-9 (2).
[3] W. K. L. Clarke, "The Use of the Septuagint in Acts" in "The Use of the Septuagint in Acts" in *The Beginnings of Christianity: Part 1* (eds. F. J. Foakes-Jackson and Kirsopp Lake; 5 vols; London: Macmillan, 1920-33), 66-105.
[4] Clarke defines a working set of books for his definition of the "LXX", but this issue can be placed to one side for our purposes; he is also working with a critical text of Acts, which is Alexandrian (Westcott & Hort), but without discussion of text-critical issues which may undermine his precise totals; again, the text-critical question can be placed to one side as we endeavour to understand the scope of Luke's Septuagintal style. Furthermore, while a modern stylometric analysis of Clarke's data would bring statistical rigor to a presentation, it is unlikely that it would overturn Clarke's basic conclusion that Luke-Acts has a Septuagintal character.

to a significantly greater extent than the other Synoptists; ii) Luke's characteristic phrases[1] are overwhelmingly found in the LXX; and iii) Luke's unique vocabulary is also found in the Apocryphal books[2] to a greater extent than the other Synoptists. The following table lists examples:

ἐπαίρω φωνή ("raised his voice")	Jud 21:2, Rut 1:9, 14, 2 Sam 13:36, Acts 2:14, 14:11, 22:22,
γνωστός εἰμί ("let it be known")	Exod 33:16, Ezr 4:12-13, 1 Esdr 2:14, Dan (Th) 3:18, Acts 2:14, 4:10
Καὶ νῦν ("and now")	Deut 4:1, 10:12, Jud 11:23, Psa 2:10, Acts 3:17,
καὶ ἰδού ("and behold")	Exod 4:14, Deut 1:10, 1 Sam 15:12, Acts 1:10, 5:28, 8:27
καὶ ἐγένετο ("and it came to pass")	2 Sam 1:1, 1 Macc 10:64, Neh 4:6, Luke 1:23, Acts 2:2, 10:13
ἐν τῷ + infinitive	Gen 4:8, Exod 34:29, 1 Macc 2:7, Luke 1:8, 24:4, Acts 2:1, 8:6
καὶ προσέθετο ("moreover")	Luke 20:11, 12, Acts 12:3, Num 22:16, 1 Macc 3:15, Isa 7:10
ἀποκριθεὶς εἶπεν ("answered and said")	Luke 1:19, Acts 8:24, 25:9, Gen 27:39, 1 Macc 15:33, Tobit 2:3

In addition to correspondences of vocabulary and style, Luke quotes and alludes to the Jewish Scriptures, and these reflect a text close to the LXX (the Old Greek, OG). Clarke lists 12 exact or substantially close quotations and 16 "freer" quotations. This reflection of the OG exists alongside knowledge of the Hebrew text.

Scholars have observed patterns in Luke's Septuagintal style. F. F. Bruce observes that Luke's use of Septuagintal phrases is more common in his

---

[1] Clarke defines a "characteristic phrase" as one that occurs at least five times in Acts and twice as often as in the rest of the NT, "The Use of the Septuagint in Acts", 71.
[2] Clarke notes particular affinities with 2 Maccabees and regards it as "highly probable" that Luke had read that work, "The Use of the Septuagint in Acts", 74.

gospel and the first half of Acts.[1] Clarke notes that the preponderance of Scriptural quotation and allusion comes in the first half of Acts.[2]

The impact of this style upon the reader is to further associate Luke-Acts with the Jewish Scriptures as the natural reading companion.

4.2.6 Salvation Historical Theology

Our final piece of evidence that Luke is writing in a "Scriptural" genre is Luke's concept of "Salvation-History": Luke discloses an understanding that God is at work in his story. In addition to the literary features of quotation and allusion, which connect his work to the Jewish Scriptures, and as well as Luke's use of typology and along with his Septuagintal style, Luke has a theology of "Salvation-History". Luke's implicit claim is that just as God has acted in Israel's past, so too he is acting in Israel's "present" through Jesus and the apostles. While this is large topic in itself, the following four points suffice to under gird Luke's "scriptural genre".

1) Luke has a notion of a "plan" of God which is being carried forward into "his era" of God (Acts 7:30; cf. 2:23; 4:28; 5:38; 13:36; 20:27). This plan is moved forward through commission statements that disclose God's purpose. Thus John the Baptist's commission statements include the angelic announcement (Luke 1:13-17) and the use of Isa 40:3-5 (Luke 3:4-6); Jesus' commission statements include the programmatic prophecies of Zacharias, Simeon, Anna and Mary, as well as the use of Isa 61 in the Nazareth episode (Luke 4:16-30); and the commission statements of the apostles include Jesus' commission (Luke 24:47-49; Acts 1:8) as well as the programmatic prophecy of Joel. Accordingly, the "plan" of God and its ongoing execution form a theological continuity with the Jewish Scriptures.[3]

2) Luke has a notion of prophecy and fulfilment. He announces in the prologue that he is describing events that have been fulfilled amongst the early Christians. He uses a verb "accomplish" (Luke 1:1, NASB, RSV), within Luke-Acts to indicate the theological sense of prophetic

---

[1] F. F. Bruce, *The Acts of the Apostles* (London: Tyndale Press, 1952), 28.

[2] Clarke, "The Use of the Septuagint in Acts", 98.

[3] For an extended discussion of the plan of God see D. P. Moessner, "The 'script' of the Scriptures in Acts: suffering as God's plan (βουλῆ) for the world for the 'release of sins'" in *History, Literature, and Society in the Book of Acts* (ed. B. Witherington III; Cambridge: Cambridge University Press, 1996), 218-250.

fulfilment,[1] given Luke's predilection for "to fulfil" in relation to the Jewish Scriptures (Luke 4:21; 21:22; Acts 1:16; 3:18; 13:27) and events (Luke 21:24, 32; 24:44). This suggestion is strengthened by the observation that Luke juxtaposes the concept of "all things" with "to fulfil" (Luke 21:22, 32; 24:44; Acts 13:29).

3) Luke deploys a sense of divine purpose driving the events of his story, and he derives this from the Jewish Scriptures. This can be seen in his use of "must" in relation to the correlation of his narrative events and Scriptural prediction.[2] Thus, Jesus predicts the necessity of his suffering (Luke 9:22; 17:25; 22:37; 24:26, 44) in accordance with the Scriptures, and Luke represents the apostles having the same perception of the necessity of fulfilling Scripture (Acts 1:16; 17:33). By association, Luke's use of "must" elsewhere can be read as implying a relationship to a divine program, both for Jesus and the apostles (Luke 4:43; 13:33; 21:9; 24:7; Acts 3:21; 14:22; 27:24).

4) Luke presents his story as *partly* tragic;[3] the hopes expressed in the "Birth Stories" are not fulfilled in respect of Israel. The "nationalistic" aspects of the initial prophecies ("throne of David", "reign" (Luke 1:32-33), "salvation from our enemies" (Luke 1:71, 74), redemption of Jerusalem" (Luke 2:38)) are unfulfilled within the narrative. Instead, Luke includes predictive material about the destruction of Jerusalem. This story is only partly tragic, however, because Luke associates the restoration of Israel with the return[4] of Jesus after the destruction of Jerusalem (Luke 21:24-27; Acts 3:19-21).

---

[1] F. Bovon, *Luke 1* (Hermeneia; Minneapolis: Fortress Press, 2002), 20.

[2] For an extended discussion of Luke's use of "must" see C. K. Rothschild, *Luke-Acts and the Rhetoric of History* (WUNT; Tubingen: Mohr Siebeck, 2004), 189-208.

[3] On this see R. C. Tannehill, "Israel in Luke-Acts: A Tragic Story", *JBL* 104 (1985): 69-85.

[4] While it is a common scholarly proposal to say that Luke-Acts presupposes a notion of "delay" in respect of Jesus' return, this thesis is controverted by Luke's pre-announced story plot-line in Luke 21. The critical events prior to the return are not fulfilled in his story which stops around 64 CE. In strict story-terms, there is no delay because there is no destruction of Jerusalem; the narrative ends before the story is concluded. Scholars have "read into" Acts a delay that they perceive from their own vantage point.

Salvation-historical readings of Luke are concerned with purpose; on a narrative plane this is the concept of *plot*. F. Kermode comments that a typological reading presents a hidden plot within "the manifest one".[1] So, for example, it is not just a question of seeing Jesus' exorcisms as a contributory factor leading to his death; there is a broader plot of salvation history. This plot requires us to set Jesus' words and actions within the context of Israelite history and the history of God's dealings with mankind. Luke's salvation-historical theology therefore is a natural sister to his typological method.

5. Conclusion

While multiple genres could be assigned to Luke-Acts and distinctly to Luke and Acts, the question arises as to whether there is a dominant genre classification.

In this essay, our argument is that the "Scriptural" characteristics of Luke-Acts are pervasive to an extent not matched by any Hellenistic historiographical characteristics. The leading Hellenistic features — the preface, the speeches, the synchronisms, and the use of sources — do not outweigh the Jewish Scriptural feel inherent in the story. These features pertain to form rather than content, but *content* carries the greater impact. In terms of the reading experience of Luke's audience, reading Luke-Acts is more likely to have resembled the reading (or hearing) of the Jewish Scriptures than the available political histories or biographies of the times. The reception history of Luke and Acts in the late second century would support this conclusion insofar as it poses the trajectory question: how did the early church justify reading Luke and Acts *alongside* the Jewish Scriptures if it wasn't written *as* Jewish Scripture in the first place. Recognition of the genre of Luke and Acts as "Scripture" as early as the writing and first circulation of the two works is an indication that this was its perceived genre. Luke's own Scriptural intertextuality is evidence that this was also his understanding of its genre.

Luke expresses a theology which has *literary* implications relating to the Jewish Scriptures and the prospect of adding to those writings. The question arises: Did Luke conceive of his writing as "Scripture"? We conclude our case with three points:

---

[1] F. Kermode, *The Genesis of Secrecy* (Cambridge, Massachusetts: Harvard University Press, 1979), 64.

1) Luke shows awareness of the historic role of prophets in Israel's history. Prophets have books recording their oracles (e.g. Luke 4:17). Luke identifies John the Baptist and Jesus as prophets (Luke 1:76; 4:24; 7:16; 26-28). He also presents their fate as typical for prophets (Luke 11:49-51; 13:33-34; Acts 7:52). Luke claims to be recording their words and deeds (Luke 1:1-4; Acts 1:1), therefore it is reasonable to assume that he viewed his writing as "Scriptural".

2) Luke records an awareness of literary periodicity in Jesus' remark, "...the law and the prophets were *until* John: since that time the kingdom of God is preached" (Luke 16:16). The content of that preaching is *prima facia* contained in Luke's gospel and as such represents the writing that comes after the "Law and the Prophets" and adds to those writings the new teaching of Jesus—a third corpus.

3) Luke narrates the presence of the holy Spirit at the beginning of the Gospel and throughout Acts. In terms of the narrative prominence of the holy Spirit, Luke positions the holy Spirit as intimately involved with witness to the gospel. W. H. Shepherd's study, *The Narrative Function of the Holy Spirit as a Character in Luke-Acts* (1994)[1] argues the case that the prominence of the holy Spirit serves to guarantee the narrative account that Luke is presenting. The Spirit is the "Spirit of prophecy" and as such confirms, not only the Word that was preached by the apostles, it confirms this Word as recorded by Luke.

---

[1] W. H. Shepherd, *The Narrative Function of the holy Spirit as a Character in Luke-Acts* (Atlanta: Scholars Press, 1994).

CHAPTER EIGHT
The Spirit of Elijah

1. Introduction[1]

The bestowal of the Spirit is not just a phenomenon at Pentecost; rather, we should see the bestowal of the Spirit beginning with Jesus, John the Baptist, and the other prophets at the birth of Jesus. John had the Spirit of Elijah, but there is also an analogy between the bestowal of the Spirit at Pentecost and the Spirit of Elijah (Luke 1:17). Such a proposal has consequences for Luke's "last days" understanding of Pentecost (Acts 2:17), as it imparts a particularly *Jewish* emphasis to Pentecost, and it requires us to apply a "last days" framework across the entire story of Luke-Acts.

2. The Bestowal of the Spirit at the Birth of John and Jesus

The bestowal of the Spirit as prophesied by Joel is fulfilled starting with the birth of John and Jesus. This is indicated in various ways:

1) Luke's distinctive use of *pimplemi* ("to fill") in relation to the Spirit is found in relation to the apostles (e.g. Acts 2:4) as well as John the Baptist, Elisabeth and Zacharias (Luke 1:15, 41, 67).

2) John the Baptist and Jesus are presented as prophets in Luke' story (Luke 1:76; 4:24; 7:16, 26; 13:33; 20:6; 24:19; Acts 3:22-23; 7:37), and as such their possession of the Spirit falls within the compass of Joel's latter day bestowal of the Spirit which is couched in terms of prophesying. The principal term for their preaching is one employed in Joel's prophecy as Joel 3:5 (LXX) uses *euangelidzo* ("they that have the good news preached to them") as the corresponding term for the Hebrew *sryd* ("the remnant"). The same verb, *euangelidzo* is used by Gabriel to announce the birth of John the Baptist (Luke 1:19), as well as the preaching of the Gospel (e.g. Luke 4:18), and the apostolic mission (e.g. Acts 5:42). This commonality ties the three ministries of Luke-Acts together as an activity directed to the same **generation** rather than separate actions belonging to different epochs.

---

[1] This essay appeared in *The Testimony* in a slightly shorter version.

3) Luke's use of the concept of "power" also suggests that he was writing the fulfilment of Joel's prophecy into the terms of his story opening. The expression, "power of the highest" (Luke 1:35) strikes an echo with Luke's later expression, "power from on high" (Luke 24:49), which refers to the bestowal of the Spirit at Pentecost. Similarly, this language of "power" is used in connection with Jesus (Luke 4:14, Acts 10:48), which suggests that Luke does not regard Jesus' anointment with the Spirit as different *in kind* to that of other characters in his story, even if there is a difference of *degree* in the range of its effects through Jesus. Accordingly, Luke retrains the same metaphor for the possession of the Spirit (*pleres* "full", Luke 4:1, *pimplemi* "to fill", Luke 1:15, 41, 67, Acts 2:4) throughout his account.

On the basis of (1)-(3), we conclude that the fulfilment of Joel's prophecy begins with the birth of John the Baptist; the bestowal continues through Jesus' ministry and extends through Acts.

3. The Bestowal of the Spirit at Pentecost

Luke anticipates the bestowal of the Spirit at Pentecost with Jesus' assertion, "And, behold, I send the promise of my Father upon you" (Luke 24:49). There is an allusion here to the terms of the Elijah prophecy of Mal 4:5, "And, behold, I send..."[1] (indicated by the LXX which uses the same Greek), and the close parallel, "And behold I send forth..." of Mal 3:1.

The use of "to send" in Luke 24:49 is distinctive on two counts. Firstly, it contrasts with the gospel of John, which uses a different Greek verb for the sending of the Holy Spirit (John 14:26; 15:26; 16:7) ; and secondly, Luke has used "I send" in relation to commissions, whether these concern the disciples and apostles (Luke 9:2, 52; 10:1, 3; 19:29, 32; 22:8, 35), prophets (Luke 11:49; 13:34), angels (Luke 1:19, 26), Jesus (Luke 4:18, 43; 9:48; 10:16), John the Baptist (Luke 7:27), or miscellaneous characters (Luke 7:3, 20; 14:17, 32; 19:14; 20:10, 20). The pattern is regular and repeated in Luke and Acts. This choice of verb therefore is distinctive because it carries a *personification of commission and delegation* in respect of "the promise of the father", i.e. the holy Spirit. This personification would be consistent with a bestowal of the Spirit upon the apostles as a bestowal of the "Spirit of Elijah".

---

[1] This is the text in Greek New Testament with the most textual support, but the word for "behold" is omitted from some important manuscripts such as Codex Siniaticus and $_p$75.

A number of elements in Luke's narrative present Pentecost as another fulfilment of Malachi's forerunner prophecy:[1]

1) The "Elijah prophet" comes *before* the messiah; the holy Spirit comes at Pentecost *before* any return of Jesus (Acts 1:11; 3:19-20). The principal function of the bestowal of the Spirit is "prophecy", as shown by the quotation of Joel; Elijah is the archetypal prophet, as shown by Luke's story of the Transfiguration. The "Elijah prophet" is a personal "messenger" ("my" messenger) from the one sending; the disciples are likewise personal messengers sent forth to preach (Acts 1:8, "witnesses unto me").

2) The "Elijah prophet" has a function of "comforting" the people (Isa 40:1). Luke reflects this when he asserts that Simeon is waiting for the "consolation" (Luke 2:25[2]) of Israel. The gospel of John (subsequent to the death of John the Baptist) describes the coming of the holy Spirit as the sending of "another" comforter (John 14:26), Luke reflects this tradition when he ascribes "comfort" to the holy Spirit (Acts 9:31).

3) The "Elijah prophet" is sent before "the great and terrible day of the Lord" (Mal 4:5), and the pouring out of the Spirit is likewise before "the great and terrible day of the Lord" (Acts 2:20; Joel 3:4 LXX).

4) The "messenger" prepares a "way" (Mal 3:1; Isa 40:3) and this is applied to the work of the Baptist (Luke 3:4). Scholars have long noted that "way" is a significant term of identity in Acts and disputed its background and sources.[3] If Malachi is the background, Luke may be

---

[1] C. F. Evans has also noted that the operation of the Spirit in the early chapters of Acts has "some counterpart in the Gospel in Luke 1 and 2, see *Saint Luke*, (London: SCM Press, 1990), 87. He describes the parallel in terms of a resumption of prophecy, but he does not explore the Elijah parallel that we propose. For example, Luke's sense of *pun* may be present in the comparison he makes between John the Baptist and the bestowal of the Spirit—in both accounts the question of "drink" and drunkenness appears (Luke 1:15; Acts 2:13).

[2] Luke is using the corresponding noun to the verb in the LXX of Isa 40:3.

[3] Thus for example, B. J. Malina and J. H. Neyrey argue for an *halakhic* background to the symbol in "First Century Personality: Dyadic, not Individualistic" in J. H. Neyrey (Ed.), *The Social World of Luke-Acts*, (Peabody: Hendrickson, 1991), 92.

using "way" as a group boundary marker[1] to identify disciples and their beliefs, and in this manner show the apostles' ministry as a continuation of the work of John the Baptist in bringing out a people from the nation

5) The role of the forerunner is to "turn the people to the Lord their God" (Luke 1:16); this was the pre-eminent work of Elijah on Mt. Carmel—to turn the people away from Baal to Yahweh (1 Kgs 18:17; Matt 17:11-12). The same purpose is prominent in Acts (Acts 3:19; 11:21). Peter asserts that were the people to turn unto God, "times of refreshing" would have come from the "face of the Lord" (Acts 3:19).

6) "Elijah" has the function of "turning" the children to the fathers (Mal 4:6). This function is applied to John the Baptist in Matthew's record (Matt 17:11), and Luke strikes an echo with the "fathers and children" aspect of the forerunner's ministry with regard to John the Baptist *and* the apostles (Luke 3:8; Acts 3:25).

On the basis of (1)-(6), we conclude therefore that what is happening in Acts is the same as what is happening in Luke's gospel. The "Spirit of Elijah" brings a broad view of the work of a prophet to Luke's whole story, whether John the Baptist or the Apostles. Even though Luke does not attribute miracles to John the Baptist, this does not diminish his participation in this "Elijah" latter day bestowal of the spirit. In the case of the apostles, the broader witness of Elijah is reflected in the accounts of their confrontation with the Jewish authorities and their miracles.

4. Conclusion
Luke narrates a historical period which has a beginning with John the Baptist, a story that concerns the "last days"; the operation of the Spirit in this time period fulfils the terms of the OT prophecies made by the eighth century prophets, Joel and Isaiah, and therefore from that perspective, however many bestowals of the Spirit on however many individuals there are, this is all part of the same phenomenon predicted by Isaiah and Joel for the "last days".

---

[1] The evidence in Luke indicates that "the Way" was used and understood by *opponents* to identify believers and in this way it acts as a boundary marker.

CHAPTER NINE
Old Testament History

1. Introduction[1]

The subject of the "Old Testament and History" is a large one and we can only engage here in a summary essay with a discussion of representative examples of the kinds of topic that comprise the area. Our interest in the subject is to outline a reasonable approach to the history in the Old Testament so that it can be read and re-read with a view to adopting and/or building up the faith that is found in the Old Testament.

We use the expression "Old Testament" because it is the Christian faith that we seeking to foster from these books of the Jewish Scriptures. For Jesus, his disciples and the early church, the "Old Testament" was simply their Scriptures; they did not use the nomenclature of "Old Testament"— this came later as the prophets of the first century church added to these Scriptures new writings that became the "New Testament". The view of Scripture held by Jesus and the first believers was a high one: the Scriptures were given by God, inspired, profitable and could not be broken (John 10:35; 2 Tim 3:16; 2 Pet 1:21). This is their witness and evaluation, and it is a witness from far nearer the historical times during which the Jewish Scriptures were written than we find ourselves today. This is an important point when we consider modern historical reconstructions that reject the "history" recorded in the Jewish Scriptures. For example, if a historian today regards Moses as a figure of legend because there is no extra-Biblical evidence for his existence, such an argument can be countered with the evidential witness of Judaism in the first century, which had no doubt about the existence of Moses.

The evaluation of the Old Testament as history is positive and/or negative according to the scholar that you consult. There are those who offer very negative assessments and those who offer the opposite; no doubt this state of affairs can be explained by pointing to the presuppositions of each kind of person: a critical scholar will have a naturalist standpoint and treat Biblical material the same way as other Near Eastern texts, although it may be suspected that there is a bias in favour of non-Biblical texts where there is a conflict between the two; in

---

[1] This essay will appear in the book *Reasons*.

contrast, a conservative scholar will treat the Biblical text with an eye on its status as a Scriptural text and favour its evidential witness.

The hypothetical and tentative nature of the business of historical reconstruction facilitates the two types of scholarship to the extent that the conservative scholar does not need to appeal to the authority of Scripture (the Old Testament) to settle an issue. Instead, s/he can use the standard methodologies of history but prefer conservative choices in the configuration of the evidence, and so the resulting historical reconstruction will be different. It is because the raw data underdetermines the historical reconstruction that conservative scholars can make conjectures, reject external sources as unreliable, and construe evidence differently to their critical colleagues; the same point applies with regard to critical scholars—they are making choices in their overall interpretation of the data.

Things get left behind, whether it is texts, walls, or pottery, and these things are the stuff of history. The Old Testament refers to many individuals and their lives but they have left no other traces of their existence. This does not cast doubt on the Old Testament because the stories in which they occur are not on the scale of the affairs of state. Thus, the stories about Abraham, Isaac and Jacob are family stories; the history of the kings of Israel and Judah, on the other hand, deals with individuals and events on a larger scale. It is not unsurprising to find corroborative evidence of the history of the kings in the records of other Near Eastern states but nothing about the Patriarchs. In this latter case, historical corroboration is about the kind of nomadic lifestyle represented—is it true for the times and the place?[1]

Absence of evidence is not evidence of absence, but it is reasonable to expect extra-Biblical evidence, the "larger" an individual or an event's presence is on the stage of history. Thus, we might reasonably expect "large" individuals and/or events in the Old Testament such as the exodus, the conquest of the land, or the reign of David and Solomon to

---

[1] The historicity of the patriarchal stories is shown in a general way by pointing to correspondences between the stories and other archaeological and textual data from the Early Bronze Age. For a recent discussion, see in D. E. Fleming, "Genesis in History and Tradition: The Syrian background of Israel's Ancestors, Reprise" in *The Future of Biblical Archaeology: Reassessing Methodologies and Assumptions* (eds. J. K. Hoffmeier and A. Millard; Grand Rapids: Eerdmans, 2004), 193-232.

be corroborated; we might not expect smaller individuals and/or events to be confirmed, such as Abraham's visit to Egypt, the existence of Aaron, the women King David married, or the ministry of the prophet Hosea. This is an important point because it narrows the range of possible conflict that has arisen or might arise about the Old Testament.

A further preliminary point that needs to be made is this: the further back in time we go, the less evidence there is to handle and the more hypothetical is the reconstruction of history. In this regard, we should make a distinction between the "primeval history" of Genesis 1-11 and the history of Israel that begins in Genesis 12 and continues to the end of the Old Testament. Rationalist historians relegate to the status of "myth" and/or "legend" the stories in Genesis 1-11 such as "Adam and Eve", "the Flood" or the "Tower of Babel". The stories about the patriarchs are treated more sympathetically by such historians even if they are regarded as largely "folklore"; yet again, such historians treat the accounts of the kings more positively. So it is that when investigating the Old Testament and its "history", the further back in time one goes, the more assumptions one finds underlying the scholar's treatment, especially philosophical and theological assumptions.

The Old Testament is a large collection of books and the historical timescale is extensive (2000 years in round numbers if we exclude Genesis 1-11). Accordingly, we have to discuss the topic of "The Old Testament and History" with representative examples. While in scholarship we can find negative appraisals of more or less any aspect of Old Testament history, it is not all of equal value or a challenge to those who have taken a positive approach. In broad terms, critical scholarship has rejected the accounts of the exodus, the conquest of the land and the establishment of the monarchy. In addition, little historical value is placed on the so-called "primeval history" of Genesis 1-11. Apart from these "big events", any number of smaller details in the historical record of the Old Testament have been questioned and rejected, but it is beyond the scope of our summary essay to make such a list.

A person who comes to the Old Testament, whether s/he is a Christian or somebody seeking faith, should read-up on what conservative scholars say about its historical content, as they will provide historical reasons for understanding why Jesus and the early church held a high opinion of the Jewish Scriptures. An even-handed stance would read what both critics and supporters have to say about the Old Testament record. In this essay we will look at the following examples: the primeval history, the conquest,

111

and the kings of Judah. We will finish the essay with a few thoughts about the relationship of faith and history. The Bible has always had its critics, but our thesis is that there is as yet nothing in the world of scholarship that prevents a reader from trusting its history and thereby adopting its faith.

2. Primeval History

The first chapters of Genesis are widely misunderstood, misrepresented and dismissed as unhistorical; instead, they are valued for their so-called "religious" truth. This observation is about interpretation: if the early chapters of Genesis are not interpreted correctly, any historical judgment is irrelevant. The notion of "history" here is one of the "pre-history" of humankind, the historical "story" that is told about the origin of human civilization on earth in the Near East, and (in Genesis 1) a part of the geological history of the planet. For example,

- If the genealogy of Genesis 5 is counted literally and consecutively, the pre-history is short and recent (including Noah), and this flies in the face of any number of scientific disciplines. If the human ages are notional and the genealogy is non-consecutive, then the length of the pre-history is undetermined.

- If the Flood is global, then the account conflicts with several branches of science. If the Flood is local to the Mesopotamian Basin, then it is to be compared with other traditions about a great flood in the region, and there isn't any necessary conflict with science; the account can be positively appraised as history.

- If Tower of Babel is a story about miraculously creating some local languages, then it cannot be verified or falsified by Historical Linguistics—it falls under the radar of that science because it is a miraculous intervention.

- If special creation is excluded *a priori* from the account of the human species, then there is no prospect that the "Adam and Eve" story could be true. If on the other hand, human ancestry is traceable to a common ancestor pair, then a point in pre-historic time has been identified for Adam and Eve. Furthermore, it is not possible to exclude special creation on a scientific basis because it involves the miraculous and divine agency.

112

- If creation week is about the origin of the universe, it places the sun, moon and stars in the wrong place on Day 4. However, if the planet and its water are, instead, presupposed by the account in Gen 1:2, and the story is about *replenishing* the earth, then it is not in conflict with current views of the universe or of geological history; the prior existence of the sun, moon and stars is implied by the prior existence of the planet. (This view is known as **Old Earth Creationism**.)

- If creation "week" is a metaphor for the actions of God in relation to the heavens and the earth over time—his being work presented in terms of the "working week" (Exod 20:11), then there is no basis for arguing that the account is in conflict with science; its truth value lies in its phenomenological descriptions[1] of the configuration of the planet for the placement of human life.

The above brief points are about the interpretation of Genesis 1-11. When someone dismisses this part of the Old Testament, it is often the dismissal of an erroneous interpretation. Any assessment of the historical value of the Old Testament should be focussed on the original intent and meaning of the narrative. What science has done for Biblical Studies is to remove older erroneous interpretations and facilitated a proper appreciation of the text. What science has not done is overturn special creation, divine agency and the miraculous, and our interpretation of Genesis 1-11 should retain these elements, otherwise it will be unfaithful to the interpretation of Genesis in the rest of the Bible, for example, with regard to the literal existence of Adam and Eve.[2]

The story narrative that we have in Genesis 1-11 is austere and brief; this is especially so for the creation account of Genesis 1, and it is precisely because that account is a high level description of creation using verbs that would be readily understood to a person working the land, that it is still believed today and valued as a true account of origins. The account

---

[1] The descriptions of Genesis 1 betray the perspective of subsistence life. For example, humans are given dominion over fish because they catch and eat fish; likewise with fowl and cattle. Or again, the seas are told to "bring forth" the fish abundantly, and the verb reflects what would *appear* to be the case for a fisherman.

[2] While this is a Biblical essay, and not a science paper, it is worth noting that to the extent the sciences do not factor in special creation, divine agency and the miraculous—to that extent they distort the story of our origins.

lacks any attempt at the "how" of things with which science is concerned and it is focused on the "that" of things which a person of faith must believe if he is to have an Old Testament faith. It is not like the somewhat fantastic myths of creation native to Mesopotamia.

However, a person coming to these stories today may find some more difficult to accept than others. The element that causes most difficulty for a first-time reader is the genealogies and their numbers. The modern reader initially takes the numbers literally and the generations to be consecutive and without gaps and finds them unbelievable. However, these two assumptions may not be correct for the primeval genealogies. We need to know about the conventions for such genealogies for pre-historic times before we can dismiss them.

3. Pre-historic Genealogies

The Old Testament scholar, K. A. Kitchen, offers a standard discussion of the genealogy of Genesis 5 in relation to the king lists and reign lengths of Mesopotamian monarchs. In Sumerian and Akkadian king lists, prior to the flood there were 8 or 10 kings stretching back until kingship was "lowered from the heavens". In the Sumerian King List, for example, the total number of years for the reigns of the eight kings is 241,000 years whereas the total number of years for the reigns of the kings after the flood is 24,510 and 2310 years for a sequence of 23 and then 12 kings.[1] Whereas the Sumerian King List documents a long pre-history before the Flood in terms of 8 or 10 kings and their reigns (depending on the tablet), the genealogy of Genesis 5 works with 10 generations and fewer years.[2] Both counts break at the Flood, each has large numbers and the years decline dramatically after the Flood. Their common "8/10" framework[3]

---

[1] ANET, 265; K. A. Kitchen, *On the Reliability of the Old Testament* (Grand Rapids: Eerdmans, 2003), 439f.

[2] This comparison is true in a general way if both Genesis and the Sumerian King List are using a decimal system; however, the King List is actually using a modified sexagesimal system. J. H. Walton, *Ancient Israelite Literature in its Cultural Context* (Grand Rapids: Zondervan, 1989), 127-131, shows how the two decimal and sexagesimal systems align very closely in their totals after conversion if the original compiler of the Sumerian King List was using the Genesis 5 genealogy and misunderstood its digits as a modified sexagesimal number. In this way, Walton makes a conclusive case for the Genesis genealogy being the older text.

[3] The use of "ten generations" as a motif to exhaust a period of time is seen in the law, "An Ammonite or Moabite shall not enter into the

allows the suggestion that we have here a **notional use of numbers** to structure an unknown and long period of time.

A second point to make here is that the genealogy in Genesis 5 is not necessarily consecutive—the father-son relationship may in some instances be a grandfather-grandson relationship or there may be a multiple of intervening generations. The opening entries of the genealogy are,

> And Adam lived an hundred and thirty years, and begat a son in his own likeness, after his image; and called his name Seth: And the days of Adam after he had begotten Seth were eight hundred years: and he begat sons and daughters: And all the days that Adam lived were nine hundred and thirty years: and he died. And Seth lived an hundred and five years, and begat Enos: And Seth lived after he begat Enos eight hundred and seven years, and begat sons and daughters. And all the days of Seth were nine hundred and twelve years: and he died. And Enos lived ninety years, and begat Cainan: And Enos lived after he begat Cainan eight hundred and fifteen years, and begat sons and daughters: And all the days of Enos were nine hundred and five years: and he died.
> Gen 8:3-1 (KJV)

We would normally read this today as a consecutive sequence without any gaps. However, the early story of Genesis 4 documents the birth of Cain and Abel before Seth. The genealogy of Genesis 5 gives no hint of a Cain or an Abel or any other sons and daughters before Seth, but a reader should take this information and use it to condition his understanding of the genealogy of Genesis 5. Seth is a first generation son of Adam (Gen 4:25), and Enos is likewise a first generation son of Seth (Gen 4:26); but Cainan may be a grandson, or a great-grandson, or a more distant "son" of Enos; the genealogy may therefore have gaps. The birth of Cainan to Enos may be the birth of a *forbear* of Cainan, the individual in whose line Cainan was born. This possibility is important as it should prevent a reader from treating the genealogy of Genesis 5 as a simple consecutive sequence of father-son relationships—there is a great deal of time after

congregation of the Lord; even to their tenth generation shall they not enter into the congregation of the Lord for ever" (Deut 23:3, KJV).

Enos and before Cainan.[1] A further indication that the genealogy of Genesis 5 could be read in a non-consecutive way is the absence of the added information of "calling the name of the son": this detail is recorded for Seth in Gen 5:3, Enos in Gen 4:26, and for Noah in Gen 5:29 but not for the other "sons"; the number of generations in the middle of the genealogy is therefore unknown.

This interpretation makes sense in the light of the nomination of only 10 generations; there are ten names that structure the family history of Noah.[2] The ten-fold stylised arrangement is mirrored in the genealogy of Cain: although it is a 6 generation framework, both end with an individual who has three sons, and both have similarly named ancestors. Such a selection from history (i.e. the reality of these individuals) supports the interpretation of the ages in the genealogy as notional.

The other difficulty that modern readers have with the genealogy is the longevity of the individuals; the oldest man lived for 969 years and this is dismissed as an unbelievable "fantastic" number. Again, a modern reader is assuming that the ages given are literal, but the modern's case against the ages being real consists simply of the estimates of death given by archaeological anthropologists of the dead that they uncover in any grave sites in the Near East from any point in the past. Furthermore, there is no basis in paleo-biology for supposing that human life-spans were much different in the last 10,000 years. If we thus assume that men and women lived to what we regard as normal ages, we should ask: *why* are long ages given here in Genesis 5 and in the Mesopotamian king lists?

One kind of response would be to reject the ages given as 'real' and regard the numbers as false; we could then reject the historicity of the genealogy as a whole, and use this conclusion to cast doubt on the historical value of the primeval history. This kind of reaction would be simplistic, and we

---

[1] In addition, we should observe that there were many sons and daughters born to each of the names before the descendent who is named; this is shown by the example of Adam and Eve with Seth and implied by the great age at which the "descendent" (forbear) is born.

[2] That we have a family history in Genesis 5 is indicated by the colophon of Gen 6:9, "These are the records of the generations of Noah" (NASB). On this see, R. K. Harrison, "From Adam to Noah: A Reconsideration of the Antediluvian Patriarchs' Ages" *JETS* 37/2 (1994): 161-168 (162); P. J. Wiseman, *New Discoveries in Babylonia about Genesis* (4th ed.; London: Marshall, Morgan & Scott, 1946), chap. 5.

should instead ask: if those who composed the genealogy knew very well how long humans typically lived (whatever we say that was; life-spans could have been longer), *why* would they employ long ages? A preliminary point would be that we are assuming the long ages given were ubiquitous among humans, but the only data we have relates to ten individuals.

Some conservative commentators do see literal ages in the genealogy and they observe that one long age is not associated with a birth or a death and that is the fact that Enoch "walks" with God for 300 years; this needs further explanation.[1] Moreover, the reduction of human ages after the Flood to between 100-200 years and then to around 70 plus years was gradual over a few generations. Thus, it is suggested that God intervened after the Flood so that human beings had shorter life-spans; the precedent for this is Gen 6:3, "And the Lord said, My spirit shall not always strive with man, for that he also *is* flesh: yet his days shall be an hundred and twenty years" (KJV). These commentators affirm that the ageing process was speeded-up.

This approach is problematic for critical scholars of the Bible because it involves the idea of divine intervention. This is a "problem" that occurs in several other places in the Old Testament where the miraculous is recorded or implied. In response, conservative scholars have tried different approaches: for example, it has been said that the Hebrew digits are not decimal (Base-10) but Base-2 or some other base; or, the numbers are aligned with an old cosmological scheme related to the planets; and, even, the years are not solar years but some other (perhaps lunar) "year". These suggestions, and others, show that scholars do not dismiss the genealogy as poor history; there is a good case[2] to be made for it being older than Mesopotamian king lists in composition. Rather, they seek to explain the *use of large numbers* in the genealogy by scribes perfectly familiar with the relatively short human life-span. Of these approaches, the best harmonizing suggestion is that the genealogy[3] is **notional** and serves the

---

[1] It could be said that God "took" Enoch and it was believed that he then walked with God for 300 years.

[2] Walton, Ancient Israelite Literature in its Cultural Context, 127-131.

[3] The genealogy uses two verbs: the days 'were' so many years and an individual 'lived' for so many years. This choice means that the names are not the names of ages, such as the 'Adamic Age' or the 'Age of Lamech', following the convention of monarchies (e.g. Tudor, Hanover or Windsor). A *lived* long age is the meaning and therefore it is the genealogy as a whole that would be notional not the individual ages.

purpose of structuring an unknown long period of time, accepting that the human life-span might have been somewhat longer than it is currently. How does this work? Is this a desperate attempt to rescue the Biblical text?

The ages that are given mostly cluster above the 900 mark—just short of a thousand years. Lamech's life is cut short just before the Flood and Enoch is a special case, but otherwise the 900 +/- pattern is carefully chosen, because the choice of a "thousand years" as a limiting period isn't arbitrary. In the "Prayer of Moses", it is said that, "…a thousand years in thy sight *are but* as yesterday when it is past, and *as* a watch in the night" (Ps 90:4, KJV). The comment is, no doubt, a metaphor for the passage of time and how the ages are marked by God. The New Testament writer, Peter, makes a comment with this verse when he says, "But, beloved, be not ignorant of this one thing, that one day *is* with the Lord as a thousand years, and a thousand years as one day" (2 Pet 3:8, KJV).

This language is relevant to Genesis 5 because in Genesis 2 God had declared that were Adam to sin, he would die in the day that he sinned (Gen 2:17). If the poetic understanding of time expressed in the Prayer of Moses is at work in Genesis 5, the limitation of the antediluvian ages to just under a thousand years is one way in which the compiler of these traditions (traditionally Moses[1]) shows the fulfilment of God's edict of death: the refrain of the genealogy is "and he died" (8x). If a thousand years are as a day in God's eyes, all these men did die in the kind of "day" that God had decreed for Adam's dying.

The understanding implicit in the Prayer of Moses is not irrelevant to our reading of Genesis 5. The prayer starts off (vv. 1-5) as a meditation on the early chapters of Genesis with its references to "all generations", "giving birth to the earth", "children of Adam", "destruction" and a "flood". If a long and unknown period of time was going to be structured with ten generations, ages just under a thousand years would be chosen to conform to God's attitude to the passage of time and the edict that Adam was to die in the "day" that he sinned. The opening verses of Moses' prayer reconcile the apparent contradiction between Genesis 2 and 5 in its meditation.

---

[1] W. C. Kaiser, *The Old Testament Documents: Are they Reliable and Relevant?* (Downers Grove: InterVarsity Press, 2001), 57-58; Wiseman, *New Discoveries in Babylonia about Genesis*, chap. 8.

The Old Testament account of creation is often ridiculed because the genealogy of Genesis 5 is totalled up to contribute to an age for the earth of around 6000 years. The historical reliability of the whole of the Old Testament is then thrown into doubt. This is a poor stance to adopt. The genealogy is "of its times" in using large numbers, if we reject the literality of the numbers, this does not mean the individuals are not historical individuals. However, once we observe that there is no name-calling from Cainan onwards until Noah, we have a basis for treating the genealogy as having substantial gaps and the pre-history of Genesis becomes an indeterminate period.[1] The genealogy itself does not engage in totalling up. Whether we then treat the genealogy in a strictly literal way or a notional way can remain an open question.

4. Exodus and Conquest

Did the exodus happen? Were the Israelites in bondage in Egypt? As a preliminary point, we might say that the exodus is integral to the witness of the rest of the Old Testament—the religion and theology of the Israelites revolves around the exodus. The exodus is also referred to many times in the New Testament. This is powerful evidence for the exodus having happened; it is not an incidental story in the Old Testament that can be dismissed. Nevertheless, critical scholars have dismissed the account as legendary, while conservative scholars have regarded the story as faithful to its historical setting and the most likely explanation of Israel's origins as a nation. The most recent full length defence of the historicity of the exodus is that of J. K. Hoffmeier;[2] here we will consider the Old Testament account of the "conquest".

The historicity of the account of Joshua's conquest of the land has been questioned from an archaeological point of view. However, critical[3] and conservative[4] scholars have given different evaluations of the evidence. This divergence of opinion is the result of the "silence" of the archaeological data—it has to be interpreted in a context. Conquest leaves

---

[1] The start of the age of civilization is usually dated to about 10,000 BCE, which is one way to estimate the time period of the genealogy.

[2] J. K. Hoffmeier, *Israel in Egypt: The Evidence for the Authenticity of the Exodus Tradition* (Oxford: Oxford University Press, 1997).

[3] M. Weippert, *The Settlement of the Israelite Tribes in Palestine* (London: SCM Press, 1971).

[4] J. Bright, *A History of Israel* (London: SCM Press, 1972); Kitchen, *On the Reliability of the Old Testament*; Hoffmeier, Israel in Egypt: *The Evidence for the Authenticity of the Exodus Tradition*.

behind evidence of destruction, but it is difficult to be certain of any alignment of archaeological data to a particular conflict; how could an archaeologist positively associate a destruction layer from the 13c. BCE with the Old Testament record rather than the outcome of a battle between native Canaanite kings? There may be distinctive weapons evidence left behind or other material remains that identify a particular attacker; a victorious attacker may subsequently occupy the conquered city and leave material remains behind in more recent layers of the site; however, equally there may be no such remains.

Conservative scholars have generally held that the exodus is to be dated to the late 13c. BCE and they have aligned the conquest with the late 13c. or early 12c. BCE destruction layers in Palestinian cities and towns such as Lachish, Ashdod and Hazor, as well as others. P. W. Lapp notes[1] that above the destruction layers of these places, there is evidence of a less advanced culture and of semi-nomadic people. We have archaeological evidence for the presence of Israel as a tribal people[2] in Canaan from the Merenptah Stele in 1209/1208 but no textual reference to their presence before that date. Thus, the historical reconstruction is that the Israelites took over the central highlands of Canaan.

The account in Joshua doesn't detail the destruction of many towns; Jericho, Ai and Hazor are the only ones noted. The various campaigns undertaken by Joshua were from a base at Gilgal. Generally, the army moved on after defeating a town, re-grouping back at Gilgal. After these initial raids, the Israelites moved to occupy the central highlands. The 13c. archaeological evidence for the destruction of Hazor has been confirmed, but not for Jericho or Ai. This allows critical scholars to query the conquest account, but some conservative commentators have argued that this shows the archaeological evidence better fits a 15c. BCE conquest (ca. 1450).

---

[1] P. W. Lapp "The Conquest of Palestine in the Light of Archaeology" *CThm* 38 (1967): 283-300 (287).
[2] The determinative marker for a "people" rather than a "land" is used in the stela, thereby indicating a tribal association rather than a monarchic land— Hoffmeier, *Israel in Egypt: The Evidence for the Authenticity of the Exodus Tradition*, 30.

An early date for the conquest would fit Old Testament chronology (1 Kgs 6:1, MT; Jud 11:26). J. J. Bimson has argued[1] the 15c. destruction layers at towns and cities such as Jericho,[2] Bethel, Hazor, Debir, Lachish, Hebron, and Dan are the Israelite "conquest" and it was limited. Settling in the highlands after the military raids and using mostly existing settlements, Israelites would have re-used Canaanite things while adding their own (Josh 24:13), and this accounts for the nature of the material remains of the 15c.-14c. BCE. The countervailing evidence of Ai remains, which most archaeologists affirm was unoccupied both at this time and in the later 13c. date, unless the identification of Ai is wrong which has also been argued.[3] Moreover, the evidence of the Merenptah Stele from 1208/9 presupposes the presence of a tribal people in Canaan, which we may suppose requires the Israelites to have "conquered" the land and to have been settled for some time. If we follow the Old Testament chronology and place the conquest around 1450 BCE, then most of the archaeological criticism of the account in Joshua is irrelevant.[4] J. J. Niehaus and K. L. Younger have shown that the narrative in Joshua is typical of Near Eastern war narratives both of the first and second millennium. Typical of such accounts is hyperbole, war oracles, and divine involvement in warfare. It is this kind of comparative evidence that gives a reader confidence in the historical trustworthiness of the Old Testament account—the account is of its time.[5]

5. Judges and Kings

Verification or disconfirmation of the Old Testament record becomes a much easier task when the kingdoms of Israel and Judah come to the

---

[1] J. J. Bimson, *Redating the Exodus and Conquest* (Sheffield: Almond Press, 1981).

[2] The case for a 15c. destruction of Jericho is also argued in B. G. Wood, "Did the Israelites Conquer Jericho: A New Look at the Archaeological Evidence" *BAR* 16/2 (1990): 44-59. Wood is cautiously supported by Hoffmeier, *Israel in Egypt: The Evidence for the Authenticity of the Exodus Tradition*, 7.

[3] D. Livingston, "The location of Biblical Bethel and Ai reconsidered" *WTJ* 33, (1970): 20-44; J. M. Grintz, "Ai which is beside Beth-Aven" *Biblica* 42 (1961): 201-216.

[4] Hoffmeier, *Israel in Egypt: The Evidence for the Authenticity of the Exodus Tradition*, 34.

[5] K. L. Younger, *Ancient Conquest Accounts: A Study in Ancient Near Eastern and Biblical History Writing* (Sheffield: JSOT Press, 1990); J. J. Niehaus, "Joshua and Ancient Near Eastern Warfare" *JETS* 31 (1988): 45-50.

notice of the Mesopotamian Empires; it is at this time (the 8c.) that the records of those empires can be consulted for any correspondence with Old Testament history. Textual evidence relevant to the Old Testament before this time is rare for several reasons:

- Royal inscriptions on stela in Jerusalem from the early kings may well have been destroyed, as Jerusalem has been repeatedly destroyed and occupied down the centuries; the same point applies to other cities, towns and villages.[1]

- Royal archives would have been recorded on papyrus, leather, etc. but the climate is not conducive to the survival of such materials.

- The texts that we have are as few as those for neighbouring nations such as the Moabites and Philistines.[2]

Nevertheless, where there has been a mention of the Israelite or Judahite kings on stela, the nomenclature and history has confirmed the Old Testament record. As the field of history is large, we will take a worked example in which there is conflict between critical and conservative historians in order to show how and why the conservative approach is more satisfactory. The example is the Assyrian blockade of Jerusalem from which the Old Testament records a miraculous deliverance— conservative scholars accept this deliverance and critical scholars reject it as legendary.

5.1 The Assyrian Blockade of Jerusalem

According to the Assyrian records,[3] the third campaign of their emperor-king, Sennacherib, in 701 was directed generally to the land of Hatti (the

---

[1] The expression 'The House of David' has been found in an inscription from Dan—A. Biran, "An Aramaic Stele Fragment from Tel Dan" *IEJ* 43/2-3 (1993): 1-18.

[2] The Moabite Stone refers to Omri and Ahab, kings of Northern Israel; it may also refer to the "House of David"—see A. Lemaire, "'House of David' Restored Moabite Inscription" *BAR* 20/3 (1994): 30-37.

[3] For a convenient listing of the sources of the blockade of Jerusalem and the dates of the inscriptions see the table in R. Becking, "Chronology: A Skeleton without Flesh? Sennacherib's Campaign as a Case-Study" in *Like a Bird in a Cage* (ed., L. L. Grabbe; Sheffield: Sheffield Academic Press, 2003), 46-72 (65).

Syro-Judean land-bridge) rather than Judah which was only a constituent country. The Assyrian records paint a picture of a wholly successful campaign. It involved action against Phoenicia, Philistia as well as Judah; Egypt, who sent an army into the region, was beaten in battle. In relation to Judah, Sennacherib mounted a blockade against Jerusalem, took 46 strong cities, countless villages, forts, a large number of captives (200,150[1]) and domestic animals; he later received a gift from Hezekiah and took his daughters and women from the palace; and he increased Hezekiah's annual tribute (ANET, 287-288).

This summary cannot be reconciled with the biblical account of a miraculous deliverance for Jerusalem, so did this happen?

- 2 Kgs 18:13 has Sennacherib come up against all the fenced cities of Judah and taking them; this agrees with the Assyrian record. 2 Chron 32:1 notes that Sennacherib first *encamped* against the fenced cities, during which time Hezekiah made preparations to strengthen his position in Jerusalem (vv. 2-8).

- 2 Chron 32:10 reports Sennacherib's view of Hezekiah's position: he was under blockade in Jerusalem. This agrees with the Assyrian record which refers to earthworks or forts cast around Jerusalem.

- 2 Kgs 18:14 sees Hezekiah submit to Sennacherib who was at Lachish, and Sennacherib imposes a tribute of 30 talents of gold and 300 talents of silver. The text says that these monies were "appointed" to Hezekiah, and he regards the monies as something "put upon" him; this is the language of annual tribute and this detail agrees with Sennacherib's note of an increased annual tribute.

---

[1] M. De Odorico, The *Use of Numbers and Quantifications in the Assyrian Royal Inscriptions* (SAAS II; The Neo Assyrian Text Corpus Project; Helsinki: Helsinki University Press, 1995), 172., states that the number is an emphasis upon the "very high" (200,000) whilst conveying truthfulness in the exactitude (plus 150). Archaeological calculations place the population of Judah well under 100,000. Y. Shiloh estimates the population of Jerusalem and its outer environs during the eighth century to be between 25,000 and 40,000 inhabitants—"Judah and Jerusalem in the Eighth-Sixth Centuries B.C.E." in *Recent Excavations in Israel: Studies in Iron Age Archaeology* (eds., S. Gitin and W. G. Dever; AASOR 49; Winona Lake: Eisenbrauns, 1989), 97-106 (98).

- Sennacherib's record notes 30 talents of gold and 800 talents of silver that were sent *later* to Nineveh along with valuable commodities, daughters, concubines and musicians, along with a personal messenger. This would have been construed as a first annual tribute payment, as well as a gift in recognition of subservience. It is the same tribute/gift recorded in Kings because the Assyrian record (Rassam Cylinder[1]) is dated to 700. It was presumably sent to Nineveh and dispatched before Sennacherib turned the Assyrian army on Jerusalem in an act of treachery (Isa 33:1). We can accept the Assyrian record of the tribute on the grounds that it is detailed, contemporary, and then reiterated in the final edition of Sennacherib's Campaigns in the Taylor Prism; there is no certain conflict with the biblical amounts because the Assyrian basis of calculation may be different or exaggerated.[2]

- The narrative in Kings then goes onto record the sending of (the) Rabshakeh and a large army against Jerusalem from Lachish. Although a new episode account begins in 2 Kgs 18:17, the mention of Lachish ties the narrative to what has been formerly recounted (the sending of an ambassador to Lachish, v. 14). The whole episode is described in great detail and it leads to the deliverance of Jerusalem through the miraculous destruction of the Assyrian army. Obviously, none of this information is in an Assyrian record.

- The Rabshakeh episode climaxes with the promise of deliverance,

    By the way that he came, by the same shall he <u>return</u>,
    and shall not come into this city, saith the Lord. 2 Kgs
    19:33 (KJV)

    This text picks up on Hezekiah's attempt to get Sennacherib to "return" from him (2 Kgs 18:14) and implicitly criticizes the giving of a gift/tribute to Sennacherib rather than reliance upon Yahweh.

---

[1] The Rassam Cylinder is the earliest note of the gift/tribute.

[2] The text in Kings has 300 talents but the discrepancy might be due to a number of factors: the Assyrians may have differently calculated the silver and included sundry goods in the tribute/gift totals. See Becking, "Chronology: A Skeleton without Flesh? Sennacherib's Campaign as a Case-Study", 67-68.

While this episode is absent from Assyrian records, we take it as genuine, and see it as in the correct sequence of events.

Scholars will select which elements of the Assyrian and Biblical records correspond to the facts.[1] While this is a loaded comment, it is nevertheless expressing the point that scholars see in historical documents an ideology that expresses the point of view of the author of the document. Certainly, Kings and Chronicles present a different selection of details and emphases on the Assyrian Crisis. The same is true for Biblical scholars who will "write up" the history of the campaign rejecting the miraculous account of deliverance: ideology affects the critical scholar as much as the biblical writer—one believes in miracle and divine intervention, the other believes in probability and the human dimension.

5.2 Miraculous Deliverance

The Assyrian records paint a picture of success against all opponents. However, it is unusual that such success did not, on its own terms, mention the capture of Jerusalem. Many other cities are noted as besieged and conquered, so we would have to ask why Jerusalem did not suffer the same fate. Sennacherib defeated the Egyptians at Eltekeh and went on afterwards to besiege and conquer further cities, but the blockade of Jerusalem did not result in it being conquered. It is rather the capture of Lachish which is celebrated in the reliefs in Sennacherib's palace (though not in the *Annals*).[2] Furthermore, E. Ben Zvi notes[3] that the *Annals* give a lot of space to the ordinary tribute gift almost as a way to make up for the lack of any report of Jerusalem's conquest. The conquest of other cities and the submission and/or replacement of their kings are perfunctory notes by comparison. It is puzzling as to why Hezekiah was not removed

---

[1] For a discussion of this issue in relation to 701 see E. Ben Zvi, "Malleability and its Limits: Sennacherib's Campaign against Judah as a Case-Study" in *Like a Bird in a Cage* (ed., L. L. Grabbe; Sheffield: Sheffield Academic Press, 2003), 73-105.

[2] D. Luckenbill, ed., *The Annals of Sennacherib*, (repr. Wipf & Stock, 2005; Chicago: Chicago University Press, 1924). The reliefs are discussed in C. Uehlinger, "Clio in a World of Pictures—Another Look at the Lachish Reliefs from Sennacherib's Southwest Palace at Nineveh" in *Like a Bird in a Cage* (ed., L. L. Grabbe; Sheffield: Sheffield Academic Press, 2003), 221-305. Uehlinger discusses other reliefs that might picture Jerusalem, but reaches no conclusion, 293-303.

[3] Ben Zvi, "Malleability and its Limits: Sennacherib's Campaign against Judah as a Case-Study", 94.

as a king given that he was a leader of the rebellion against Assyria. These details support the view that Jerusalem was delivered miraculously and that this has been omitted for obvious reasons from the Assyrian records.

The nature of the miraculous deliverance is not stated (2 Kgs 19:35; 2 Chron 32:21). The number given for the Assyrians killed is 185,000 but the accuracy of the number is set within the canons of the historical reporting of the day;[1] it is a visual impression of the huge size of the army encamped outside Jerusalem. It is easy enough to hypothesize a natural means for a virulent (water/air borne) virus to sweep through the camp. Such deliverance would not, however, be a defeat from Sennacherib's point of view: there is obviously no acceptance of a miraculous intervention by Yahweh in his records. Interpreted naturally, a water-borne virus, say, (or one borne in a new delivery of wine to the camp), having decimated the army, would weaken his military presence in the region and cause him to return to Assyria. His decision not to complete the capture of Jerusalem was a military and logistical decision.

The deliverance by the Angel of the Lord is unusual and is reminiscent of the exodus from Egypt. It is unusual because Israel and Judah had experienced similar crises and threats in their history, but none of these were resolved through such a dramatic intervention. As R. E. Clements says, "The report that the dire consequences threatened by the confrontation between Sennacherib and Hezekiah were averted by direct divine intervention is highly unusual in Old Testament history-writing";[2] accordingly, some scholars regard the account as legendary.[3] However, the book of Isaiah includes several oracles about the safety of Jerusalem and her deliverance, and this kind of witness indicates that the historical account of 2 Kgs 18:17-19:37 is not a one-off legend. Furthermore, the account coheres with the themes of Samuel and Kings with its interest in the Davidic monarchy, and the choice of Jerusalem as the place where Yahweh would set his name. We cannot therefore dismiss the account in 2 Kgs 18:17-19:37 without dismissing other aspects of Kings, Chronicles and Isaiah.

---

[1] Following De Odorico's analysis in *The Use of Numbers and Quantifications in the Assyrian Royal Inscriptions*, 172.

[2] R. E. Clements, *Isaiah and the Deliverance of Jerusalem* (Sheffield: JSOT Press, 1980), 11.

[3] Clements, *Isaiah and the Deliverance of Jerusalem*, 15.

6. Conclusion

By way of conclusion, we will consider the relationship of faith and history. Critical and conservative scholars have argued their cases in monographs and journals. A reader coming to the Old Testament asking the question whether its history can be trusted can infer that its historical record has not been overturned—conservative scholars have provided historical reconstructions of the Near Eastern archaeological and textual evidence that fits the Old Testament account. These are not partial or *ad hoc* but are comprehensive even if there are points of detail where they express uncertainty and a lack of knowledge.

A historian is free to reconstruct the evidence in whatever way s/he chooses; the result is then presented for peer appraisal. There is no burden of proof on a critical or a conservative scholar—the process is a matter of handling some hard data (such as ceramic dates), but there is also a fair amount of subjective interpretation; the critical scholar tends to reject the Old Testament evidence for theological and philosophical reasons—the conservative scholar accepts the Old Testament as evidence and attempts a harmonization of its evidence with the relevant archaeology and any other texts.

In the past, before the rise of Biblical Criticism in the Enlightenment, a Bible commentator might have appealed to theology and/or philosophy to support the Old Testament—he would say that it was divinely inspired and part of the canon of the church. Today, conservative scholars do not *assume* any status for the Old Testament and treat it simply as textual evidence for historical reconstruction. They do not cast it aside for any theological and philosophical reasons, which ironically is the situation with critical scholars. In rejecting any inherent authority for the Old Testament, the Enlightenment replaced such authority with a set of theological and philosophical assumptions which created a sceptical starting point for a scholar working within academia. It was in effect the replacement of one authoritarian structure (church) for another (an academia defined by an Enlightenment philosophy of rationalism, naturalism and scepticism).

For this reason, the better scholarship in Biblical Studies is conservative, and this is because it accepts all the archaeological and textual evidence, making an attempt to reconstruct the history in a maximal way. A reader, looking to see if the Old Testament can be trusted, should therefore give preference to the arguments and the reconstruction of conservative scholars. There is an ideological bias in the work of critical scholars which reflects the philosophy of the times; conservative writing is much more self-conscious about the influence of presuppositions on historical research. Conservative scholars value the Old Testament text because it is a substantial witness to the history.

A factor which we have not yet mentioned is the dating of the Old Testament texts. This is a large subject, particularly affected by the shifting sands of hypothesis and theory. Theories of late dates for the texts are likely to be the concomitant luggage of a sceptical view of the Old Testament account of history. The tendency to late-date the Old Testament texts is bound up with source critical theories of composition and theories about the development of religious ideas in Israel and Judah. The point here is that critical scholars then downgrade the evidential witness of books like Joshua or Judges precisely because they regard them as late and etiological[1] in purpose.

Again, the clash between critical and conservative scholars that we have seen in respect of the historical value of the Old Testament is also present in regard to literary theories about the Old Testament. It is beyond the scope of this essay to consider this topic, except to observe that conservative scholars have persuasively argued that the attempt to record and pass on history (orally and then in writing) is early and infused with an integrity that is apparent on the page. Unless there is tangible evidence to the contrary, we should respect this integrity in the text.[2]

What then can we say about faith? The history of the Old Testament cannot be rejected as irrelevant to faith simply because Christian faith is historical in nature—it is about divine intervention in the affairs of humanity. Moreover, the Old Testament cannot be rejected in favour of the New Testament simply because the New Testament writers evidently continue the historical story of the Old Testament in the Gospels and Acts. Furthermore, their witness to the Old Testament and their usage of the Old Testament makes it integral to any expression of the Christian

---

[1] There is a further irony here in that critical scholars will suspect the Old Testament narratives because they are etiological, but accept unquestionably Near Eastern texts even though they may well be etiological.

[2] For example, see W. Hallo, "Biblical History in its Near Eastern Setting: The Contextual Approach" in *Scripture in Context: Essays on the Comparative Method* (ed., C. D. Evans, W. Hallo, and J. B. White; Pittsburgh: Pickwick Press, 1980), 1-26.

faith. While there is a lot of clutter for a reader to work through in the writings of those who have commented on the Old Testament as history, there are reliable guides to the jungle in conservative historians who have refused to reject the Old Testament as evidence for philosophical and theological reasons. While they may believe, as a matter of faith, in the authority of the Old Testament as a work of Scripture, they argue for a harmonic approach to Biblical and non-Biblical evidence because this makes for the best historical reconstruction.

CHAPTER TEN
Old Earth Creationism

1. Introduction[1]

Many scientists will say that Science has disproved the Bible, and consequently dismiss the Bible. Other scientists however do not think science has disproved the Bible. Most people give up "doing science" when they leave school, and they do not have the expertise to evaluate the pros and cons of this argument. Many follow the "experts" who dismiss the Bible, while others become agnostic—they are not sure whether the Bible conflicts with Science. Still others reject those parts of the Bible that science has "disproved" and keep what is left.

The main motivation for doubting the early chapters of Genesis stems from our scientific culture. This culture claims to have overturned the historical frame of reference within which Jewish and Christian doctrine is placed.

Science is multi-faceted, embracing experimental sciences as well as more theoretically descriptive science. Success in science however is infectious—success in experimental science creates a climate in which the more theoretical sciences benefit in many ways. Science is a worldwide enterprise, and the development of evolutionary theory is part of this enterprise.

Scientific theories need to be carefully considered. Success in experimental science imparts confidence in the associated scientific theory. This success can confer on scientific theories in general a presumption that they will be confirmed. As a result an aura can surround the activity of science, but where science constructs theories about the past this aura needs to be checked. In the fabric of astrophysics and evolution theory there lie fundamental assumptions upon which the theoretical base is built. In this area, more than others, what is taken as 'experimental' confirmation of theory is itself described in theory-laden terms, and this should make us cautious.

---

[1] This article (somewhat shorter) appeared in a magazine, but the details are lost; it also appears in another form in my book *Beginnings and Endings* as an appendix; that book is a study of Genesis typology.

Even though we may be cautious (and sceptical) about the particular claims of evolutionary science, how do we answer the general claim made by Science that the Genesis creation account cannot be considered historical? One answer to is say that scientists, and in particular the popularisers of Science, have misconstrued the Genesis account. It is this answer that we want to examine in this appendix.

2. The Scope of Creation

When considering the interpretation of Genesis 1 in the light of Science, it is the scope of the Genesis account that is usually questioned by scientists. Does Genesis record the creation of the universe? Does it state that creation took place over six literal days? Does it say when creation took place - a few thousand years ago, or millions (billions)? All these questions are about the scope of the account.

Scientific theory may well be wrong, but this does not affect the question. It is a Biblical question whether the scope of the account is local or universal.

Hebrew scholars are divided on whether the opening verse of Genesis 1 is an introductory statement for the narrative (as in the KJV), or a relative clause prefacing God's first pronouncement, 'Let there be light'. That is, we either have the statements,

> In the beginning God created the heaven and the earth.
> And the earth was without form and void...

or we have the more complex sentence,

> When God began to create heaven and earth, and the earth was then welter and waste and darkness over the deep and God's breath hovered over the waters, God said, 'Let there be light'. (E.g. Alter)

These translations lend themselves to different interpretations. The more complex series of relative clauses requires the earth to be initially without form, covered by water, and in darkness. It does not include a separate statement to the effect that the planet or water was created. Creation took place with an **old earth** in place.

The KJV has been interpreted differently to refer in v. 1 to the absolute beginning of the universe. It is said there is a gap between v. 1 and v. 2

which allows for the evolution of the universe. However, equally, it can read it as a *summary statement* of the ensuing account and, on this reading, we have the earth presented to us in an initial state with which God works; there is no reference to the beginning of the universe. The account proper then begins in v. 3 with the creation of light, and we have in the following verses a description of the fashioning of the local heavens and the earth.

It is this reading of Genesis 1 that we want to present. Our proposal is that the first verse is either a summary statement of the creation account, or part of series of relative clauses (with v. 2) that preface God's first utterance, 'Let there be light'.

Our reason for making this suggestion is that the main body of the account includes a description of the making of 'heavens' and 'earth'. The expanse between the waters is called 'heavens' and the dry (land) is called 'earth' (vv. 8-10). Both of these areas subsequently become the focus of further configuration work—the 'earth' for vegetation, and 'heavens' for the appearance of the Sun and Moon.[1] This reading is indicated by Exod 20:11,

> For [in] six days the Lord made heaven and earth, the
> sea, and all that in them [is], and rested the seventh day...[2]

The 'heavens' and 'earth' are configured within the compass of the six days, but it is clear from that account exactly what 'heavens' and 'earth are - an expanse between waters, and dry (land). We cannot then separate the

---

[1] The mention of the stars in connection with the making of the two great lights (v. 16) is actually a parenthesis and not a statement that the stars were made or created on Day 4.

[2] This text supplies an answer to the question as to why there are two creation accounts and why we have the first creation account. Although it is not often asked as to why we have the first account, it being thought obvious that the Bible should have such a beginning, this misses the point. We have such an account to justify the Sabbath. Opposing a social order where there is no seventh day of rest, but each day is the same kind of work day as the previous one, God presents his own work of creation as six days of work with a seventh for rest. Such a presentation is therefore a *metaphor* of the Adamic creation, so used to establish the Sabbath law for the people.

opening verse from the rest of the narrative and make it refer to the creation of the universe at some point prior to creation week.

We can usefully compare the account of the New Creation. John's Gospel quotes Gen 1:1, 'In a beginning was the Word...', and John relates this beginning (re-stated in John 1:2) to his following description of the New Creation. In other words, we cannot de-couple a mention of the beginning from the creation account that ensues in the case of John. If we cannot do this for the anti-type, we should not do it for the type. In Biblical typology 'beginnings' are closely related to what is begun.

Our proposal limits the scope of the creation account, for it excludes from the account an explanation of how the planet was created. What are the consequences of making this exclusion? The main one would seem to be that if we assume the earth already exists as a planet in v. 2, this may reasonably imply the existence of the universe. As for the planet itself, its description in v. 2 may suggest the absence of the current configuration of our atmosphere; there was just a dark 'covering' over the earth. The later creation of the expanse of 'heaven' would be part of the fashioning of our atmosphere. This makes 'heaven' a local concept, because the expanse is clearly the sky.

We should not think then of the 'universe' when we read of God's creation of 'heaven' in v. 1 or v. 7. When we read that God configured the sun and the moon "in" heaven (v14), these bodies are made apparent or "set" in heaven (through atmospheric configuration). The language used is of an observer on earth. Such a placement would require the prior existence of space and our solar system and come about with the fashioning of the atmosphere from dark to light.

Current astrophysics makes the formation of solar bodies and their planetary satellites all part of the same process—an evolutionary process beginning with the Big Bang. The proposal that Genesis 1 describes a local fashioning of the earth and its atmosphere is not inconsistent with this current theory.

3. Gap Theory
Some commentators have suggested that there is a 'time gap' between v. 1 and v. 2, such that 'heaven' and 'earth' were created first, many aeons before the creative work of the creation week. Many have speculated about a 'pre-adamic' creation during this 'time-gap', and it has been suggested that this pre-adamic creation was destroyed (or came to an end),

and the earth was brought to chaos. It has been proposed that it is this chaos which God addresses in his work - which ought then to be considered as a re-creation.

I have argued that a gap is not indicated between v. 1 and v. 2, but rather v. 1 is an integral part of the creation account as a whole - as its opening summary. However, this does not mean that God's work of creation (as it is described) did not address prior conditions. A period before creation is implied; it is just that this is not implied by any break in the account between v. 1 and v. 2. What indicates these initial conditions is the description of the earth in v. 2. Hence, creative work prior to the account in Genesis is not excluded on any level (as required by Science).

We need to look at the first two verses of Genesis 1 as set off from the rest of the account. This is indicated by the structure of the account. Each day of creation is opened with 'And God said' and concluded with 'And the evening and morning were the...day'. This means that the account of what God did on Day 1 begins in v. 3 with 'And God said, Let there be light'. We should not think of the account of Day 1 as beginning with either of the first two verses. The opening verse summarises the account, and the second verse sets the scene for the first day. A parallel can be drawn with the New Creation: John is careful to note that there was a world into which the Light came (John 1:9-10), and this world was 'dark' (John 12:46).

4. Conclusion

Several branches of Science come into apparent conflict with the Bible. Astrophysics is one branch which is highly theoretical and evolutionary. It is often assumed that this branch of Science has shown the Bible's account of creation to be false, because it is said that this account describes the creation of the universe. What we have tried to do in this essay is indicate how the Genesis account is actually more localised.

CHAPTER ELEVEN
Heaven

1. Introduction[1]

The word 'heaven' is perhaps an old-fashioned word. In a culture that is accustomed to talking about space, the air, the atmosphere, the solar system, galaxies, and the universe, there doesn't seem to be very much of a place for a "heaven" or, for that matter, "heavens". Accordingly, it is usually assumed that this place is only appropriate in the cosmological schemes of bygone cultures, and as such it can be discarded from everything but the poetry and mythology of religious belief. Such a view is not taken in this essay.

2. The Local Concept of Heaven

It is perhaps overlooked that heaven itself, the firmament, was a created space, *and as much a created place as the earth*. It was an area made by the angels, since the work of creation was the especial work of the angels. Hence, the closing verse of the Genesis 1 creation account is,

> These are the <u>historical origins</u> of the heavens and of the
> earth <u>when they were created</u>... Gen 2:4ᵃ; cf. Matt 1:1

A popular harmonization of Science and the Bible says that heaven and earth were created in some primeval past before the general creation described in Genesis 1. Such an approach takes the 'heaven' of Genesis 1:1 to be the "universe". The theory postulates a "gap" between Genesis 1:1 and the subsequent verses, which describe a more local creation. But Genesis 2:4ᵃ embraces the *whole of the Genesis 1 account*. Whatever was created in Genesis 1 was created at the same "time" and much more *local* in scope.

The beginning of the second creation account confirms this reading. This starts in Genesis 2:4ᵇ,

---

[1] This article appeared in a magazine, but the details are lost; it is a variation on the previous article (Chapter Ten).

...in the <u>day</u> that the Lord God made the earth[1] and the heavens, and every plant of the field before it was in the earth... Gen 2:4b-5

This opening clause encapsulates the making of the earth and the heavens in the time span of a 'day', although this period of time is longer than the days of creation.[2] From our point of view, it shows that heaven and earth are made at the same time.

The creation of heaven and the earth at the same time is also implied by Exodus 20:11 in the command about the Sabbath:

> For *in* <u>six days</u> the Lord made heaven and earth, the sea, and all that in them *is*, and rested the seventh day: wherefore the Lord blessed the Sabbath day, and hallowed it. Exod 20:11

The Genesis 1 account of creation includes details about the making of a local atmospheric 'heaven' in Genesis 1:6-8, using the same word as that found in Genesis 1:1, so it seems incongruous to reconcile the Bible and Science by making Genesis 1:1 refer to the "universe". It seems more appropriate to take the scale of creation needed to create 'heaven' to be the same scale as that needed to create the conditions on the 'earth'. Thus God's work with a local planet included not only the planet surface but also a local sky.

The opening verse of Genesis can be read in an absolute way as in the KJV, or it can be read in a relative way,

> In the beginning God created the heaven and the earth..."

> "In [a][3] beginning, <u>when</u> God created...when the earth was without form and void...God said...

---

[1] Note the reversal of 'heavens and earth' into 'earth and heavens'.
[2] We may be intended to read "our" type of days as an analogue of the days of creation. This makes the days of creation into an "anti-type" to our "typical" days. This will be my assumption.
[3] The absence of a definite article is confirmed in the quotation of John 1:1.

Regardless of which reading[1] we take, what seems clear is that darkness and waters are *not* created as such in Genesis 1 and the planet is presented in an initial state of chaos.[2] The existence of the universe is therefore also implied. The use of a relative clause as a translation of the Hebrew brings this sense out clearly.

3. Heaven and the Universe

The Bible is not a scientific textbook on astrophysics, and it is often assumed that its talk of heaven is unscientific. How then do we evaluate Biblical talk about heaven with the scientific description of the universe? How is Outer Space related to the Genesis 1 local concept of 'heaven'? How are the sun, moon and stars "in heaven"?

God *names* the expanse of the sky as 'heaven', and this is one of several naming choices that are made in Genesis 1. The sun, moon and stars are mentioned in connection with Day Four.

> And God said, Let there be lights in the firmament of the heaven to divide the day from the night; and let them be for signs, and for seasons, and for days, and years: And let them be for lights in the firmament of the heaven to give light upon the earth: and it was so. And God made two great lights; the greater light to rule the day, and the lesser light to rule the night: *he made* the stars also. And God set them in the firmament of the heaven to give light upon the earth, and to rule over the day and over the night, and to divide the light from the darkness: and God saw that *it was* good. And the evening and the morning were the fourth day. Gen 1:14-19

There are two points to note about the work of this day: the first point is that when the text says the God *made* the sun and the moon to be lights in the sky, the Hebrew doesn't mean that God made these bodies out of nothing, rather the sense is of God doing or working at something, and of working with existing materials. The account states that the sun and the moon were "to be lights in the firmament", and this implies that God's work concerned the atmosphere (e.g. cloud cover, air composition,

---

[1] The NEB and the NRS translate the first two verses in a relative way.
[2] This approach opens up the possibilities of a (destroyed) pre-Adamic creation, with evidence in the fossil record.

refraction indices), and how the sun and the moon were *to be seen* in the firmament.

The penetration of the dark covering of the earth introduced light, and the already existing rotation of the planet meant that day-time and night-time could be designated on Day One. God's work with vegetation on Day Three implies the existence of an orbital relationship between the sun, moon and the earth. On Day Four God appointed the sun and the moon to be lights "ruling" the day and the night (Ps 74:16, 104:19); what Day Four concerns therefore is how time can be measured by mankind using the sun and the moon, in terms of signs like "the passing of a year", the "passing of a season", and the "passing of a day"; this is why the sun and the moon are brought **into view** on Day Four.

The second point to note is that the mention of the stars in Genesis 1:16 has been misinterpreted. It doesn't say that God *created* the stars on Day Four. In fact what we have is a parenthesis in the text:[1]

> And God made…the lesser light to rule the night (the stars also)…

The point of this clause and the parenthesis is that the work that God is carrying out in respect of the atmosphere, making the moon to appear as a light at night-time, has the same effect for the stars.

Although we know that the sun, moon and stars are at a very great distances from the earth, they *appear* to be "in" heaven, and this is the achievement of the work of Day Four. There is therefore an association in Scripture between the sun, moon and stars and the local heaven, and it is this association that explains why 'heaven' embraces what we have called 'Outer Space' and the 'Universe' in later books of the Bible.[2]

It is a western cultural assumption that Biblical cosmology has been superseded by modern cosmology. There are two broad points of apparent conflict: the first is the age of the universe, which modern

---

[1] The parenthesis is indicated by the fact that v. 17 refers just to the sun and moon.

[2] The laws of physics describe the atmosphere, the solar system and the universe. The Bible does not deploy the laws of physics in a description of heaven, but it does present heaven in relation to the earth in the same way that the universe is described *relative* to the earth in astrophysics.

estimates[1] place in billions of years; the second is the big bang evolutionary model. We have argued for a local view of creation on exegetical grounds, and therefore current estimates of the age of the universe are not contradicted by the Bible.

Furthermore, a local view of the creation account doesn't conflict with the big bang model. This model places a point of singularity *first* in the order of things and stellar evolution is taken to proceed from this point, with galaxies [etc.], solar systems and planets following on in due course. The Biblical account is geocentric, with the planet presented *first* as without form and void, dark, and covered with water. What brought about the universe is not described, because the focus of the Genesis account is purely local.

4. Visions of Heaven
The Bible describes a natural heaven on the one hand, but it also presents us with a view of what we might call a "real" heaven as the dwelling place of God. Man cannot see the (real) heaven for what it is, because heaven is veiled from sight and revealed only in vision. What is the relationship between our natural heaven and the real heaven?

The Bible visions seem to represent heaven as *directly above* the earth (e.g. 1 Chron 21:16). There doesn't appear to be any space travel involved in getting to heaven. Heaven is not presented as beyond the current position of the expanding universe. Heaven is closer to mountains, and angels come down from heaven and meet with individuals on mountains. The prophets look up (into the middle distance, as it were) and see visions of heaven. They are transported to heaven and see events worked out on the earth. Modern popular science has no place for such a view of heaven. However, science fiction does deploy notions of multiple dimensions, alternate universes, and an infinite level of sub-space domains to articulate its story lines. Sceptics cannot therefore allege that heaven is an *inconceivable* realm. But why can't we see the real heaven?

The speed of light is a fundamental constant in standard theories of the universe.[2] Nothing material in the universe can move faster than light.

---

[1] This estimate is very dependent on assumptions as to the constancy of the speed of light.
[2] We are not saying that the speed of light has always been constant, or that it is the same speed everywhere in the universe. We are just following a standard model.

This makes the universe a closed system in that we cannot move beyond the universe or observe beyond the universe. We need light (or more broadly, the electro-magnetic spectrum) to see and the waves are bound by the laws of the universe: to get beyond the universe, the waves would cease to be waves, as we know them, and cease to function as 'light'. The Bible informs us that God dwells in unapproachable light (1 Tim 6:16), which suggests a different sort of light to the light that is bound into the universe. This light is part of a set of dimensions that we can't see in the normal way.

5. Conclusion

The natural structure of the atmosphere and space-time is a screen that prevents us observing heaven itself with natural means. However, the natural phenomena of the atmosphere are used to mark out the presence of God in heaven. God uses such phenomena to indicate his control over the earth.

God created heaven and earth; he gave the earth to men and took heaven to himself:

> The heaven, [even] the heavens, [are] the Lord's: but the earth hath he given to the children of men. Ps 115:16

> Know therefore this day, and consider [it] in thine heart, that the Lord he [is] <u>God in heaven above</u>, and upon the earth beneath: [there is] none else. Deut 4:39

The most common (rabbinic) view of the heavens is that there are *three* heavens (cf. 2 Cor 12:2). They proposed that the sky was the first heaven; and then there was the wider heaven beyond, where there was the sun moon and stars; beyond this there was the 'third heaven', which is the eternal dwelling place of God and the angels. It is a speculation whether there are three heavens or not, and the fact that the original for 'heaven' is often plural does not settle the matter. In this essay, we have argued for a local concept of heaven with which the sun, moon and stars are associated. It is another study to consider what it means to talk of a "third heaven". However large we conceive heaven to be, *all* the natural phenomena of heaven declare the glory of God.

140

CHAPTER TWELVE
Creation Types in Exodus

1. Introduction[1]

Scripture is full of allusions to the work of creation. It would be impossible to discard the Genesis account and keep the rest of the Bible. Moreover, it is the details of creation that reverberate throughout the narratives, and these echoes confirm the Scriptural creation accounts. Not all details occur together in later Scriptures, but selections are made by each of the writers (under inspiration). In this essay we will explore some of these allusions as they appear in the account of the tabernacle-sanctuary.

There are three sections of the book of Exodus that deal with the tabernacle-sanctuary. The first (Exodus 25-31) covers the instructions for building the tabernacle-sanctuary and aspects of the priesthood; the second deals with the making of the structure itself (Exodus 35-39); and the third describes the erection of the tabernacle-sanctuary by Moses (Exodus 40). In each passage there are overtones of the Genesis creation account.

2. Narrative 1 - the Building Plans

There are echoes of the creation account in the instructions for the tabernacle (Exodus 25-31). For example, they are punctuated by seven utterances of the Lord: "And the Lord spake unto Moses..." (Exod 25:1),[2] and this is like the "And God said..." utterances of the creation account. Although there are more than seven "And God said..." utterances in Genesis 1, they are tied to a seven day sequence, and this is the *echo* being struck in the Exodus narrative. The building instructions themselves are ordered in a particular way to reflect the creation accounts of Genesis:

> i) The *seventh* utterance concerns the Sabbath (Exod 31:12). The sixth utterance had concerned *work* - the work of constructing the tabernacle and sanctuary. The

---

[1] This article was rejected by magazines; it was written in the early 1990s as part of an unpublished book called *The Doctrine of Salvation: Volume Two*.
[2] See also Exod 30:11; 30:17; 30:22; 30:34; 31:1, 31:12.

natural follow-on to this command is the command to rest. This is linked to creation, which is designed to teach the Israelites that their work was comparable to God's work of creation. This way of ending the instructions matches the way creation was ended - with a day of rest on the seventh day of creation.[1]

ii) The creation accounts began with the spaces of heaven, earth and waters, and culminated with the creation of man on the sixth day. Similarly, the *sixth* building instruction for the sanctuary concerned *man*, in particular the man who would have the spirit of God (Exod 31:3; cf. Gen 2:7), and be empowered to construct the sanctuary. With this man there was to be a helper "given" to him (cf. Gen 3:12), a type of Eve. This sixth utterance mirrors the creation account in Genesis.

The first and longest instruction deals with (in order) the ark, the mercy seat, the table of shewbread, the candlestick, the tabernacle and its vail, the *placement* of the tabernacle furniture mentioned so far, and then the altar and outer court. Finally, in this "instruction" we are given commandments concerning the man. This is the order of Genesis: a garden is created for the man and then the man is placed in the garden. The man is dressed for "glory", picking up the detail that man was created in the image and *glory* of God (1 Cor 11:7). He is filled with the spirit of God (like Bezaleel), picking up the detail that God breathed into Adam the breath of life. In Genesis there is a concern with fruitfulness and *naming*, and in the account of Aaron's garments,[2] names of the "children" feature prominently on the breastplate (Exod 28:9-10, 21, 29). Once Aaron has been introduced, the focus of this long instruction changes, and it concludes with the command concerning the altar of incense.

---

[1] The Sabbath is a sign, and such signs accompany God's creative work. The Sun, moon and stars were for signs, and the bow was another sign. The created order in Israel was to have no physical sign, but rather a temporal sign. Their work was to be structured according to the same time period as God's initial work of creation. Their working week would be a continual reminder of God's work of creation, and this reminder would be especially poignant on the Sabbath.

[2] It needs to remembered that the Genesis pattern is being applied in a context where there is sin. Whereas Adam was the "image and glory" of God, with Aaron, it is the garments that are for "glory" (Exod 28:2).

We might ask why it is that the altar of incense is mentioned last in this long first instruction. It would seem that it is mentioned last because it is an instruction that revolves around Aaron. It is significant that it is only after Aaron has been mentioned that he then appears as the subject of further instructions. He is not mentioned in the earlier details about the ark or the table of shewbread.

The long first instruction is followed by six more fairly short commandments. The first two of these read like footnote instructions picking up on two of the main features of the long first instruction. It mentions the "children" of Israel and their tabernacle half-shekel as a "memorial unto the children of Israel" (Exod 30:16). This is picking up on the role of the stones on the Ephod as a "memorial unto the children of Israel" (Exod 28:12), and giving a further symbolic memorial for the "children of Aaron". The second "footnote instruction" mentions a further item of furniture—the laver in connection with "Aaron and his sons"—they were to wash in this water recepticle.[1]

It is *as if* by the expressions "memorial unto the children of Israel" and "Aaron and his sons" two superscripts were placed and supplementary instructions were given. However, in the absence of such formal devices in the Hebrew, the narrative has placed the instructions in a specific sequence, and advertised their subordination by making them pick up on previously mentioned details.

In the same vein, the fourth and fifth instructions read like an "endnote" with a "footnote". They concerns the "spices for anointing oil" and the "spices for sweet incense" (Exod 25:6), but the fourth instruction refers to the anointing of all the sanctuary apparatus including the laver, which makes it a natural "ending" instruction. But having mentioned the "spices for anointment", the narrative naturally follows onto mention the "spices for sweet incense" to be placed "before the testimony" on the altar of incense (Exod 27:21; 30:6, 36).

The sixth instruction breaks this pattern of footnotes and endnotes we have been describing in a significant way. It reads as follows,

---

[1] Notice that this is the *third* instruction, and the third day of creation saw the separation of the waters.

> And the Lord spake unto Moses, saying, See, I have
> called by name... Exod 31:1-2

The word "see" picks up the word "look" in "And *look* that thou make [them] after their pattern..." (Exod 25:40), and its function is to turn Moses' vision around. At the start he has looked at a pattern shown in the mount, but now he is invited to *look* down from the mount to Bezaleel, the man who would carry out this work. However, although it breaks the pattern, it is still part of the sequence of seven instructions as it includes in the description of Bezaleel's work all the elements of the earlier instructions including the object of the third instruction (the laver), the subject of the fourth instruction (the anointing oil) and the sweet incense (instruction 5).[1]

3. Narrative 2 - the Work of Building

The description of the construction of the tabernacle-sanctuary follows the incident of the Golden Calf. This incident developed during Moses' sojourn on the mount, and it interrupts the natural flow from instruction to construction. The narrative, however, marks this interruption by *repeating* the last Sabbath instruction as the prelude to the commencement of building the tabernacle-sanctuary (Exod 35:2).

Bezaleel and Aholiab are the named workers, but this work of building the tabernacle-sanctuary was carried out by many hands (Exod 36:1). In this typology Moses represents God, from whom they receive *all things* (Exod 36:3), and Bezaleel is "the man" around whom the work of construction revolves. (Compare how Aholiab drops out of the picture and Bezaleel is the focus of the third person singular pronoun throughout Exodus 36-38, and see Exod 38:22). After the work was done, "Moses *looked* upon all the work and, behold, they had done it as the Lord had commanded" (Exod 25:40; 39:43). This echoes the conclusion of God's creative work in Genesis, "[God] *saw* all that he had made, and found it very good" (Gen 1:31). The summary, "Thus the heavens and the earth were *finished*, and all the host of them" (Gen 2:1), has its counterpart in "Thus was all the work of the tabernacle of the tent of the congregation *finished*" (Exod 39:32). And a blessing concludes both kinds of work (Gen 2:3, Exod 39:43).

---

[1] Notice that the order of Bezaleel's schedule roughly reflects the order in the previous five instructions.

144

4. Narrative 3 - the Erection of the Tabernacle

The erection of the tabernacle is also described in terms that evoke the record of creation. The erection takes place in the *beginning* of the year on the first day of the first month. The narrative begins by stating that on this day the tabernacle was reared up. The creation account is similar: it opens with a beginning and states what was done in that beginning.

The account of the tabernacle erection is punctuated by seven references to "as the Lord commanded Moses".[1] And the account is a matter of fact description of what Moses (n.b. not the people) did at each stage. The account concludes, "So Moses *finished* the work" (Exod 40:33), and this is another echo of God finishing his work, "God *ended* his work" (Gen 2:2).[2] After this, the tabernacle and its vessels were to be anointed, and this matches God blessing the seventh day and making it a sanctified or "set apart" time (Gen 2:3; Exod 40:9). Once the tabernacle and its vessels were anointed, Aaron was to be prepared and then allowed into the tabernacle (Exod 40:12, 32), and this matches God's placement of Adam in the Garden of Eden.

5. Conclusion

We have examined the Exodus account of the construction of the tabernacle-sanctuary and found deliberate echoes of creation. The work of the people was a reflection of God's work in creation. A pattern for a sanctuary was delivered to Moses (Exod 25:9, 40), as one would be later delivered to David and Ezekiel. This pattern was based on the heavenly tabernacle (Heb 8:2; 9:24). This fact explains why we have these echoes of creation—the tabernacle-sanctuary was a microcosm of heaven and earth. The facts of God's creation were presented to Israel in miniature in the arrangements of the sanctuary. It is no wonder that the psalmist would later declare, "Oh how I love thy law! it is my meditation all the day".

---

[1] See Exod 40:19, 21, 23, 25, 27, 29, 32.

[2] Compare here the "finished" of Gen 2:1, with the "finished" of Exod 40:33 and Christ's words, "It is finished" on the cross (John 19:30; cf. Jms 1:15).

CHAPTER THIRTEEN
Noah's Flood

1. Introduction[1]

This essay discusses a topic in Biblical Apologetics: Noah's Flood. There are those who argue that Noah's Flood was global; here we present the alternative view that it was a **local** catastrophic event in history.

2. Geographical Perspectives in Genesis 2-6

A common objection against fundamentalist Christians is that they believe in a "god of the gaps". Non-believers accuse fundamentalists of shifting their interpretation of the Bible in respect of the creation and the flood accounts to avoid scientific objections. They credit God with what Science has not explained. The counter-argument to this accusation is that while Science has shown some interpretations of Genesis to be untenable, this does not mean that the Genesis account is untrue *per se*. In the 19c., as uniformitarian geology argued the case for an "old earth" and a long period of time for the geologic column, Flood Geology fell by the wayside and the "global flood" interpretation was challenged by the interpretation that Genesis in fact described a local flood. This development might look like a retreat to the "gap" of an unproveable or "easier to prove" local flood theory, or it might be a false interpretation finally dying the death and thereby allowing a true interpretation to emerge. This is a matter of spin.

Whether the Genesis flood was local or global is just a matter of biblical interpretation. The case for a local flood is centred on the analysis of "perspective" in narrative. There is the perspective of the narrator and that of the principal characters—Yahweh and Noah. These perspectives are their respective horizons and points of view on the situation of which they are a part. The perspective to determine when deciding for or against a local flood is geographical, both human and physical.

2.1 Narrator Perspective

The "narrator" tells the story and the author writes the narrator into his story. With Genesis, scholars identify sources and hypothesize about a

---

[1] This article was published in the *Christadelphian EJournal of Biblical Interpretation*; it also appears as an Appendix in *Beginnings and Endings*.

long transmission of story from oral to written form with editorial work along the way. Unless we work with the final form in the MT, such a transmission affects what can be said about the "narrator". That person may evolve as the story evolves. However, we do not need to enter into source-critical issues about the flood account. We can attribute to the earliest incarnation of the narrator a post-flood perspective in matters of geography when describing the situation prior to the flood.

This result in analysis is significant for the question of the scope of the flood. The effect of a global flood would not leave the geography intact across this event. Without speculating about the mechanisms of global flood theories (e.g. plate tectonic theories, water canopy theories), the changes envisaged are *all-encompassing* as regards any possible geographical continuity. It would seem then that the inclusion of a *local geographical perspective* in the opening account (Gen 6:1-4) on the part of the narrator is an indicator to the reader to adopt a local view.

1) Continuity in geography is implied before Genesis 6 in the story of the Garden of Eden. Eden is described in terms of later naming conventions and economic activity. For instance, the name of "Assyria" or "Ashur" (Gen 2:14) is one that derives from the history following Nimrod's descendants in Mesopotamia (Gen 10:8-11), and the name of "Cush" reflects the same post-flood development of nations in which "Cush" is a regional name in Northern Mesopotamia rather than its later denomination of the lower Nile. In addition, the courses of the rivers applied in the Edenic story are those of the post-flood world, which again suggests continuity in such aspects as the location of mountain ranges, watersheds and basins. The economic activity of the regions also betrays a later point of view, and this is one in which gold and precious stones are valued. Such valuation implies trade and commerce, and given the use of the names of nations, the description of Eden is complete as one given from the post-flood (post-Babel) point of view. This is an illustration of the harmony of the various stories in Genesis 1-11.

The perspective of the narrator is from a later time, and the continuity implied is one that permits the application of names and descriptions to regions and their characteristics. This kind of continuity is about physical geography rather than human geography. It is not implied that Assyria or Cush existed as nations in the days of Adam and Eve. For our purposes an implication about continuity of topography is a significant for how you read the flood account. It directs the reader to suppose that the gross physical geography was unaffected by the flood. Rivers remained where

147

they were before and after the flood; land was in the same place, mountains, *and so on.*

The traditional ascription of authorship of Genesis to Moses is not required by our argument. In any event, such an ascription does not preclude Moses' use of earlier traditions handed down by the patriarchal family. All our argument so far achieves is the identification of a narrator who has a post-flood outlook on the earliest primeval history.

2) The next perspective of the narrator to consider is the "father of" perspective. Necessarily, when a text attributes to an individual the distinction of being the father of a people or a way of life, then this implies that sufficient time has passed for such a people to come into existence or a way of life to become characteristic of a group of people. In the story of Cain and Abel we have "father of" statements. Jabal is the "father of" tent dwellers and cattle (Gen 4:20). This implies a time gap between the narrator's position and the birth of Jabal—sufficient time for a people to grow up and choose a way of life centred on domestic husbandry. The same point applies to Jubal who is the "father of" all who handle the harp and organ (Gen 4:21): there is distance between the narrator and Jubal because not only has Jubal to be born and give rise to a people, musical instruments have to be invented and economic activity has to be such as to support the leisure activity of music.

The position in time of the narrator in this account is not necessarily after the flood. As far as the detail goes, the narrator's perspective could be centred from before the flood—these characteristic groups could well be pre-diluvian. There is sufficient time before the flood for such developments. There is an absence of geographical indicators which would give away the later post-flood perspective which can be seen in Genesis 2. The only candidate is the reference to the "land of Nod" which carries the meaning "land of wandering" and is symbolic of Cain's wandering; this is not a geographical term that appears in later scripture.

Of course, if Moses was the author of the Cain and Abel account, and did not use early tradition, the perspective of the narrator would plausibly be ascribed to him. It would be his point of view that Jabal was the father of tent-dwellers. This seems an unlikely viewpoint for Moses given that the patriarchal family and the Israelites were tent-dwellers. There is therefore an argument here that if Moses authored Genesis in some sense, he was using early traditions.

148

While critical scholars would not argue that Moses was "the author" of Genesis, this does not affect the value of our observation about the narrator in Genesis 4. If first century Jews believed that Moses was the author of Genesis, our argument about the narrator in Genesis 4 is the sort of argument that they could have developed to show that Moses used earlier traditions. Thus, if we were first century readers of the Torah, we could well have regarded the Cain and Abel story to be older than the second creation account, while accepting that the whole tapestry was inspired and from the hand of Moses in some final sense.

2.2 The Face of the Eretz

It is well known that the Hebrew *eretz* can be "earth, land, ground or country". How it is translated affects the reading of a story and gives the reader a false or true perspective.

1) The first occurrence of the phrase, "face of the *eretz*", is in Gen 2:6 and, given the agricultural context in v. 5, the correct reading is "face of the ground" or "face of the land". It is important to note the agricultural context of v. 5 as this sets the scope of *eretz* to be "the land" viewed as that which is tilled and under cultivation.

In agricultural terms, rain is critical and drought is a serious problem. From this perspective, the narrator is describing the situation in Eden as one of drought in terms of rainfall, but one in which there arose each day a mist from the ground,[1] suggesting a damp fog arising from a high water table or dew. In his view, there was no man to till the *ertez*.

When Cain says, "Behold, thou hast driven me this day away from the face of the ground" (*eretz*, Gen 4:14, RSV), he is betraying his perspective of "the land which my family farms" (to use modern terms). The expression "face of the *eretz*" is the land which men farm. This interpretation is in keeping with the emphasis of the curse that men should till the ground, although in Gen 3:17 the word translated "ground" is *adamah*.

2) The land can support people who live "off the land"—subsistence farmers. The next occurrence of "face of the *eretz*" is Gen 6:1, "when men began to multiply on the face of the land". This detail continues the perspective of men living off the land, but the detail also echoes the fact

---

[1] It needs to be stressed that the mist rises from the ground and is close to the ground; it is not a water canopy around the planet.

that Cain had been banished from the face of the land. The intimation of the text is that there was pressure on the land to support the growing population.

At this time "the daughters of men" are taken by the sons of God and God's spirit in his prophets strove against this practise. The continuance of their behaviour led to God's pronouncement limiting their days.

3) Those tending the land are not the only group on the scene in Genesis 6. There are also the "giants" (KJV) but this is a misleading translation. Although the KJV has translated the Hebrew as "giants", this is a reflection of the LXX translation of the Hebrew *nephilim*, and a more accurate rendering would be something like "those who fall upon", i.e. marauders. This kind of person is precisely the opposite of those who tend the land and they are traditional enemies of those who farm. They are those who prey upon the settled populace, murder and steal arable produce and livestock in order to live. Their presence in Genesis 6 is a typical concern of a narrator whose outlook is agricultural rather than, say, nomadic.

We can see the narrator's post-flood perspective in his mention of the "sons of God" before the flood and also *after* the flood:

> And it came to pass, when men began to multiply on the face of the land, and daughters were born unto them, that the sons of God saw the daughters of men that they *were* fair; and they took them wives of all which they chose...

> ...There were giants in the earth in those days; (and also <u>after that</u>, when the sons of God came in unto the daughters of men, and they bare *children* to them, the same *became* mighty men, which *were* of old, men of renown). Gen 6:1-4 (KJV revised)[1]

The passage says "and also after that" – i.e. after those days before the flood – there were sons of God who came unto the daughters of men and who subsequently bore "mighty men of old" and "men of renown". These mighty men are compared to the "marauders" before the flood. This remark indicates the narrator's perspective in that he is aware of

---

[1] I have added brackets to make the mention of the second group clearer.

marauders in his day and he is aware of the earlier sons of God and what happened to their agricultural way of life.

If we adopt a first century perspective on the Torah, this observation can be used to support the proposition that Moses used early traditions. An agricultural perspective and a concern about marauders would be typical for a settled community rather than the wilderness Israelites. The narrator of the opening flood account reflects such a background and this indicates something of the scale of the flood—it affected the land upon which his characters depended for their livelihood.

2.3 The Nephilim

The Hebrew *nephilim* only occurs elsewhere in Numbers:

> And there we saw <u>the giants</u>, the sons of Anak, *which come* of <u>the giants</u>: and we were in our own sight as grasshoppers, and so we were in their sight. Num 13:33 (KJV)

This passage states that the sons of Anak were of the *nephilim* as well as being the *nephilim*. Are these related to the *nephilim* of Genesis 6? Against an equation is the fact that the locale for Genesis 6 is Mesopotamia whereas in Numbers 13 it is Canaan. Further, the *nephilim* are now settled dwelling in cities rather than marauders. However, these differences are not decisive because after Babel there was migration and a settling of nations. The *nephilim* of Numbers 13 could be the descendants of Mesopotamians.

A detail is added in Genesis 6—the *nephilim* after the flood are "mighty men of old". This is another indicator for the perspective of the narrator and, plausibly, of the author. From his vantage point, the *nephilim* after the flood were "of old". This places the narrator at some distance from the generation that gave birth to the *nephilim*, but "of old" is an elastic expression.

The "days of old" in Deut 32:7 are the days of Babel; in Josh 24:2 they are the days of Terah and Abraham. In both these cases the days of old are Mesopotamian days. Does the narrator see the "mighty men of old" as men from the Mesopotamian days of Babel? The argument in favour of this conclusion is a comparison between Babel and the flood:

151

(i) In both cases there are two genealogical strands – Cain and Seth in Genesis 4-5 and Shem, Japheth and Ham in Genesis 10- 11.[1]

(ii) There is violence in Genesis 6 and there is a beginning of violence with Nimrod who is described as a "mighty one" — "And Cush begat Nimrod: he began to be a mighty one in the earth" (Gen 10:8).

(iii) Imagination and thoughts are features of both times (Gen 6:5, 11:6).

We can suggest therefore that the perspective of the narrator in Gen 6:1-4 is of someone after Babel looking back upon the flood and seeing a comparison between the mighty men before the flood who pillaged the landed community and the mighty men who had built the cities of Mesopotamia; these men were scattered after Babel and some ended up in Canaan. This is a very local perspective on the flood.

2.4 Conclusion

The opening of the flood account is Mesopotamian in perspective. This is indicated by the expression "face of the land" which indicates an agricultural view. The geographical perspective of the narrator is local to the Near East and the days of old in Mesopotamia. While English versions use "earth" for *eretz*, and thereby contribute to a global view of the flood, the key opening Hebrew phrase of the account suggests a flood local to Mesopotamia.

3. Mesopotamian Local Floods

The local flood interpretation of Genesis 6-8 has biblical and non-biblical support. In this section we will set out the case for a local flood using an historical argument. It will be evident that we regard the Genesis story as true, but this point of view is not presupposed in our analysis.

The Genesis story is set in a Mesopotamian locale insofar as the "foothills of Ararat"[2] are mentioned as the resting place of the ark (Gen 8:4). This indicates to the reader the fact that the flood concerned Mesopotamia. The existence of other accounts of a great flood in this region supports this presumption; these other accounts do not betray a global perspective. We can see this if we compare the various accounts.

---

[1] They also follow the same formula as with the ante-diluvians.
[2] We discuss this expression below.

While the Mesopotamian flood stories have been dismissed as non-historical and categories such as "myth" and "legend" have been applied to them, this is a discussion that we do not need to enter for our purposes. Our argument is that they are evidence for the *fact* of a catastrophic flood in the region, whether or not we regard any or most elements in the story as a-historical. Their witness to the fact of a local widespread flood is a strong argument for the view that the Genesis account is likewise a story a local flood.

3.1 Gilgamesh

The Babylonian Gilgamesh Epic is well known and we cannot review its content here; our purpose is to point up the local perspective of that part of the story that relates to a Mesopotamian flood.[1] The following points indicate the local perspective:

- Utnapishtim, the hero, is a resident of Shuruppak, a city on the Euphrates. The gods responsible for the deluge were worshipped in this city (XI.11-14).

- Utnapishtim asks about the reasons for the forthcoming deluge and is informed by Ea, his god, that another god, Enlil, hates him and he has to leave the city and go to a subterranean place where Ea dwells; he cannot go to the land of Enlil. The rain of the flood will come upon the men of Shurippak (XI. 38-47).

- Utnapishtim states, "Whatever I had of the seed of all living creatures [I loaded] aboard her" (XI.83); that is, the animals local to him were loaded on a ship.

- A violent storm begins the deluge and the gods are involved. For example, Ninurtu, the god of the wells and irrigation works causes the dykes to give way (XI.102). The involvement of this god gives a local scope to the flood insofar as it is important to state that the irrigation canals were overrun.

---

[1] Our text is taken from the convenient edition of A. Heidel, *The Gilgamesh Epic and Old Testament Parallels* (2nd Ed.; Chicago: University of Chicago Press, 1949).

- The scope of the flood is "the land"; the "land" is broken like a pot (XI.107); the "land" is lit up by lightening (XI.104); the flood overwhelms the "land" (XI.128).

- After seven days, the flood "subsides", a description which indicates a local flood receding (XI. 130).

- After the storm, Utnapishtim looks out of the window of the ship and sees on the horizon a stretch of land; the ship sets down on Mount Niṣir, a mountain known to Utnapishtim before the flood (XI.139-140). Utnapishtim comments that "all mankind has turned to clay" (XI.133).

- After the flood, and after sacrificing to the gods, Utnapishtim says of Enlil, the god who brought about the deluge—"...without reflection he brought on the deluge and consigned my people to destruction" (XI.168-169). His focus is *his* people.

- Ea discusses the action of Enlil in bringing about the flood and says to Enlil at one point, "instead of thy sending a deluge, would that a famine had occurred and [destroyed] the land" (XI.184). The possibility that a famine could have served the purpose indicates a local scope.

- Utnapishtim is made to settle down after the flood at the "mouth of the rivers" (XI.195).

These details show the local scope of the flood and this delimits the scope of statements like "all mankind has turned to clay" (XI.133) and the "seed of all living creatures" was loaded onto the ship (XI.83).

There are many details in the Gilgamesh story of the flood that parallel the OT account as well as details that do not correspond.[1] The similarities are about the sequence of events, story details such as the window, the raven, the sacrifice; the differences are in details such as the size of the

---

[1] L. R. Bailey comments, "The similarities between the biblical and the Mesopotamian flood stories are so striking and so numerous that it is impossible to escape the suspicion that they are somehow related", *Noah: The Person and the Story in History and Tradition* (Columbia: University of South Carolina Press, 1989), 20.

ship, the length of the storm and how many were aboard the ship. The relationship between the two accounts is outside the remit of this essay. Our point is that there is a *fact* of the flood indicated in the two accounts and Gilgamesh is clearly a local flood. This suggests that the Genesis story is likewise a local flood account.

3.2 Story of Ziusudra

This Sumerian account is very fragmentary, but it tells the story of Ziusudra a king-priest of the Mesopotamian city of Shuruppak.[1] The "Sumerian King List" lists Shuruppak as one of the five cities of Sumer, and after listing eight kings over these cities it states, "(Then) the Flood swept over (the earth). After the Flood had swept over (the earth) (and) when kingship was lowered (again) from heaven, kingship was (first) in Kish"; it then lists post-diluvian kings.[2] This gives a chronological placement of the flood in relation to Sumerian kings and the land of Sumer. As evidence of the *fact* of the flood, it bears some weight as the mention of the flood is unencumbered by the story-teller's art.

The local detail that we have in the Story of Ziusudra is as follows:

• The flood sweeps over the "cult-centres", i.e. the five cities' temples.[3]

• The flood sweeps over "the land"; a term used to refer to Sumer.[4]

• The rain lasts for seven days and seven nights.

Again, as with the Gilgamesh Epic, there are correspondences with Genesis which we have not noted as well as differences.[5] Our point is that

---

[1] The city is stated in the account and a connection is made with the Gilgamesh Epic in the text known as "The Instructions of Shuruppak" which contains instructions from Shuruppak to his son Utnapushtu, see J. B. Pritchard, *Ancient Near Eastern Texts* (Princeton: Princeton University Press, 1969), 594; hereafter ANET.

[2] ANET, 265. Bailey documents a similar citation, *Noah*, 14, from British Museum Tablet 2310, which lists rules of the city of Lagash (a Sumerian city) and begins the list, "After the Flood had swept over and had brought about the destruction of the land".

[3] ANET, 43-44.

[4] ANET, 43 n. 6.

[5] See Bailey, *Noah*, 14-16.

the account is of a local flood, of what happened to the local cult-centres; it is perhaps obvious that Sumerians would pass down a story about "what happened to *them*". Embellished in the re-telling, it still bears witness to the fact of a local catastrophic flood.

3.3 Atrahasis Epic

This epic concerns an "Exceeding Wise One", which is the meaning of the name, 'Atrahasis'. As with the Gilgamesh Epic and the Story of Ziusudra, the account is fragmentary,[1] but the flood is clearly local to Mesopotamia.

- The text begins by stating that the cause of the flood was that "The land became wide, the peop[le became nu]merous".[2] This suggests population pressure and migration widening the borders of the land; it does not suggest a global scope.

- The epic describes aborted attempts by the Mesopotamian gods to quell the noise of mankind, including famine. The thought that famine *could have* solved the problem that humanity was creating for the gods indicates a local scope.[3] The mention of famine and land in the story gives an agricultural setting—a farming community supporting cities.

- The animals are "the beasts of the field" and the "fowls of heaven", as many as "eat herbs". Family, relations and craftsmen are taken into the ship.[4] This suggests domestic beasts and local inhabitants.

---

[1] The latest text of the epic has been presented in A. R. Millard and W. G. Lambert, *Atra-Hasis: The Babylonian Story of the Flood* (Oxford: Clarendon Press, 1969). See also W. G. Lambert, "New Light on the Babylonian Flood" JSS 5 (1960): 113-123. An older less complete text is presented in ANET 104-106, 512-514, and Heidel, *The Gilgamesh Epic and Old Testament Parallels*, 106-116, and the Millard-Lambert text has been excerpted in W. Beyerlin, *Near Eastern Religious Texts relating to the Old Testament* (London: SCM Press, 1978), 90-93.

[2] ANET, 104.

[3] ANET, 104.

[4] ANET, 105.

- The flood is caused by the storm-god Adad; the god Ninurtu assists by bursting the dykes.[1] The specific detail of dykes being burst indicates a local concern in the story.

- The storm and flood last for seven days and seven nights.[2] There is no mention of the fountains of the deep bursting. The quantity of rain is clearly a local indicator.

Again, these details show a parochial focus for the story. There are corresponding details with Genesis that we have not noted, as well as divergent details.[3] Nevertheless, the world-view of the narrator is Mesopotamian rather than global.

3.4 Summary

The genetic relationship between the Genesis account and the Mesopotamian accounts is not important for our argument. The differences between the accounts do not prevent a synchronic comparison and do not disprove a relationship of some sort. The weakest theory describing that relationship would be that they share a common oral root. Our argument is that the three accounts and other incidental references to the flood in the king-lists point to the *fact* of a local flood. Moreover, given that the Mesopotamian plain was subject to flooding,[4] as shown by the archaeological record, the flood of these traditions and the king-lists must have been exceptional to give rise to the stories. Contrary to Bailey who asserts[5] that Gilgamesh and Atrahasis imply a world-wide flood, we have seen that the terms of these stories are *local* in scope. Bailey's reading seems influenced by Christian readings of the Genesis Flood.

4. The Rainbow in Genesis

A common reading of the story of the flood is that it describes the *origins* of the phenomenon of the rainbow. Such a phenomenon is global in nature – rainbows appear anywhere on earth given the right conditions. The beginning of such a phenomenon at this time is part and parcel of a global flood reading of Genesis 6-9. It requires that the meteorology of

---

[1] Lambert, "New Light", 118.
[2] Beyerlin, Near Eastern Texts, 93.
[3] Bailey, *Noah*, 14-16.
[4] Bailey, *Noah*, chap. 3, sets out the evidence.
[5] *Noah*, 17.

the earth was changed after the flood to bring about this phenomenon.[1] In this paper we will question this reading.

4.1 The Text
The text states,

> And God said, This *is* the token of the covenant which I make between me and you and every living creature that *is* with you, for perpetual generations: I do set <u>my bow in the cloud</u>, and it shall be for a token of a covenant between me and the earth. And it shall come to pass, <u>when I bring a cloud over the earth, that the bow shall be seen in the cloud</u>: And I will remember my covenant, which *is* between me and you and every living creature of all flesh; and the waters shall no more become a flood to destroy all flesh. And <u>the bow shall be in the cloud</u>; and I will look upon it, that I may remember the everlasting covenant between God and every living creature of all flesh that *is* upon the earth. Gen 9:13-16 (KJV)

The Hebrew for "bow" is the ordinary word for a bow—a weapon.[2] We might ask why the phenomenon we call a "rainbow" should be called a "bow" rather than, say, a "rain-arch", or a "rain-arc", and it might be difficult to think of a reason, except to point out that a "bow" was a weapon and God calls the phenomenon that he places "in the cloud"— "my bow". A militaristic echo is not inappropriate as the flood has demonstrated that God is a God of judgment and he has wrought judgment in the land against the (bow-using?) marauders of the land.[3] That God has a bow is shown by Hab 3:9-11 and Ps 7:13.

However, this is an aside, and the main point for comment has to be on "my" in "my bow". Why does God call the phenomenon something that belongs to him? Is this phenomenon just a rainbow? There is no word for

---

[1] Many commentaries interpret the bow as a rainbow. For example, C. Westermann, *Genesis 1-11* (Minneapolis: Fortress Press, 1994), 473.
[2] G. von Rad, *Genesis* (London: SCM Press, 1961), 130, and *contra* Westermann, *Genesis 1-11*, 473.
[3] *Contra* von Rad, *Genesis*, 130, who says that the signification is that God has put aside his bow of war; rather, the bow is in a cloud and this represents what has just happened: God has destroyed mankind with storm-clouds.

"rain" in the text, and it is an ordinary word for "cloud"; we might ask then do rainbows *always* and *only* appear in clouds? The meteorological answer would be that this is not the case. The text asserts, "…when I bring a cloud over the land, that the bow shall be seen in the cloud", and we might ask whether this is the case with clouds—do they *always* carry rainbows that are seen? Again the meteorological answer would be in the negative. If the phenomenon is not a spontaneously occurring rainbow, then is it something comparable to a rainbow, something that God brings about in a cloud from time to time?[1]

The Hebrew "in the cloud" or "in a cloud" occurs eight times outside Genesis 9 (Exod 16:10; 34:5; Lev 16:2; Num 11:25; Ps 78:14; Lam 3:44; Ezek 1:28; 32:7). Four occurrences relate to the theophanic cloud; for instance:

> And it came to pass, as Aaron spake unto the whole congregation of the children of Israel, that they looked toward the wilderness, and, behold, the glory of the Lord appeared <u>in the cloud</u>. Exod 16:10 (KJV)

> And the Lord descended <u>in the cloud</u>, and stood with him there, and proclaimed the name of the Lord. Exod 34:5 (KJV)

> And the Lord said unto Moses, Speak unto Aaron thy brother, that he come not at all times into the holy *place* within the vail before the mercy seat, which *is* upon the ark; that he die not: for I will appear <u>in the cloud</u> upon the mercy seat. Lev 16:2 (KJV)

> And the Lord came down <u>in a cloud</u>, and spake unto him, and took of the spirit that *was* upon him, and gave *it* unto the seventy elders: and it came to pass, *that*, when the spirit rested upon them, they prophesied, and did not cease. Num 11:25 (KJV)

Two occurrences relate to God manifestation but not directly to the theophanic cloud:

---

[1] The presence of God in a cloud through the wilderness might suggest that after the flood there was a similar journey to a new land.

In the daytime also he led them <u>with a cloud</u>,[1] and all the night with a light of fire. Ps 78:14 (KJV)

Thou hast covered thyself <u>with a cloud</u>, that *our* prayer should not pass through. Lam 3:44 (KJV)

The only divergent text is Ezek 32:7,

And when I shall put thee out, I will cover the heaven, and make the stars thereof dark; I will cover the sun <u>with a cloud</u>, and the moon shall not give her light. Ezek 32:7 (KJV)

There are two points to note in the first four texts that bear comparison with Genesis 9:

1) Genesis 9 associates the bow and the cloud with a token of a covenant. Similarly, God's presence in the cloud on Sinai was how he manifested himself during the covenant-making of that time.

2) God's "glory" appears in the cloud *or* he appears in the cloud and this visible presence is a kind of light (or fire) in the cloud. Similarly, God places "his bow" (of glory) in the cloud before Noah.

The theophany of Ezekiel 1 seems to offer an exegesis of Genesis 9:

<u>As the appearance</u> of the bow that is in the cloud in the day of rain, so *was* the appearance of the brightness round about. This *was* the appearance of the likeness of the glory of the Lord. And when I saw *it*, I fell upon my face, and I heard a voice of one that spake. Ezek 1:28 (KJV)

This text compares the appearance of the glory of the Lord around the chariot throne to that of a rainbow. What Gen 9:13 is saying to Noah then is: You are used to seeing rainbows when there are storms — I will now set "my bow" in a cloud — this cloud in front of you that manifests my presence, and in future when I manifest my presence in a cloud you will see my glory in the cloud.

---

[1] The same Hebrew preposition can be "in" or "with".

There is irony in Genesis 9. The text does not say that God's bow would be in the cloud when there is rain, and appearances of the theophanic cloud have not involved rain. The irony is that the flood was brought about in part through sustained torrential rain. The bow of the *rain-less* theophanic cloud is therefore a reminder that God would not bring about a flood and destroy the land, but he would remember the covenant with Noah.

If this construal of the "bow" is correct, then it implies that there was no change in climate conditions before and after the fall vis-á-vis the *fact* of rainfall.[1] The occurrence of rainfall prior to the flood is implied in a comment that at the time of the creation of Adam, there was no rainfall *because* there was no man to till the ground (Gen 2:5). Once there was a man to till the ground, the implication is that this brought about rainfall again in Eden (Gen 3:23). The Gilgamesh Epic[2] mentions a similar phenomenon at the end of the flood,

> As soon as the great goddess arrived [i.e. Ishtar] , she lifted up the great jewels which Anu had made according to her wish: 'O ye gods here present, as surely as I shall not forget the lapis lazuli on my neck, I shall remember these days and shall not forget (them) ever! XI.162-165

This event takes place after Utnapishtim has offered the sweet smelling savour sacrifice (XI.159-160). Anu, the patriarchal god, gives Ishtar great jewels and this is taken to be a necklace represented as a rainbow in the sky. Ishtar then promises to remember the days of the flood which is comparable to Yahweh remembering the flood (Gen 9:15).

There are differences here with Genesis, but the similarities are notable. The manifestation of Ishtar was inferred from the presence of a bow described as "the great jewels"; the manifestation of God was seen in his bow in the cloud. However, the Gilgamesh Epic is too thin to support the proposition that the phenomenon of rainbows *began* at this time; it only records the fact of a bow. The Genesis account includes detail linking the

---

[1] A hydrological cycle is implied in the common river geography before and after the flood (Gen 2:10-14).

[2] Casting the net wider, some non-Mesopotamian flood stories mention a rainbow at the end of the account and the existence of these stories has been seen as evidence of a worldwide flood—Bailey, *Noah*, chap. 1; Westermann, *Genesis 1-11*, 477.

bow to the future manifestation of God in a cloud, and this precludes the reading that rainbows began at this time; the bow of Genesis 9 is a very specific manifestation of God.

4.2 Conclusion

The bow of Genesis 9 is a theophanic manifestation of the God of Israel confirming a covenant with Noah. This form of manifestation is distinctive to Israel's traditions; hence, clouds are not noted in the Gilgamesh Epic. It may have taken the form of something like a spectacular cloud-bow, a glory, a coronae, or an iridescent cloud. Jewish interpretation of the first century makes the bow a rainbow (e.g. *Jub*. 3:12), and this has been the common Christian interpretation.[1] However, it is a mistake in this interpretative tradition to suppose that rainbows *began* at this time or that any rainbow seen today is a manifestation of the God of the covenant.

5. Reversing Genesis

The global interpretation of the Flood account is very old and very common in Jewish and Christian thought. It rests on a straightforward reading of the "global language" of the account. Today, the strength of the local flood reading is often seen to lie in the scientific objections to a global flood, which come from diverse but converging disciplines. The fact that many different scientific subject areas have something to contribute against a global reading means that such a reading requires wholesale revision of *a lot* of scientific conclusions. In this section, we will examine the argument that the flood is a global reversal of the Genesis creation.

5.1 Reversing Genesis

The argument to consider is that the language of Genesis 6-9 is a reversal of Genesis 1, and therefore the planetary scope of Genesis 1 should be the same in Genesis 6-9. While it is conventional to consider Genesis 6-9 in terms of two sources (very much like Genesis 1-3 contain two creation accounts), we are examining the *final form* of the narrative and ignoring scholarly source criticism. There are number of points of contact between Genesis 1 and Genesis 6-9 that we need to consider in this argument. Our

---

[1] D. A. Young, *The Biblical Flood: A Case Study of the Church's Response to Extrabiblical Evidence* (Grand Rapids: Eerdmans, 1995), 25. The standard treatment of early Jewish and Christian interpretation is J. P. Lewis, *A Study of the Interpretation of Noah and the Flood in Jewish and Christian Literature* (Leiden: E. J. Brill, 1968).

counter-argument will be that Genesis 6-9 includes points of contact with the *local* creation account of Genesis 2, and so the flood is not a simple reversal of Genesis 1.

1) Yahweh looks from heaven and sees that the wickedness of man was great in the earth (*eretz*, Gen 6:5), and he repents regarding his "making" of man upon the earth (Gen 6:6). The common verb for "making" links to Gen 1:26 where the intention of *elohim* to "make" man is stated. The argument is put that as there is global intent in Genesis 1 so too there is in Genesis 6.

However, there is no statement about *Yahweh* making man in Genesis 1 and it is well known that the name "Yahweh" is characteristic of the second and *local* creation account; here we read of Yahweh "forming" man and "making" his helpmeet (Gen 2:7, 22). This raises a doubt over the *global* reading of Genesis 6-9—the echo implied in the use of the name "Yahweh" is with the local creation of the Garden of Eden. When we read therefore of Yahweh looking and seeing that man's wickedness was great, he was *looking upon a land* and repenting of the fact that he had made man upon the earth.

Is God looking and seeing the planet, or is he looking and seeing a land? Yahweh states that he will destroy man from off the "face of the *adamah*" ("ground" (RSV), "land" (NASB), Gen 6:7). This links with Gen 4:14 which has the first occurrence of the expression, "face of the *adamah*". Cain's use of the expression does not signal a planetary perspective. Cain had offered the fruit of the *adamah*, and so his remark that he has been cast out from the face of the *adamah* is a reference to the cultivated land. It would seem therefore that Yahweh is not looking at the planet in Genesis 6. He has created man on earth, but when he looks and evaluates man he is looking at the *land* where man lives.

Man is to be destroyed from the face of the ground i.e. the *adamah*; this is a significant detail insofar as its focus is not the *eretz*. The "ground" is the leading motif of the second creation account: Adam is created from the *adamah*. This would imply a local scope for the destruction that God intends to bring with the flood.

Yahweh states that he will destroy man, beast, creeping thing and fowl of the air (Gen 6:7, KJV). The term for "beast" is *bᵉhemah*, which is translated "cattle" in Gen 2:20, which is also where the expression "fowls of the air" occurs first in conjunction with *bᵉhemah*. This link is a further indication

163

that the local creation account of Genesis 2 forms the backdrop to Genesis 6-9. This creation related to Eden and a garden; hence, the animals that Yahweh forms out of the *adamah* (Gen 2:19) are domestic beasts of the field and these are brought to Adam for naming. The bringing of animals to Adam is reflected in animals being brought to Noah (Gen 6:20).

However, it needs to be noted that "creeping things" are *not* mentioned in the second creation account and this detail is from Genesis 1. Further, the notion of "kinds" of animal is a link with Genesis 1 (Gen 6:20). Nevertheless, these links and the connections we have noted with Genesis 2 show that the flood account is not a simple reversal of the creation of Genesis 1.

2) A definite link with the first creation account lies in the phrase "the fountains of the great deep" (Gen 7:11); the first mention of "the deep" is Gen 1:2. Here the argument is made that in the beginning the planet was covered by the deep and the flood is a return to that state—it is a reversal of Genesis 1.

However, this interpretation is not secure: Genesis 6-9 does not say that "the deep" covered the earth, which would give the reverse picture to that in Genesis 1. Further, the account describes the waters as *covering the hills* (Gen 7:19-20) rather than the earth. It does not seem therefore that the narrative is seeking to portray a reversion to the primordial state of Gen 1:2.

The narrator's perspective is displayed in the description, "fountains of the great deep". If this was a description used by Yahweh, it might refer to the ocean(s) of the planet. In the perspective of the narrator, "the great deep" is the local sea—the local open sea. Isaiah uses the expression "great deep" to refer to the Red Sea (Isa 51:10); the psalmist contrasts the mountains of Judea with the great deep of the Mediterranean (Ps 36:7); and Amos uses the expression as a metaphor for a political power (Amos 7:4).That the "great deep" is the local open sea is shown by Gen 8:1-2 where it states that the fountains of the deep were stopped.

3) The initiation of the end of the flood is by a wind (*ruach*) passing over the earth (*eretz*, Gen 8:1). There is an echo here with Gen 1:2 where the Spirit (*ruach*) hovers over the face of the waters. It is argued that as one *ruach* is global, so too the other *ruach* is global.

But does the statement in Gen 8:1 relate to the whole planet? Is the new creation in Genesis 8 of the same global scope as Genesis 1? The dissimilarity with Genesis 1 consists in the fact that there the dry land appears upon the separation of waters; in Genesis 8 there is no such "separation" of waters and the appearance of dry land as a result. Further, in Genesis 1 the *ruach* is not linked to any separation of waters. If the flood was global, and the new creation consequent upon the end of the flood, exactly analogous to the creation of Genesis 1, the terminology of the "separation" of waters would have been entirely appropriate. On a global scale the separation of waters described the appearance of land in Genesis 1. In Genesis 8, the notion of the "assuaging" of the waters is not the idea of "separation". Waters assuage or recede (or abate or subside) from *existing* land masses: the flood waters therefore reached up to a certain point on the land mass and assuaged from that point. Winds are indigenous and local and do assist the assuaging of flood waters.[1]

This detail of the waters assuaging sets the *scope* for the "fountains of the deep". The Hebrew word for "fountains" is not an uncommon word and denotes a "spring" on land. What the "fountain" might have been *in the deep* is a matter of speculation,[2] but that they were local fountains seems clear.

4) The final detail which is said to reflect Genesis 1 is the "fruitful and multiply" theme (Gen 8:17; 9:1). This is a clear echo of Gen 1:28 as the motif is absent from the second creation account. This shows that the new creation after the flood is comparable to the Genesis creation.

However, this does not require a global perspective for the *destructive element* of the story. It is just as possible that Noah is commanded to replenish the land and to consider this a new creation analogous to the command to the male and female of Genesis 1. In later scripture, Israel is a "creation" and a "heaven and earth"; they are also to consider themselves in the light of Genesis 1—but they are not global creations.

---

[1] Current weather systems do not allow for a single wind to pass over the whole planet; there are multiple wind systems in place.
[2] Repeated tidal waves caused by undersea volcanic activity would be one scenario. The Arabian Plate has one edge running along the east coast of the Persian Gulf. Any undersea volcanic activity here could produce repeated tidal waves inundating the top of the Mesopotamian basin.

The above points, (1)-(4), make the case for a local flood reading of the allusions to Genesis 1 and 2 in Genesis 6-9.

5.2 Summary

The "global" language of the flood story is not global. What appears global is in fact local. Nevertheless, there is a design in the story which makes the flood a reversal of creation. This design, however, is for example and for teaching—the flood that came upon Mesopotamia is compared to creation (Genesis 1) as an event of equal significance for that region.

6. Global Language

An inference of global scope is made from the use of terms and expressions such as "all flesh", "every living substance", and "every living thing of all flesh".[1] The catalogue appears comprehensive. The problem with the argument is that it is vulnerable to a scope qualification: the counter-argument is that "all flesh" is destroyed from the *country* in which Noah lived and not the planet. When this qualification is made, a stalemate is created between those who argue for a global flood and those who advocate a local flood.

6.1 Interpreting All

At various points in the narrative a comprehensive "all" or an "every" is used. The number of uses of these quantifiers gives rise to an impression of totality. Coupled with the common translation of *eretz* as "earth", the interpretation of a global flood is naturally suggested to a reader. However, closer reading should dislodge first impressions.

1) Yahweh repents of the fact that he has made man and cattle, creeping thing and fowl of the air and he proposes to destroy them from the face of the ground (Gen 6:7). This is not a comprehensive catalogue, as indicated by the choice of *bᵉhemah* ("cattle") which links to the Genesis 2 creation of "beasts of the field" rather than the more general "beasts of the earth" from Genesis 1. We can be certain about this link because it is from the *ground* (not the earth) that the beasts of the field are formed (Gen 2:19-20) and it is the destruction of beasts from the face of the *ground* that is the focus of Genesis 6. We might ask why cattle (domestic beasts),

---

[1] C. A. Hill, "The Noachian Flood: Universal or Local", Perspectives on Science and the Christian Faith 54/3 (2002): 170-183 (171) calls this the best argument, biblically speaking, for a worldwide flood. She argues for a local flood.

creeping things and fowl are included while marine life and the beasts of the earth are excluded. To this we can say: the reason for the flood is the wickedness of man rather than the anything to do with cattle, creeping things, and birds. Their inclusion is puzzling until it is realised that they are part of man's *habitat*.

If we pose the question: why would God *repent* of making cattle, creeping things and fowl, the detail of the story suggests that these resources in man's habitat were being plundered by marauders raiding the farming communities. The violence that God sees leads to him to pronounce that he will remove both the perpetrators and the underlying causes of the violence.

2) The expression "all flesh" is used by God when speaking to Noah about what he proposes to do (Gen 6:12). The text says that "God looked" and this echoes the creation account of Genesis 1 where the phrase is used several times. There is a contrast between God looking and seeing that things are good in Genesis 1 and looking and seeing that "all flesh" had become corrupt in Genesis 6. The question to pose is: when God "looks", does he look on those with whom he is working out his purpose? Elsewhere the expression "God looked" only occurs in Exod 2:25 in relation to Israel's distress in Egypt. This suggests that for God to look upon the earth is for him to look upon those with whom he is working out his purpose. In the case of Genesis 6 these are the "sons of God".

The perspective of the narrator is different to that of God. God looks down from *heaven* upon the *earth*; the narrator describes the state of affairs *in the land*. Hence, a narrator can describe the land as corrupt "before God" and "filled with violence" and God can *say* that the earth was filled with violence. This is an important distinction to bear in mind, as God can speak of "the earth" while the scope of the reference is still a land.

The Hebrew expression translated "before God" indicates matters of obedience and worship as this is the constant use of "before God" elsewhere (e.g. Exod 18:12; Josh 24:1). Such things had become corrupt before God. All flesh had corrupted his way, i.e. God's way (cf. 2 Sam 22:31). This is obviously a different issue to the fault of violence. There is a pun in the Hebrew at this point: the text records God's words as, "The end of all flesh is come *before me*, because the earth is filled with violence from *before them*". What has come "before" God addresses what has come "before" all flesh.

167

The text states that God looked upon the earth and saw that "all flesh" had corrupted his way. This sets up an obvious restriction of scope on "all flesh". It is trivially true that Noah is excerpted from the scope of "all flesh", but more importantly, the scope of "all flesh" is contextual in that it is determined by the topic of discourse. Thus within the Prophets, there are discourses where the scope of the expression "all flesh" is Israel and/or her neighbours (e.g. in Isa 40:5; 49:26; Ezek 21:4; Joel 2:28: Zech 2:17). In some texts, "all flesh" is more general in scope (e.g. Deut 5:26; Job 34:15). In Genesis 6 the scope of "all flesh" comprises those who were coming before God and those filling the land with violence. In terms of the groups in the story, there are three: the sons of God, the daughters of men and the Nephilim. The "sons of God" are those who would have been coming before God (cf. Job 1:6), and the account blames them for consorting with the daughters of men. The Nephilim are, as the expression suggests, marauders—men of violence. In God's address to Noah then, it is these groups who comprise the "all flesh".

3) The expression "all flesh" is qualified in Gen 6:17, "all flesh, in which there is the breath of life, from under heaven; and everything that *is* in the earth". The argument is put that this has global scope—*eretz* must mean "earth" as it is put in apposition with "from under heaven".

There are three points to make regarding this argument. First, the motif of the "breath of life" is not used in Genesis 1 but in Genesis 2. The Hebrew in Gen 6:17 is "spirit of life" and in Gen 2:7 it is "breath of life" (Gen 7:22 has "breath-spirit of life"), but the expression in Genesis 2 is used of human beings and not animals. This delimits "all flesh" to be human beings rather than animals. Secondly, the assertion is a threat and the figure is hyperbole. The figure of destroying *a people* "from under heaven" is consistently used elsewhere in threats (Exod 17:14; Deut 7:24; 9:14; 25:19; 29:19; 2 Kgs 14:27). Thirdly, given the focus on human beings, the second clause "everything that *is* in the earth" also does not cover animals.

There is a perspective implied in the threat that is made by God. In communicating with Noah, God adopts Noah's perspective which would have concerned the land. When God says to Noah that he will "bring a flood of waters upon the *eretz*", Noah's perspective would have been the land where he was living. This is indicated by the language of *bringing* a flood that God uses with Noah. This is a natural way of describing both river-based floods and floods caused by tidal inundation. A high tide or a tidal wave *brings* a flood upon the coastal land; heavy rain and/or a snow melt in the mountains *brings* a flood when the river downstream bursts its banks. The language of *bringing a flood upon the land* is not the language that describes a global flood.

4) The expression "every living thing of all flesh" in Gen 6:19 covers birds, domestic beasts and creeping things. They are of various kinds and to be preserved as male and female pairs. The scope of "every living thing of all flesh" is set by the further specification of clean and unclean beasts and fowl that were to be taken into the ark. It could be held that a specification of "clean and unclean" is not explicitly made for creeping things (Gen 7:2-3, 8), but this is probably an over-literal insistence and the distinction is ranging over beasts, birds and creeping things. In the Law (Lev 20:25), the three categories were included in the clean/unclean regulations (e.g. Lev 11:31). These three categories then seem to "go together" in Gen 6:19-20 and are categories of "every living thing".

This specification of "clean" and "unclean" is restrictive in scope. Within the Law the classification pertained to *eating* and it included marine life (Lev 11:46; 20:25). This law is the only guide to the interpretation of Genesis 6 and the question of what animals were taken on board. The classification in the Law is not comprehensive for all animal life and broadly speaking we can say that it covers a restricted range of animals, birds and creeping things of which the Israelites had knowledge and were in the habit of eating. The Law sought to regulate their eating. Similarly, in Noah's case, the animals and birds (clean and unclean) would be that range known to him and classified with regard to eating.[1] The storybook image of elephants and tigers on an ark is not implied by "every living thing of all flesh".

The expression "every living thing" translates a common and flexible Hebrew phrase (*kal hai*) and the word for "living thing" (*hai*) is also often translated "beast". We should always note what Hebrew word is translated as "beast" as it could be *b*hemah* or *hai* and a distinction is made between the two words in Gen 1:24. The phrase *kal hai* occurs in Gen 1:28 in relation to the dominion of humankind over "every living thing",

---

[1] Hence, the command in Gen 9:3 is an *extension* of the range of what animals were permissible for eating and not the *introduction* of a permission for eating meat. The command has a practical relevance to the story of Noah's flood if, as we have argued, one of the underlying causes was the violence of marauders towards the farming communities. Relaxing a restriction on eating would ease future pressure on food supplies.

169

but in Gen 1:30 the Hebrew expression is translated as "every beast". In Gen 2:19-20 and 3:14 it is used in the expression "every beast of the field" and Gen 3:1 has "any beast of the field" using the same phrase. When the distinction "clean" and "unclean" is in focus the word *behemah* is used which would be more appropriate for a domestic distinction.

The expression "every living thing" can have a wide or narrow scope. In Gen 2:19-20 and 3:14 its scope is narrowed by the addition of "of the field" and it covers domestic beasts. The scope is similarly narrow in Gen 1:28 as it covers just "creeping things". Moreover, Gen 1:28 is part of a general statement of animal husbandry ("dominion", Gen 1:26-30) and focuses on the animals that humankind would husband. Here it is worth noting that Gen 1:30 is a practical direction for the first human pair about their husbandry. They are directed to both feed themselves and the animals over which they have dominion with plants (i.e. the produce of arable farming).[1] It is noteworthy that grass (Gen 1:11-12) is not specifically mentioned, but perhaps grass, as such, was not farmed.[2]

There is therefore an implication of arable and animal farming in the account of creation in Genesis 1, and this is an important detail to bear in mind when considering the scope of the flood. The global scope of the opening days of creation changes in Gen 1:24 when the sixth day begins. Commands are given to the human pair to have dominion over plants and animals; they are "given" the work of arable farming and animal husbandry.[3] This narrowing of focus in the account reflects the local scope of the second creation account in Genesis 2. This account bookends the creation and fall of man with comments about their tilling of the ground (Gen 2:5; 3:19). The account of flood has symmetry here with the account in Genesis 1 and 2: after the flood Noah becomes a tiller of the ground. The local focus of Gen 1:26-30 and 2:4b-3:24 sets the local scope for the reading of Genesis 6-9.

---

[1] Of course, fish are not mentioned within such husbandry as the feedstuffs specified are arable and related to land husbandry.
[2] The mention of arable farming does not imply that humans were not meat eaters. A *positive direction* to farm necessarily does not imply a *negative prohibition* regarding animal husbandry or hunting. Rather, the direction to have dominion over animals would have embraced all aspects of husbandry; *contra* Whittaker, *Genesis 1-2-3-4*, 1986), 43-44.
[3] Hence, Gen 1:30 is not saying that all animals were vegetarian; rather, it is directing the first human pair to feed the animals that came under their dominion with arable produce; *contra* Whittaker, *Genesis 1-2-3-4*, 43-44.

5) While there is a miracle implied in the unclean and clean animals *coming* to Noah, the record states that Noah was to *take* "all food" on board for the animals (Gen 6:21). This detail implies a local scope for the flood with the food taken on board being agricultural produce for what would have been any (clean and unclean) animals fed on arable produce. This food would have come from the surrounding area and be the sort of produce that could sustain the animals *of that area*. There is no need to hypothesize that Noah sought bamboo from China to feed Giant Pandas.

This restriction of scope implied by the practicalities of feeding is an important detail. The purpose of the ark was to "keep seed alive upon the face of all the earth" (Gen 7:3). This compares with the corresponding statement in the *Gilgamesh Epic*, "Whatever I had of the seed of all living creatures [I loaded] aboard her" (XI.83).[1] The expression "face of all the earth" is quoted from Gen 1:29, in connection with God's assignment of plant bearing seed and trees to the male and the female for food. This connection indicates that the correct translation of the Hebrew is "face of all the land" and that the stress is on the "face" where these things grow. This implies that the purpose of the ark in keeping seed alive was not to replenish the globe but the local and now devastated country in which Noah lived and off which the people and animals had lived. Certainly, a local scope for "the face of the whole earth" is required for the story of Babel (Gen 11:4, 8-9), and elsewhere the expression denotes the extent of the Promised Land (Deut 11:25) and regions of Judah (1 Sam 30:16; 2 Sam 18:8).

6) A new expression of totality is introduced in Gen 7:4, 23, "every living substance that I have made will I destroy from of the face of the ground" (7:4) "every living substance was destroyed which was upon the face of the ground" (7:23). In Gen 7:23 the scope is delimited by "both man, and cattle, and the creeping things, and the fowl of the heaven". There is no new information in this scoping that we have not already considered. The use of "ground" (*adamah*) rather than "earth" or "land" (*eretz*) draws in the background of the local creation of Genesis 2 rather than the global one of Genesis 1.

The figure of a "face" of the ground is an import detail which conveys the idea of supporting life. We have noted the use of "face" in Gen 1:29 in relation to the land (*eretz*) and the contextual mention of plant bearing seed and trees. In Gen 2:6, the "face of the ground" is mentioned in an

---

[1] Our text is taken from the convenient edition of Heidel.

explicit agricultural context. Gen 3:19 contains a pun on "face" such that Adam will till the ground in the sweat of his "face". Cain is driven from the face of the ground which, as a tiller of the soil, he feared. He was turned into (initially) a wanderer—the opposite of a farmer. The circumstances that gave rise to the flood revolve around the face of the ground: men multiply on the face of the ground (Gen 6:1, 7) and this leads to pressure on the land's resources and consequent violence.

When we consider "every living substance that I have made will I destroy from of the face of the ground" we should do so in the light of this consistent pattern in the concept of a "face"—the scope comprises those living off the land, man and beast. The term "substance" is rare in the Hebrew and only used elsewhere in Deut 11:6 for the substance of a man's household. Its use here in Genesis is a further pointer to the motif of a farming community: the living substance of each of the farming households would be destroyed in the flood. There is no indication in this language of a global flood in which kangaroos and tigers are involved.

7) In Gen 7:14, the animals that go into the ark are "every beast" (*kal har*) after its kind, "all the cattle" (*kal b'hemah*) after their kind, "every creeping thing" after its kind, "every fowl" after its kind, and "every bird" of "every sort" (Gen 7:14). The text echoes Gen 1:24 in its distinction of "beast" (*har*) and "cattle" (*b'hemah*) and the use of the idea of a "kind"; "male and female of all flesh". We have argued that the scope of *kal b'hemah* is restricted to the clean and unclean beasts (*b'hemah*, Gen 7:2-3, 8). The categories of "clean" and "unclean" are also applied to birds and unless we are over-literal, to creeping things. The expression "every beast" unqualified by "of the earth" or "of the field" has its first occurrence here in Gen 7:14.

In Gen 6:19, we have "*kal har* of all flesh", but the Hebrew is better translated "every living thing (*kal har*) of all flesh", as Gen 6:20 has the corresponding verb "to keep alive (*hayah*) in the *inclusio* position. Accordingly, Gen 7:14 and its *kal har* should be "every living thing". It is broader than the domestic scope of "all the cattle" (*kal b'hemah*).

In Gen 6:19-20, we have the "two by two" instruction which is later expanded in terms of clean and unclean beasts, fowl and creeping things (Gen 7:2-3, 8). This suggests that "every living thing" (*kal har*) is an expression of general scope for whatever is being denoted by "all the cattle" (*kal b'hemah*), "every creeping thing", "every fowl", and "every bird" (Gen 7:14)—whatever was classified as "clean" and "unclean". This reading is supported by Gen 8:1 which just has *kal har* and *kal b'hemah*.

8) A new phrase is used in Gen 7:21, which is best rendered, "all swarming creatures that swarm upon the land". This specification is found in the Law in describing the class of "flying creeping things" (Lev 11:20-23), as well as other "creeping things" (Lev 11:29, 41-44). A number of creatures are identified in the Law under this description as clean and unclean. In the flood account, it would seem that the creeping things *that swarm* are a more precise identification of the "creeping things" so far mentioned. As such, "all swarming creatures" is as restricted as the other living things categorized as clean and unclean.

9) There is a distinction to draw between an expression of intention to destroy all flesh and any description of what actually happened. The description of the destruction of life in Gen 7:21-22 restricts the area affected to "the dry land" (NASB, RSV). The underlying expression is not very common and used elsewhere only of dry river beds (4x) and dry sea beds (2x) (Exod 14:21; Josh 3:17; 4:18; 2 Kgs 2:8; Ezek 30:12; Hag 2:6). We can infer then that the term for "dry land" does not denote the planet, or the land-masses of the earth; rather, the dry land here is that land related to river basins and delta basins—land susceptible to river flooding or the ingress of the sea. It is here that all flesh died rather than elsewhere on the earth.

10) The "new creation" after the flood is described in language that evokes the Genesis 1 account of creation (Gen 1:24-30). This makes the new creation a *type* of the Genesis creation and this intention of the narrative explains the "global appearance" of the language of "all". Thus, "every living thing", fowl, cattle and creeping thing after their kinds are to be "fruitful and multiply" in the land (Gen 8:17). This new creation is a *microcosm* of the Genesis creation; it is the Genesis creation established in Mesopotamia.

11) The final note of totality concerns the edict about animal life after the flood. In Gen 9:2 the expressions "every beast of the earth" (*har eretz*) and "all the fishes of the sea" appear for the first time in the flood account. These creatures would now live in "fear and dread" and this raises the question of why this consequence should be imposed.

The mention of every "beast of the earth" and all the "fishes of the sea" at this point in the text should be compared with the terms of the covenant made with Noah in Gen 9:10.

> And with every living creature that *is* with you, of the fowl, of the cattle, even of every beast of the earth with you; from all that go out of the ark, to every beast of the earth. Gen 9:10 (KJV revised)

There are three scope statements in this assertion. The first is "every living creature that is with you, of the fowl, of the cattle"; the second is "even of every beast of the earth with you"; and the third is "from all that go out of the ark, to every beast of the earth".

The second scope statement uses "beast of the earth" for the second time in the flood account. It is not saying there were some wild beasts in the ark; rather it is a repetition for emphasis of the first scope statement: "even of every beast of the earth with you". The third scope statement is a further repetition embracing the same fowl and cattle and every living creature in the ark. It is better rendered "out of all[1] that go out of the ark, in respect of[2] every beast of the earth".

In Gen 9:2 there are "beasts", "fowl" and "creeping things". This is disguised in the KJV because it translates the relevant Hebrew as that which "moveth" rather than "creepeth" upon the earth. Along with the mention of fish, we have a fourfold division of creatures.

In Gen 9:3 there is an extension of the food chain for humankind to include every creeping thing over and above those previously classified as "clean". The food chain is extended to include "every beast of the earth" in addition to clean beasts of the field. The giving of "every" living thing for food is compared to God previously having given "every" green plant for food. Prior to the flood, humankind ate of every green plant (the arable crops) but was restricted to eating clean animals; after the flood, just as they had eaten of every green plant, now they could eat of every living thing. The reason for this extension lies in the circumstances that

---

[1] The Hebrew prepositional phrase occurs in Gen 6:19 translated as "of" and "out of".
[2] The Hebrew preposition is used in a similar way in Gen 23:10 and compare Lev 11:42 and 16:21.

gave rise to the flood, viz. the pressure on the resources of the land and the violence that this caused.

6.2 Summary

In this article we have examined the "all" and "every" expressions of the flood account. There are a large number and they give the impression of totality. There are many indications in the text that the scope of "all" and "every" is restricted and local to Noah and the land in which he was living. Nevertheless, the narrative has been written to signal to the reader the type that the old creation was being destroyed and a new creation was being created. We should not mistake language designed to convey a *type* for language describing a global flood.

7. Mountains, Rivers and Land

Genesis 6-9 describes the flood with comparatively little physical detail. The global flood interpretation has substantial opposition from many scientific disciplines; the local flood reading has considerably less (if any) problems. The Mesopotamian region is known for extensive flooding throughout the ages.[1] Nevertheless, there is some physical detail that we can examine and thereby evaluate whether the flood account is a reasonable description of a catastrophic local flood in Mesopotamia.

7.1 Mesopotamia

S. Pollock notes that "Mesopotamia is, geologically speaking, a trough created as the Arabian shield has pushed up against the Asiatic landmass, raising the Zagros Mountains and depressing the land to the southwest of them. Within this trench the Tigris and the Euphrates Rivers and their tributaries have laid down enormous quantities of alluvial sediments, forming the Lower Mesopotamian Plain...Today the Lower Mesopotamian Plain stretches 700 kilometres...to the west of the Euphrates, a low escarpment marks the southwestern boundary of the alluvial plain and the beginning of the Western Desert".[2] The Mesopotamian Basin can be divided into the Upper Plain above Baghdad, the River Plain below Baghdad and the Delta Plain in the south.[3]

---

[1] Bailey, *Noah: The Person and the Story in History and Tradition*, chap. 2.

[2] S. Pollock, *Ancient Mesopotamia* (Cambridge: Cambridge University Press, 1999), 29. Pollock's chapter 2 should be consulted for the geography of Mesopotamia in ancient times.

[3] Pollock, *Ancient Mesopotamia*, 30.

This description of an extensive flood plain satisfies one of the conditions of the physical description of the flood, viz. that it extended beyond the visual horizon of Noah "under the whole heavens". If we place Noah in the south, on the Delta Plain, between the Tigris and Euphrates rivers, where the Gilgamesh Epic places Utnapishtim,[1] then the "high hills" (Gen 7:19, KJV) on the plain would have been covered "under the whole heaven" from Noah's vantage point. As the waters prevailed upon the land by overflowing the river channels of the Tigris and Euphrates and their tributaries in the south, the high hills on the surrounding plain would have been covered. The Hebrew for "hills" is the same as for "mountains" (Gen 7:20), but the use of "mountains" in English versions gives an impression of global proportions for the flood. This fails to take into account the question of perspective implied by "high" in relation to a plain. The Hebrew word involved can be equally "hill" or "mountain".

The Hebrew for "high hills" is necessarily of relative perspective. A "high hill" to a dweller on a flood plain is not a high hill to a dweller in the Zagros Mountains. Within the alluvial floodplain there would have undulating hills of low proportions (sand hills, sedimentary deposits, old levees,[2] low ridges[3] and abandoned city-mounds for the flood waters to overflow. The "high hills" would not denote the Zagros Mountains or the foothills of these mountains. They are the hills local to the ark's point of departure in the south of the Mesopotamian flood plain.

The waters "prevailed" upon the land; they increased gradually and lifted up the ark above the ground (Gen 7:17). The depth of the waters is given as 15 cubits above the high hills,[4] a measure which is a significant indicator of the local proportions of the flood. This sort of measure would be taken by soundings and such a short measure only makes sense in a local situation.[5] Alternatively, the measure might have been determined from the draught of the ark. More importantly, this measure is

---

[1] Our text is taken from the convenient edition of Heidel and the reference is XI.11-14.
[2] Pollock, *Ancient Mesopotamia*, 33.
[3] Pollock, *Ancient Mesopotamia*, 29.
[4] The Hebrew and the LXX allows the 15 cubits' measure to be above the land rather than the high hills, and if this were the case, the high hills would be river embankments.
[5] C. A. Hill, "The Noachian Flood: Universal or Local", 174.

taken *at the point where the ark becomes buoyant*.[1] This measure should not be applied by a reader elsewhere in the Mesopotamian Basin, where the river channel, the associated floodplain, and the local topography would have produced different measures. Thus, water may have been deep around the river channel but less so at further distances in other areas. In the south, where the flood plain of the Tigris and the Euphrates is extensively flat, the depth of the flood need only be shallow by this measure. Thus, for example, a 40 foot undulation would require a 70 foot flood depth.

A. E. Hill has proposed a geometric model for the flood. He includes a diagram (Diagram 1)[2] which offers a proposal on how extensive the flood could have been progressing up the Mesopotamian Basin and how varied the flood depth could have been extending out from the river channels. He locates the ark launch point at Shuruppak in the south a city on the Euphrates, following the Gilgamesh Epic. The Bible account does not locate Noah, but such a location would fit the flood account, and in this case the high hills such as levees and city mounds nearest the river are those that would be the ones covered. Hill locates the resting place of the ark in the north near Cizre, which has substantial traditional support, however, the Bible does not state where in the region of Ararat the ark rested.

7.2 Ararat
The ark landed "upon the mountains of Ararat" (Gen 8:4, KJV). Ararat is a region that extends south into northern Iraq (2 Kgs 19:37; Jer 51:27),[3] but the account does not indicate where in Ararat the ark grounded.

No inference can be drawn from the word translated "mountains" as to the depth or extent of the flood in Ararat. The account implies that the flood was extensive in the south where the ark was launched, but there is no statement of extent for the resting place of the ark. Further, as already noted, "mountains" in Hebrew could mean "hills". The geographical perspective of the text could well mean the *foothills* of Ararat that set the boundary of the Upper Plain. The flood waters beyond the Upper Plain could therefore have been narrowly confined and the ark could have travelled within the deeper water of a river channel and come to rest upon

---

[1] A. E. Hill, "Quantitative Hydrology of Noah's Flood", in *Perspectives on Science and the Christian Faith* 58/2 (2006): 130-141 (130).
[2] Hill, "Quantitative Hydrology of Noah's Flood", 132.
[3] Bailey discusses the shifting extent of the region of Ararat down the centuries, *Noah: The Person and the Story in History and Tradition*, 55-61.

the banks of the Tigris *besides* the foothills of Ararat. The Hebrew preposition translated "upon" in the KJV and other versions has a wide variety of senses including a locative sense of "besides, by" (e.g. Gen 14:6; 16:7; 29:2; Num 3:26; Job 30:4).[1]

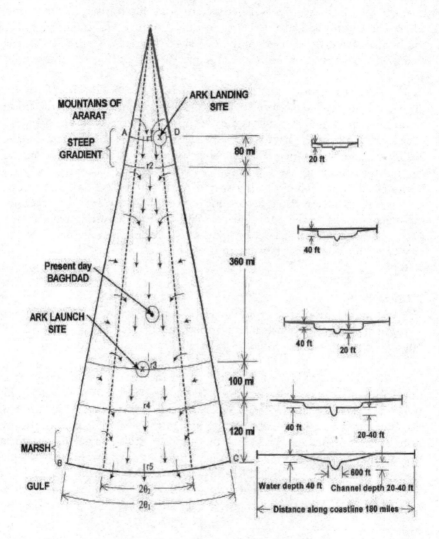

Diagram 1

[1] See BDB 755, note 6, for more examples.

7.3 Water

A local flood satisfying the measure of 15 cubits above the high hills requires a great deal of water in the south. Two sources are stated: rainfall and the "fountains of the deep" (Gen 7:11). This expression "fountains of the deep" has been taken to denote subterranean water but it is more likely to indicate tidal wave inundation from the Gulf. The Arabian Plate is subtended under the Asian plate along the western side of the Gulf (See Illustration 1) and any underwater volcanic activity (or quakes) could have led to tidal wave surges to extend inland over the Delta Plain for a considerable distance. With rainfall swelling the river system in the north and overflowing river channels in Upper Plain and the River Plain in all directions as it moved south, incoming tidal water (with eroded deposits off the Delta) would have seriously impeded water flow to the Gulf by creating widespread dams. This would have slowed the assuaging of the waters, thereby adding to the depth of the flood waters and their extent in the south on the Delta Plain. The whole delta lowland south of Baghdad is extremely flat and rises only a few metres from the Persian Gulf to Baghdad, so that Baghdad is still less than 10 metres above sea level; in effect the flood would have extended the Gulf.

Weather systems that could give rise to extended rainfall are known for the region. Exceptional cyclonic rain,[1] coinciding with spring snow melt in the mountains that feed the Tigris and Euphrates valleys, along with geologic disturbance at the boundary of the Arabian Plate creating tidal waves, can account for the flood.[2] The resulting flood would have been most extensive in the Delta Plain but less so in the Middle River Plain and the Upper Plain.

The scale of the flood on a local reading is large, as is the volume of water. But there is nothing in the biblical account itself that is implausible for the region in terms of these hypothetical weather conditions or the inundation of the sea that would exclude the explanation of a local flood for Genesis 6-9.

The size and construction of the ark is that of an exceptionally large river barge, assuming a standard Israelite measure for the cubit. The stresses that the ark could bear and the water seepage that the ark would bear

---

[1] The Mesopotamian flood accounts mention "wind-storms" and "south-storms"; see ANET, 44, 94.
[2] Hill, "Qualitative Hydrology of Noah's Flood" discusses the weather requirements.

preclude a violent global flood. We do not know the number of animals or the volume of food in the ark; all we can do is guess at relatively small numbers and volumes given the implicit land husbandry of the "clean" and "unclean" directions.

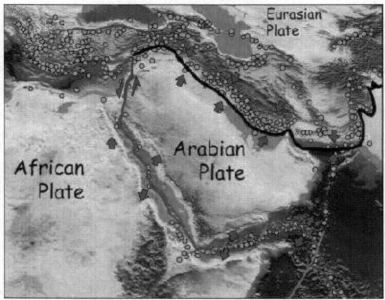

Illustration 1

As floods leave deposits and erode material, and the Mesopotamian Basin has always been subject to flooding, the physical evidence for Noah's flood will have been affected in subsequent smaller floods, changes in sea level, and the shifting course of the rivers. Archaeological digs have found flood deposits in levels for various Delta Plain cities around 2900 BCE, and some have postulated that this may be evidence of Noah's flood. Others have argued that 3500 BCE is a likely date and have pointed to other flood deposits as evidence.[1]

7.4 The End of the Flood
Having stated that the waters prevailed for 150 days (Gen 7:24), the account next describes the fortieth day of the flood and why the waters prevailed for 150 days (Gen 8:1-4). This can be inferred because Gen 8:3

---

[1] Bailey, *Noah*, chap. 3, sets out the evidence.

mentions the end of the 150 days. The explanation given is that although on Day 40 the rain was restrained, and the windows of heaven[1] and the fountains of the deep were stopped, the waters prevailed for 150 days because the waters receded slowly. The Hebrew uses the verb "to go/to walk" in the infinitive (Gen 8:3) to describe the recession, so that we can say, the waters receded *walking*. During this period of 150 days the ark travelled to Ararat. For this to have occurred against the flow of water downstream, wind would have to have driven the ark north up the river channels.[2] It is perhaps noteworthy in this connection that the account mentions a wind as the mechanism whereby the waters were assuaged (Gen 8:1), however, such a wind would have been opposite to that required to push the ark north. A southerly wind is necessary to move the ark; the journey may have been long or short during the 150 days.

In Gen 8:5, a time period of 73 days is implied after the 150 days in which waters continued to decrease after which the tops of the hills that had been covered (Gen 7:19) were seen. The text here is not saying that they were seen *by Noah*; rather, this is a narrator's statement that the hills that had been covered in the Delta Plain were now revealed. At this point in the story, Noah is hundreds of miles to the north of his former homeland. The narrative has symmetry in its second mention of 40 days. As the catastrophe draws to a close, a period of 40 days sees Noah wait before sending out a raven and a dove. Noah sends out a raven and then a dove or, more likely, a homing dove (Gen 8:9).[3] A homing dove would be trained to return to home (in this case the ark).

On the first flight, the dove returned almost immediately unable to find rest for its foot in the vicinity of the ark. On the second flight it was able to stay out all day, until evening, and bring back a plucked olive leaf. The

---

[1] The "windows of heaven" may be a figure for violent rainfall thus allowing more restrained rainfall to have continued during the 150 days.

[2] Hill, "Quantitative Hydrology of Noah's Flood", 137-139, offers an estimate needed for the speed of the wind. The variables are the weight of the ark, the gradient, and the flow of the water downstream. He offers 4 possible cases, the "lightest" of which would be for a wind of between 54 mph and 70 mph.

[3] The Hebrew term is translated as both "dove" and "pigeon" in the KJV. E. Firmage in his article "Zoology" in *ABD*, 6:1145, treats doves and pigeons together but states that homing pigeons are not attested for Mesopotamia *so far*. The story of Noah could be the only evidence of homing birds for Mesopotamia.

mention of the "plucking" of an olive leaf indicates fresh growth and this is another indicator that the flood was local to the Mesopotamia Basin. The dove would have had to have found olive trees on well-drained low ground unaffected by the flood, as olive trees would not have sprouted fresh growth under water for the year of the flood. Noah's inference from the freshly plucked olive leaf that the waters had abated rests upon his knowledge that the dove needed rest during all day flight, rather than any presumption that flood waters had receded to reveal freshly sprouting trees.

After the waters had abated, Noah and the animals disembarked to a devastated landscape unable to support life. The land would need to spring back to life; Noah would need to re-introduce animal husbandry and arable farming. The non-domestic animals that were not going to be kept by Noah would migrate to the areas unaffected by the flood. Noah himself would migrate to such a region. In time, the devastated land would be replenished.

8. Conclusion

In this appendix, we have offered a physical description of the flood based on the text. The key ideas have been i) identifying the source of the water; ii) explaining the slow recession of the water through tidal wave deposits; iii) allowing for extensive flooding in the south and less extensive flooding in the north; iv) postulating a river barge driven by a wind northwards against the flow of water and following the river channels; and v) explaining the olive leaf as vegetation from an unaffected area.

There are many websites arguing for a local flood and a global flood. This appendix has presented the case for a local flood. It lies outside the remit of the book to argue the scientific aspects of either view. In respect of a local flood, the scientific argument revolves around i) whether an ark of the stated size could have been constructed at that time and been weather-proof; ii) whether the loaded weight of the ark and its draught in the water is realistic; iii) whether the wind velocities necessary to drive the ark north against the direction of water flow are feasible; iv) whether the rate of water flow and recession of the flood towards the *open* Gulf makes a Mesopotamian flood implausible; and v) whether erosion can account for any absence of flood deposits today. The relevant scientific disciplines here are marine engineering, hydrology, climatology and geomorphology.

Biblical interpretation can only interpret the text and make sure that possibilities are clearly stated. Thus the text cannot settle the question of whether an ark of the stated dimensions could have been constructed at that time. The text allows for any construction to be proposed by a marine engineer that satisfies the contextual requirement of a very large river barge. In terms of the weight and draught of the ark, the key variable of the number of animals is unknown and the text's stipulation of "clean" and "unclean" suggests a small number. Likewise, the depth of the main river channels is unknown and how far they were navigable. The depth of the flood was relatively shallow by the one measure given, but also unknown. The Delta Plain is extensive and the speed of water flow and drainage would have been affected by the high water table, marshland vegetation, and the extent of the water. Tidal wave inundation and any tidal deposits would affect water flow to the Gulf. Similarly, sedimentary deposits from the riverine flood waters would have affected flow. Rises in sea level are also possible. These factors are the variables which affect the judgment as to whether the "open end" of the Mesopotamian Basin would have allowed the flood waters to decrease slowly as the text requires.

These are the sort of scientific issues that arise in discussion of the theory of a local Mesopotamian "Noah's flood". This remains the most common "local" reading because the biblical account bears many similarities to Mesopotamian flood accounts.[1]

Biblical objections to a local flood arise from i) the question as to why an ark was built: why was Noah not told to simply migrate away from the flood area; ii) the question of whether the account allows for there to be human and animal life unaffected by the flood outside Mesopotamia; and iii) the question of whether a local flood in Mesopotamia could have achieved the objective of destroying life *even in that region*.

As with any differing interpretations, dialogue proceeds via proposal, objection, revised proposal, counter-objection, *and so on*. So it is with the local reading of Genesis 6-9. Thus the choice of salvation through an ark is just that—it is a choice that resonates with Genesis 1 and serves as a typology of salvation in a way not possible in a story of "migration to another land". As for the possible existence of human and animal life outside Mesopotamia, the local scope of the flood is shown in the

---

[1] Hence, proposals of a flood in the Mediterranean Basin, the Black Sea Basin and the Caspian Sea Basin have garnered little support.

genealogy of Genesis 10; the peoples that come from Noah's sons migrate from Mesopotamia. The "rest of the world" is an unknown quantity in biblical terms. Would a local flood have destroyed life even in the Mesopotamian Basin? This question depends on how violent we imagine any tidal-wave inundation in the Delta Plain, but what is known from recent times of the rapid and destructive power of tidal waves makes the "fountains of the deep" coupled with cyclonic rain a plausible force for a total destruction of the Delta Plain.

CHAPTER FOURTEEN
The Historical Jesus

1. Introduction[1]

In this summary essay we will briefly review what scholars have said about the possibility of describing the historical Jesus. After this we will consider how we can evaluate the earliest written records about Jesus for historical reliability. Finally, we will discuss how and why history is important for the Christian faith. Our argument is that there are good reasons to trust the canonical gospels for historical information about Jesus, even if we come to the gospels with reservations about the extraordinary details such as the virgin birth, the miracles and the resurrection. In trusting the gospels about the ordinary things about Jesus, we take the first step towards belief in the extraordinary claims about Jesus made in the gospels. The full grounds for belief in the extraordinary are broader than that which historical arguments can furnish a reader. The role of this essay is one of encouraging a reader to get to know about Jesus in the gospels and to not let any initial doubts about the extraordinary to get in the way.

2. Scholarship

Scholars have been self-consciously aware of the business of researching and writing about the historical Jesus since the Enlightenment. Since that time scholarly debate in the area has waxed and waned and many accounts of the life of Jesus have been produced. Those who write histories of Bible interpretation typically record three periods or "quests" for the historical Jesus during the last two hundred years or so, periods interspersed with "quieter" times when scholars were not so occupied with deciding what can be known about Jesus.[2] During this time conservative scholars were positive in their appraisal of the gospels as historical records and critical scholars were more negative.

---

[1] This essay will appear in a book called *Reasons* directed at those investigating the Christian faith.

[2] Two accessible recent reviews of the field are, D. B. Gowler, *The Historical Jesus?* (New York: Paulist Press, 2007). See also P. R. Eddy and J. K. Beilby, "The Quest for the Historical Jesus" in *The Historical Jesus: Five Views* (eds. P. R. Eddy and J. K. Beilby; London: SPCK, 2010), 9-54.

The catalyst for inquiry into the historical Jesus is **doubt**: can the gospels be trusted as historical accounts? The basic methodological presupposition that defines the modern era of Gospel Criticism is that the gospels are to be treated like any other historical record. The doubt arises from the distinction between the Jesus of History and the Christ of Faith: it is asked to what extent the gospels are coloured by a later story-telling fabricated by believers and to what extent they record an accurate portrayal of Jesus of Nazareth. German critical scholars in the nineteenth century concluded that the gospels contained many legendary stories and that they also give expression to common myths of the day. They also took the view that many stories were fabricated by the early church and then included in the gospels. As a result the critical "Lives of Jesus" that were written tended to reflect just the liberal moral values of the German Enlightenment.

The German scholar Albert Schweitzer is credited with bringing to a close this first "quest" for the historical Jesus with the publication of his book, *The Quest of the Historical Jesus* (1906).[1] In reviewing the work of German scholars of the nineteenth century, he observed that they had created a Jesus in their own image, which was Jesus as a liberal moral teacher stripped of the supernatural. After Schweitzer, critical scholars focused on the analysis of the individual units of narrative and sayings in the gospels, and they sought to explain their origins and their placement in the gospels as a result of the needs of the early church. This approach, known as "the form critical study of the gospels", went hand in hand with less interest in producing a "Life of Jesus". Of course, "Lives of Jesus" were produced during this time, and from conservative and critical scholars, but as a trend, German critical scholarship moved into other areas of research.

The reason why critical scholars have been sceptical of recovering the Jesus of History has been their predilection to see the **agenda of the early church** in the gospels. Conservative scholars have been more ready to see in the gospels an attempt to record an accurate history of Jesus, something similar to a biography. While critical scholarship has waxed and waned in its interest in the Jesus of History, conservative scholars have been more consistent in defending the historicity of the gospels. Subsequently, it was not until the 1950s that critical scholars once again focused their attention upon determining what can be known about Jesus from the gospels. Thus, the German scholar Ernst Käsemann in his essay,

---

[1] A. Schweitzer, *The Quest of the Historical Jesus* (ed. J. Bowden; London: SCM Press 2000).

The Problem of the Historical Jesus (1953),[1] argued that scholars were duty bound to find the continuity between the Jesus of History and the Christ of Faith and that therefore they must determine what can be known about Jesus if they were to preserve the doctrine of his humanity. Accordingly, such scholars renewed their efforts to find the historical Jesus in what has come to be known as a "second quest". In addition to analysing the individual stories and sayings of gospels, they did so with a renewed sensitivity to the role of the author in bringing the individual units together in a gospel, a method of analysis that was dubbed "redaction criticism".

This second quest was again driven by German critical scholars but as a scholarly fraternity it gradually lost its significance in the 1970s as American critical scholarship gained greater prominence. As a result, in 1982, the scholar N. T. Wright coined the phrase "third quest" to refer to the work that mostly American scholars were doing in recovering the Jesus of History from the available records.[2] This trend is still ongoing today and it is characterized by the use of new methodologies involving the archaeology, sociology and cultural anthropology of Jesus' times.[3] There is among these scholars less emphasis on the analysis of the canonical gospels and more an emphasis on situating their record within a plausible context. This latest quest has been inter-disciplinary and overtly conscious of the role of method in reaching historical conclusions. To some extent, during this period there has been a coming together of critical and conservative scholars in a more positive appraisal of what can be known about the Jesus of History.[4]

In the history of scholarship there have been both conservatives and liberals. A layman coming to the question of what can be known about Jesus is faced with a wide choice of opinion. The movements in the

---

[1] E. Käsemann, *Essays on New Testament Themes* (London: SCM Press, 1964), 14-47.
[2] N. T. Wright, "Towards a Third 'Quest'? Jesus Then and Now" *ARC* (Montreal, McGill In-house Journal) 10 (1982): 20-27.
[3] G. Theissen and A. Merz, *The Historical Jesus: A Comprehensive Guide* (London: SCM Press, 1998), 1-15.
[4] For an overview of recent research into the historical Jesus, and a review of key scholars identified with the so-called 'third quest', see D. S. Du Toit, "Redefining Jesus: Current Trends in Jesus Research", in *Jesus, Mark and Q: The Teaching of Jesus and its Earliest Records* (eds., M. Labahn and A. Schmidt; Sheffield, Sheffield Academic Press, 2001), 82-124.

discipline have been dominated by critical scholars; these have formed fraternities in which a common goal has been sought, and historians have identified such fraternities as "a liberal quest", "a second quest" or "a third quest" for the historical Jesus. Conservative scholars have only really been part of the last fraternity and have positively assessed what can be known about the Jesus of History from the *realia* of history. Their writings have offered plenty of reasons for trusting the canonical gospel records.

3. Historical Analysis

Although it may seem an odd thing to affirm, the consensus is that Jesus did exist; we have several notices of his existence in contemporary histories of the times. The contemporary Jewish historian, Josephus, mentions Jesus when describing Pilate's governorship of the region. He was a "doer of wonderful works",[1] opposed by the Jewish leaders and crucified (*Ant.* 18.63-64). The Roman historians, Tacitus and Suetonius also mention Jesus as 'Christ' (*Annals* 15, 44; *Life of Claudius*, 25, 4).

Luke refers to the existence of various written accounts[2] about Jesus in his day.

> Forasmuch as many have taken in hand to set forth in order a declaration of those things which are most surely believed among us, Even as they delivered them unto us, which from the beginning were eyewitnesses, and ministers of the word; It seemed good to me also, having had perfect understanding of all things from the very first, to write unto thee in order, most excellent Theophilus, That thou mightest know the certainty of those things, wherein thou hast been instructed. Luke 1:1-4 (KJV)

We have four canonical gospels but other gospels of later dates are known.[3] Scholars have long observed literary relationships between the

---

[1] The consensus of scholars is that this particular expression is original to Josephus and that in this respect his text has not been altered by later Christian copyists—see G. Vermes, "The Jesus Notice of Josephus Re-examined" *JJS* 38/1 (1987): 1-10.

[2] Luke's prologue has an emphasis on written accounts although, no doubt, there was oral tradition that he took on board.

[3] Scholars have tended to date the canonical gospels after AD70, except perhaps Mark which is often dated to the mid-60s C.E.; for a critical

first three gospels, and the most common view is that Mark was used as a source for both Matthew and Luke. Consequently, scholars approach the gospels with a view to establishing their sources. Luke's comment about his own gospel is a statement of an historical method, an attempt to set things in order using eyewitness testimony. He states,

- Tradition was preserved and delivered by eyewitnesses and "ministers of the word" to second generation believers.

- There were other written records, from which it was possible to gain an accurate understanding of Jesus' life.

- New converts were instructed in the things of Jesus' life, and this was supported by written accounts, of which Luke's gospel was to be a 'perfect understanding'.

The scholar H. J. Cadbury asserted that,

> ...it is the bare fact of his [Luke] using a preface rather than in its details that Luke's relation to literature is apparent.[1]

Cadbury also argued that Luke's "prefaces and dedications at once suggest classification with the contemporary Hellenistic historians".[2] The use of prefaces was common in the Hellenistic era (but not earlier), for example, *Dionysius: Roman Antiquities*,[3] and *Polybius: Histories*.[1] Thus, the presence of a

---

review see J. A. T. Robinson, *Redating the New Testament* (London: SCM Press, 1976), who dates all the NT writings to before AD70. The most recent scholarship argues a date for Mark just twenty years or more after the death of Jesus— J. G. Crossley, *The Date of Mark's Gospel* (London: T & T Clark, 2004). For an introduction to the non-canonical gospels see H. Klauck, *Apocryphal Gospels* (London: T & T Clark, 2003).

[1] H. J. Cadbury, *The Making of Luke-Acts* (London: SPCK, 1968), 196, 344.

[2] H. J. Cadbury, "The Greek and Jewish Traditions of Writing History" in *The Beginnings of Christianity: Part 1: The Acts of the Apostles: Vol. II: Prolegomena II: Criticism*, (eds., F. J. Foakes-Jackson & K. Lake; London: Macmillan, 1922), 7-29 (15).

[3] Dionysius: *Roman Antiquities* (trans. E. Cary; Loeb Classical Library; Cambridge: Harvard Univ. Press, 1937), Bk I.1-8. All citations are from this edition.

preface in Luke and a brief recapitulation[2] in Acts is taken to be evidence that Luke-Acts was meant as a species of a single genre — Hellenistic history writing. Classic and Hellenistic historians such as Herodotus, Thucydides and Polybius advocated an objective historiography which is reflected in Luke.

This is important information for someone investigating the gospels for reliable historical information about Jesus; it is significant because one of the gospel writers has stated that an historical record was his intention and that other historical accounts existed (which he may have used). Matthew and Mark are sufficiently like Luke to be placed within the same genre, as something like a "biography"[3] of Jesus.

The priority of Mark gives it precedence in evaluating the gospels as historical accounts of Jesus' words and deeds; further, early church tradition records that it was written under the direction of Peter, an eyewitness and close disciple of Jesus.[4] Luke was a companion of Paul the apostle, while Matthew and John are held by early church tradition to be of the original disciples and therefore eyewitnesses.[5] Since Luke refers to many prior accounts about Jesus, we can surmise that Matthew and Mark were also aware of a variety of sources—other eyewitnesses, oral traditions,[6] as well as written accounts—all close in time to their subject

---

[1] Polybius: *The Histories* (trans. W. R. Paton; Loeb Classical Library; London: Heinemann, 1925), Bk I.1-5.

[2] The preface to Acts is not sharply delimited and a matter of scholarly dispute; we will take vv. 1-3 as the preface, with v. 4 beginning a new scene; vv.1-3 have a summarizing quality indicated by the time period of forty days.

[3] Scholars debate whether the gospels are formally to be classified as "biographies"; see Aune, *The New Testament in its Literary Environment*.

[4] The fourth century church historian, Eusebius, cites the testimony of Papias, an apostolic father (c. 115 C.E.), on the relationship of Mark and Peter in his *History of the Church*, 3.39.14-16 (ed. A. Louth; trans. G. A. Williamson; rev. ed.; London: Penguin Books, 1989).

[5] See D. Guthrie, *New Testament Introduction* (Leicester: Apollos, 1990), 43-53; 113-125; 269-275, who discusses Papias' mention of Matthew (*History of the Church*, 3.39) and another early church father, Irenaeus (c. 120-200 C.E.), who mentions the common view that John the disciple was the author of the Fourth Gospel.(*Adv. Haer.* Iii. 1).

[6] The transmission of oral traditions is indicated in Luke's prologue, incidental comments by Paul—1 Cor 15:1-3; 2 Thess 2:15, as well as the

matter, Jesus. This gives a reader confidence in the historical veracity of what s/he is reading in the first three gospels.

4. Criteria of Authenticity

It might be thought that Jesus' ordinary words and deeds cannot be proved to be authentic or inauthentic. How could anyone prove or disprove whether Jesus visited Bethany or caused a commotion in the temple. It is claimed that the ordinary everyday happenings in Jesus' life and the words that he spoke cannot be historically verified by any independent measure. This is trivially true but irrelevant to the business of historical reconstruction. There are several criteria which can be used to authenticate the records:

1) First, we might ask whether the ordinary things that happened in Jesus' life were common for an itinerant preacher. Are his attributed words **of their times**? These two questions articulate criteria of assessment[1] for the authenticity of Jesus' ordinary words and deeds and they need to pass muster if we are to accept the gospel records as historically accurate. Thus, scholars assess whether Jesus' message is consistent with the Judaisms of his day. Generally speaking, even critical scholars judge that Jesus' words are of their times as a prophet who preached a message about the last days of the Jewish state and the need to repent and turn to God. Jesus' thought only makes sense within Judaism before AD70; early church writers have not made changes to reflect their needs after the destruction of the temple and the Jewish state.

2) In the same way, if Jesus' message is to be judged authentic, it needs to be consistent with early Christian writings; if Christian teaching in the letters, Acts or in Revelation was different to that of Jesus, we would have reason to question either the Christian teaching or the record of the words of Jesus. This issue is really about the degree of any difference and whether we can see a **trajectory** from Jesus' words and deeds to the preaching and teaching of the early church. Again, even critical scholars do not see anything that decisively casts doubt on Jesus' words and deeds when we apply this criterion.

---

character of the first three gospels themselves, which at times have a certain oral quality. For further reading see J. D. G. Dunn, *A New Perspective on Jesus* (London: SPCK, 2005), chap. 2.
[1] For a recent study of such criteria see S. E. Porter, *The Criteria for Authenticity in Historical-Jesus Research* (JSNTS 191; London: T & T Clark, 2000), 63-102.

These two criteria, (1)-(2), are about whether we can exclude any of Jesus' preaching as inauthentic, but they are not absolute rules. Jesus should be of his times but this does not mean that he cannot be original. The early followers of Jesus should be faithful to his message, but they themselves may have written about different things. The criteria are useful as ways to counter the critical rejection of Jesus' words as recorded in the gospels, but they do not license the inclusion of such words in a canon of authentic words.

It would be somewhat sceptical to hold the opposite point of view—to say that we can only accept as authentic those sayings that cannot be attributed to the gospel writers (the early church) or to the general cultural environment of the day. This would be to focus on the original to the detriment of what would be familiar to Jesus' contemporaries. Identifying the **dissimilar** may give us greater confidence that this is what Jesus said, but identifying what is **similar** should not suffer as a result.

We have four canonical gospels and three give **multiple attestations** to the same words and deeds of Jesus. This is important as corroborating evidence for the authenticity of the records when it is clear that the gospels are independent of each of other in their record of a particular episode. However, from another point of view, a literary relationship among the first three gospels is a validation by the writers of the material they are using; moreover, these writers are close in time to their subject matter. So, with Luke's and Matthew's use of Mark, we have a confirming use of Mark as a reliable early source for Jesus' words and deeds. The same point applies if we consider Matthew or Luke to have used each other's gospel or any other sources.[1] Furthermore, if we consider not just written sources but the forms in which traditions were passed on orally, we find that they are mutually supportive.

The choice of the four canonical gospels by the church of the second century is also confirming evidence of their value as historical records provided we can show that the church used the gospels as an historical record about Jesus rather than as just the story of Jesus; the church could have chosen other gospels or more gospels. As such, **their canonical**

---

[1] There is a large body of scholarship on the sources of the gospels. When considering the historical veracity of the gospels, it is held that the use of disparate early sources adds to their credibility; see Guthrie, *New Testament Introduction*, chap. 5.

choice is a witness to the quality of the records in terms of their teaching.[1]

One way that you can build up your picture of Jesus from the gospels is, having accepted basic facts about his words and deeds, you then accept what **coheres** with the basic story that you have already accepted. Critical scholars accept that Jesus was crucified, but having accepted this, they are required to consider the causes that led to his execution. This throws up the question as to whether Jesus' conflict with the Jews and the authorities is coherent and plausible in the light of their lobbying for his death. The answer is that it is a coherent and likely cause of his crucifixion, and in this way, a historian would ascribe greater credence to the gospel accounts in this regard; another test of coherence would be to ask whether the story reflects the Palestinian environment or the legal framework in Jerusalem at the time—again, the gospel account passes this test.

Another criterion that can be used to validate some stories in the gospels stipulates that **unfavourable material will likely be genuine**—material that casts Jesus in an unfavourable light. This kind of material creates a tension with material that presents Jesus favourably. The inclusion of both kinds of material in the gospels is best accounted for if we infer that the intention of the gospel writers was objective and historical. For example, in the story of the healing of Jairus' daughter, the synagogue leader is portrayed in a favourable light, yet other stories place Jewish leaders in opposition to Jesus, and the early church was persecuted by the Jewish authorities. These considerations speak to the authenticity of the story of the healing of Jairus' daughter.

Another example of the inclusion of unfavourable material is the Beelzebub Controversy. The gospels record in different places the accusation that Jesus was able to perform miracles because he wielded the power of the devil; in addition, the story also recounts how his friends thought that Jesus was mad (Matt 12:24; Mark 3:21-30; Luke 11:15). It is significant that Jesus' opponents did not deny the miracles but attributed them to the devil or, in the second century, to magic (Irenaeus, *Adv. Haer.* Ii.32.3-5). There is also recorded Jesus' failure to perform miracles albeit because of a lack of faith in his home village (Matt 13:58).

---

[1] For an introduction to the formation of the canon, see A. G. Patzia, *The Making of the New Testament* (Downers Grove: InterVarsity Press, 1994).

It is not possible here to consider each of the stories in the gospels and argue for their authenticity using criteria of assessment; some combination of criteria will be used in each case and conservative and critical scholars will offer different assessments which reflect their differing presuppositions. What is noteworthy in the debate is not that there are those who reject and those who accept the gospel records but that there are so many different lines of argument to support a positive evaluation of the gospels.

5. Historical Difficulties

The difficulties that are had with the gospels' portrait of Jesus lie in the areas of putative factual inaccuracies; inconsistencies within and between the gospels; Jesus' nature miracles; his healings; and his resurrection. Otherwise, there are no decisive historical objections to the "ordinary" in the gospel accounts. Those who investigate the life of Jesus are more likely to disbelieve the "extra-ordinary" than the "ordinary" and therefore those happenings require separate comment.

5.1 Factual Inaccuracies

There are many characteristics of the gospels that indicate their accuracy; additionally, there are a small number of well-known so-called inaccuracies. Positive assessments of the nuts and bolts of the gospel records have been written by conservative scholars. Since the gospels are a social history of a charismatic teacher and his followers, any inaccuracies would be limited to the "public" side of Jesus' ministry—names, dates, places and the cultural environment. Thus, for example, we are able to verify Luke's political facts—the emperor Augustus, Herod the Great, Quirinius and Pilate, or Annas, Caiaphas and Ananias. Furthermore, we are able to verify Luke's reliability as a historian by examining his follow-up book, Acts.

Inaccuracies in historical texts are expected by the historico-critical method; there is no presumption that the gospel texts are divinely inspired in such a method and so historians will point out errors where there is other evidence that points to different facts of the matter. For example, the reference to a tax census of Quirinius sometime in 6-4 BCE has been dubbed an error because he is known to have become the legate of Syria in 6 C.E. and initiated a census in that year (Josephus, *Ant.* 18.1.1; cf. Tacitus, *Annals* 3.48).[1]

---

[1] This view is defended in the standard academic Bible dictionary—D. S. Potter, "Quirinius" *ABD*, 5:588-589.

There are two preliminary points to make about this "error": first, it is representative of the type of error that could be identified in the gospel records, i.e. errors to do with the more public facts of names, dates and places—the possible errors in this regard are very few indeed; secondly, where there is a conflict between two different sources (Josephus and Luke), critical scholars will favour the non-Biblical evidence and conservative scholars will favour the biblical evidence.

It is accepted by conservative scholars[1] that Quirinius was a legate of Syria in 6-7 C.E. and that there was a census then, which caused unrest in Judea (a province of Syria), and which is referred to by Luke in Acts 5:37 "After this man, Judas of Galilee rose up in the days of the census and drew away *some* people after him; he too perished, and all those who followed him were scattered" (NASB). Luke's use of the expression "the census" and his reference to Judas the Galilean establishes that he is referring to the census of 6-7 C.E. against which Judas led a rebellion.

The census at the time of Jesus' birth is mentioned in this way:

> And it came to pass in those days, that there went out a decree from Caesar Augustus, that all the world should be taxed. (*And* this taxing was <u>first</u> made when Quirinius was governor of Syria.) And all went to be taxed, every one into his own city. Luke 2:1-3 (KJV revised)

In this narrative aside[2] Luke refers to a first census, or a former or earlier census than the one made in 6-7 C.E. This is an important qualification as it coheres with Acts 5:37 which refers to the later and more famous census. Since there is no record of any more census enrolments happening after 6-7 C.E. in relation to Quirinius, we can deduce that the census of Luke 2:2 is not that of 6-7 C.E. but an earlier one. Because Josephus does not record two such census enrolments, critical scholars work with just one and infer that Luke makes a mistake with his placement of a first census at the end of the reign of Herod the Great.

However, an incidental detail of Luke's account makes it unlikely that he is making a simple mistake (after all, his chronology in Luke 3:1 is

---

[1] A representative treatment is that of W. Brindle, "The Census and Quirinius: Luke 2:2" *JETS* 27/1 (1984): 43-52.
[2] For a discussion of this narrative aside see S. M. Sheeley, *Narrative Asides in Luke-Acts* (JSNTSup 72; Sheffield: JSOT Press, 1992), 102-103.

flawless). Mary and Joseph travel to Bethlehem of Judea to enrol for tax purposes. Just before the birth of Jesus, Herod was ruler of Judea and Galilee and a census initiated in his region could have been one that required travel to Judea for those born in the south. After Herod's death, the kingdom of Judea was divided and Galilee came under the jurisdiction of Antipas. In the census of 6-7 C.E. there is no particular reason why those residents in the north would have been required to travel south for enrolment. This makes the census of Luke 2:2 more likely to have been a different and earlier one than that of 6-7 C.E.

Although no extant record other than Luke's requires the suggestion, some scholars have therefore proposed that Quirinius could have been a special military legate anytime between 6-4 BCE in addition to the domestic governor of Syria at the time (who was Sentius Saturninius until 6 BCE and thereafter Quintilius Varus between 6-4 BCE[1]). It is known that Quirinius was conducting a long campaign from the north of Syria (and maybe Galatia) against the Homonadensus at this time and had been since about 10 BCE. He could have assumed a temporary legateship in Syria during any interim period between the two documented governors.

Upon hearing of Jesus from the Wise Men, Herod sought to kill the children in Bethlehem up to two years of age, but Mary and Joseph had been warned to flee this danger. They fled to Egypt and only returned when Herod had died which is dated to 4 BCE. The inference therefore is that Jesus was born most likely in the years 6-5 BCE and that the census Luke mentions took place in one of these years.[2] A temporary military governorship on the part of Quirinius is not implausible. Herod's relationship with Augustus had broken down by the end of his reign and a direction from the military legate of Syria to conduct a census would have been heeded.

Our discussion of Luke's chronology is an example of the kind of discussion that conservative and critical scholars have about the reliability of the gospel records. It is a choice to allow Luke's evidence to stand in a reconstruction of Roman History, but it is because Luke shows himself to be reliable on other names and dates that it is best to do so in this case

---

[1] It is known from Josephus (*Ant.* 10, 9-10) that Quintilius Varus was legate until at least 4 BCE and the death of Herod but not thereafter—when it is next known that Gaius Julius Caesar was the governor in 1 C.E.
[2] Tertullian, *Adv. Marc.* 4.19, dates the census to the governorship of Sentius Saturninius.

and conjecture a second interim legateship on the part of Quirinius. In the relatively few cases where the historical veracity of the gospels can be challenged with apparently contrary external evidence,[1] conservative scholarship has provided plausible harmonisations of the data.

5.2 Inconsistencies

We have four canonical gospels and several non-canonical ones. As a matter of historical method, the main reason for preferring the canonical gospels lies in the second century witness to their authorship among the apostles or their disciples—the dispute over which gospels were accurate and reliable took place in the church towards the close of the second century and the canon is their settlement of the question. The non-canonical gospels proliferated during the second century but were rejected as authoritative by the church.

Critical scholars point to inconsistencies between the gospel records and thereby cast doubt on the picture of Jesus in a given gospel. Historians are used to handling discrepancies between different accounts of the same person and his/her life. The problem raised by such putative inconsistencies was known as early as the second century and "harmonies" of the canonical gospels were produced at the time addressing the problem.[2]

It is beyond the scope of a summary essay to discuss this area in detail. We will take two examples of "inconsistencies" in order to illustrate how conservative scholars disagree on the historical veracity of the gospels.

1) The wording above the cross is given as, variously, "THIS IS JESUS THE KING OF THE JEWS" (Matt 27:37), "THE KING OF THE JEWS" (Mark 15:26), "THIS IS THE KING OF THE JEWS" (Luke 23:38), and "JESUS OF NAZARETH THE KING OF THE JEWS" (John 19:19). This different testimony could be described as an inconsistency between the records; on the other hand, the gospel writers could be selecting their words from "THIS IS JESUS OF NAZARETH THE KING OF THE JEWS" in order to convey the accusation.

---

[1] A. N. Sherwin-White, *Roman Law and Roman Society in the New Testament* (Oxford: Oxford University Press, 1963), 162-171 (162) observes that the presence of Quirinius' name has caused the most controversy in Luke's Roman History.

[2] See Tatian, *Diatessaron* (ed., S. Hemphill; London: Hodder & Stoughton, 1888).

Whether we see an inconsistency is a matter of our attitude to the evidence. This example is typical insofar as a reader will find differences in the wording of what Jesus says in several places. Such differences are due to Jesus having spoken the same things on different occasions and/or the gospel writers recording *what* Jesus said rather than the actual words of Jesus.

2) A second example concerns sequencing events in Jesus' life. Luke opens his gospel narrative with Jesus' confrontation in Nazareth (Luke 4:16-30). This episode is placed in a different place in Matthew and Mark (Matt 13:53-58; Mark 6:1-6). Did the confrontation occur at the beginning of Jesus' ministry as in Luke or later as in Matthew or Mark? We could see this as an inconsistency between the gospel records in terms of the sequence of events in Jesus' life, although the three witnesses testify to the historicity of the actual episode. However, equally, it is possible that Luke has moved the episode to the beginning of his gospel narrative to form a prologue of two episodes in Jesus' life: the temptation in the wilderness and the rejection of Jesus at Nazareth. The point of such a prologue would be to introduce the character of Jesus' ministry as Luke will go on to narrate. Alternatively, it could be that there are different episodes of conflict being recorded: Luke records a rejection at Nazareth while Matthew and Mark record a conflict "in his own country" (Matt 13:54; Mark 6:1). The conflict is similar because the same sort of questions and objections to Jesus will have occurred throughout the villages of Galilee.

These two examples, (1) and (2), illustrate the kind of discussion that critical and conservative scholars have about the consistency of the gospel records. Conservative scholars have produced harmonies of the gospels that show how they are consistent.

5.3 Legend and Myth
It is argued by rationalist historians that some stories in the gospels are legendary and overlaid with contemporary mythology. Of itself, this does not detract from the historicity of the gospels because the mythology is of "of the times". Thus, some historians further embed the gospels in their first century milieu with this kind of argument. This is an important point of evaluation for the historicity of the gospels. The claim that a given story is legendary is a claim about historicity—the story is not a true account—and it is a claim about currency—the story is being told to enhance the reputation of the hero. Given the brief time that has elapsed between Jesus and the writing of the gospels, it is not certain that any stories can be properly regarded as "legend" on any cultural

anthropological measure. The claim that stories reference mythological beings such as Satan or Beelzebub, however, is credible and it enhances the historicity of the accounts.

5.4 Miracles

One area where historians reject the gospel accounts as factual is that of the miracles.[1] In terms of historical plausibility, there are differences to note in the evaluation of miracles. Jesus' exorcisms and healing miracles are deemed more likely than the nature miracles, because Jesus was viewed by his contemporaries as an exorcist and healer. Some scholars will offer rationalist explanations of the nature miracles, for example, it might be said that the account of Jesus walking on water has its basis in an optical illusion: Jesus was walking in shallow water and appeared to be walking on water and a historian might say that the story was embellished in its telling.

Rationalist explanations can be offered for each of the nature miracles in the gospels, but to do so is a philosophical choice; it reflects a philosophy of history in which such miracles are ruled out *a priori*. This is a form of naturalism that assumes natural law cannot be contravened, but such an assumption begs the question as to whether the God of Jesus exists and **intervenes** in the world. The Gospel writers would certainly have had such a view and therefore do not misrepresent their thought world with the accounts of Jesus' nature miracles. If you do not subscribe to the naturalist assumption, then you must remain open to the possibility that Jesus performed nature miracles.

Jesus' miracles are attributed to his possession of the Spirit of God (Matt 12:28; Luke 4:14) and they are presented therefore as acts of God through Jesus; they represent divine intervention in the natural order. As such, the gospel writers do not present miracles as happenings that contravene laws of nature; nor are they presented as inexplicable according to contemporary standards of knowledge; they are simply presented as the outcome of Jesus' actions. Depending on how you make the count, there are about 30-40 miracles in the gospels, with the vast majority occurring in Mark, who is then used by Matthew and Luke. This is historically significant as Mark is the earliest gospel and his re-use by Matthew and Luke is a confirmation of his account by contemporaries.

---

[1] The classic expression of this view is that of D. Hume—see "On Miracles" in *Hume on Religion* (ed. R. Wollheim; London: Fontana, 1963), 205-229.

It is a modern point of view to take the presence of miracle in an historical narrative to be something that detracts from the evidential value of that narrative for constructing a portrait of Jesus. The gospels would have had a more favourable reaction in their own day on this score; we know this because miracles appear in histories around at the time. For example, the classical historian, Herodotus (5c. BCE), accepted a role for the gods in human affairs as unseen forces in some events, and attributed natural events to the actions of the gods. For example, victory at sea with the enemy ships destroyed by a wind from Poseidon (*The Histories*, VII. 189-192); or again, victory over an enemy through a thunderstorm and a fall of rocks from Parnassus (History, IX. 64)—in both cases oracles predicted the victory.[1] Plutarch (50-120 C.E.) is another historian and man of letters who believed in the intervening activity of the gods in the affairs of men. With the examples of Herodotus and Plutarch in mind, we can see that first century readers of the gospels would not have had the same difficulty in believing Jesus performed miracles as a modern person; we have already noted above that Josephus records that Jesus was a wonder-worker. In assessing the historicity of the account of a miracle, certain points support a positive appraisal of the evidence:

- Miracles are attested in different and early sources (Mark, John); the earliest source (Mark) is re-used by other gospels (Matthew, Luke).

- Within the gospels, miracles are described and referenced in sayings, parables, controversy stories, as well straightforward narrative accounts. The variety of material shows that the gospel writers are incorporating the oral traditions of the first generation of Christians; two of the miracle stories contain obvious Aramaisms[2] which shows the use of the original and early oral tradition (Mark 5:41; 7:34).

- Various characters in the gospels, sympathetic and hostile, acknowledge Jesus' miracles (Mark 6:2, 14; John 3:2).

---

[1] A. H. Macdonald, "Herodotus on the Miraculous" in *Miracles* (ed. C. F. D. Moule; London: Mowbray, 1965), 83-91; see Herodotus, *The Histories* (ed. A. R. Burn; trans. A. De Sélincourt; London: Penguin Classics, 1972).
[2] While the gospels are in Greek, scholars have noticed evidence of the use of Aramaic—see M. Black, *An Aramaic Approach to the Gospels and Acts* (3rd. ed.; Oxford: Oxford University Press, 1967).

- The accounts are not included for entertainment as in a novel;[1] the gospels have a serious purpose—a miracle is not incidental or *ad hoc* to the narrative. Luke's prologue states that he was careful to record Jesus' words and deeds.

- Miracle accounts have a teaching purpose; they are signs for those can see their significance (Luke 11:29; John 20:30); they demonstrate the power of God associated with coming kingdom (Luke 11:20).

- Miracles continued with the disciples and the early believers (Mark 16:17; Acts 2:43; 2 Cor 12:12).

- There are later "third-party" witnesses to Jesus' miracle-working including, as we have noted above, Josephus, but also the Babylonian Talmud (*Sanh.* 43a)

These considerations encourage a reader to accept the accounts of miracles, but in the first instance a reader will consider whether the ordinary facts of Jesus' life as presented in the gospels are reliable.

5.6 Healing, Exorcism and Cosmic Mythology

Historians observe that Jesus' exorcisms are detailed using a contemporary mythology, viz., one that involves Satan and his demons. There are some distinctions to be observed with this proposal: Jesus mentions Satan and his demons in dialogue with others; he doesn't engage in any teaching on the subject; further, his remarks are very brief. We do not have any basis for asserting that Jesus believed in demons. The case for such a belief is more likely for the disciples and the Galilean populace, and this reflects the history of the times. Whether the gospel writers believed in demons at the time of their writing their accounts is not known.

The narrative accounts reflect the language of the day and are consistent with Jewish rather than Hellenistic thinking. The dimension that Jewish literature adds to Hellenistic ideas about demons is the nomination of a leading demon: the Devil and Satan. In Greek religion, demons might be the intermediaries of the gods, but no one particular "god" is signalled out

---

[1] This has been defended by R. I. Pervo, "The Ancient Novel becomes Christian" in *The Novel in the Ancient World* (ed., G. Schmeling; Leiden: E. J. Brill, 1996), 685-711.

201

as a leader of demons.[1] So, for example, in the Jewish work *Jubilees* (c. 161-149 BC), Mastema or Satan is given a recurring adversarial role in Israelite history.[2][3] This is confirmatory evidence for the accuracy of the gospels account of Jesus' exorcisms.

There are other aspects of Jesus' exorcisms that cohere with his times. In *Ant.* 8.46-48, Josephus describes an exorcism that bears comparison with Jesus' practice. In Josephus' example, Solomon's name is invoked and a ring with a root attached is placed into the nostrils of the demoniac. The demon is adjured to depart, and the exorcism is then demonstrated by the disturbing of a basin of water. Jesus' exorcisms likewise involved adjuring demons, and in the case of the Gaderene demoniac, the exorcism was demonstrated by an external sign—pigs went down a hill (Mark 5:13); Josephus' exorcist commands the demon to enter no more into its victim, and this is what Jesus does with an epileptic boy (Mark 9:14).

Another example that bears comparison with Jesus' exorcisms is in the fragment 4Q560 from the Dead Sea Scrolls which contains a Jewish incantation against various demons associated with various ailments. The text mentions a fever-demon and this can be compared with Jesus' healing of Peter's mother-in-law, as Jesus likewise adjured and rebuked this fever (Mark 1:30: cf. Luke 4:39). Other examples of similarity could be given but these are enough to illustrate that the gospel records are "of their times" in their account of Jesus' exorcisms. There is therefore no basis for doubting their historicity on the basis of their use of a cosmic mythology.

J. Robinson comments on Mark that "the exorcisms, rather than being the nearest point of approach to history in a myth, are the points in a historical narrative where the transcendent meaning of that history is most clearly evident".[4] Robinson is referring to the cosmic aspect of the exorcisms in which Jesus is portrayed as in conflict with Satan or the demons under his command. This aspect is transcendent in the sense that Jesus is not just healing a possessed man, but the possession is

---

[1] W. Burkert, *Greek Religion* (Oxford: Basil Blackwell, 1985), 179-181, 329-332.
[2] See Josephus, *Jubilees* 11:15, 17:15-18:13, 23:29, 46:1-2, 48:2, 12, and 50:5.
[3] See further A. Perry, *Demons and Politics* (2nd ed.; Sunderland: Willow Publications, 2010).
[4] J. Robinson, *The Problem of History in Mark* (London: SCM Press, 1957), 33. This cosmic conflict is also seen by some scholars in Pauline Christianity, e.g. in Eph 6:12, Col 1:16, 2:16.

symptomatic of a struggle between God and Satan over Israel, and Jesus, as representative of God, is confronting the enemy. The Beelzebub controversy interprets the exorcisms in this light. Robinson's argument is that apart from the interpretative context of the Beelzebub Controversy, the exorcisms would resemble other exorcism stories from the Ancient World, but "in the Markan presentation they depict a cosmic struggle in history to inaugurate the eschatological reign of God".[1]

5.7 Resurrection

This essay will not consider the resurrection in detail; here it is only necessary to make three brief remarks. The resurrection is an act of God in history; it is something that was done for Jesus—it is not part of his life. The issue for a questioning reader is whether the God of the Jews exists and acts in history, and the only way to answer this question in respect of the resurrection is to look at the **after-effects of Jesus' death** to determine how they are best explained.

1) The main after-effect is the existence of the Christian church; we could account for this phenomenon in terms of ordinary factors such as the ethical and social teaching of the first Christian preachers and leaders, or we might explain it in terms of their message of religious hope. So, for example, the early Christians gave greater freedoms to women in the church than other Jewish sects, and this would explain the attraction of the church to women; or again, Christians promoted a view of the church as the focus of worship in contradistinction to the temple in Jerusalem— there was then a ready understanding that could handle the dissolution of the Jewish state. However, such explanations of the growth of the church do not necessarily explain the **conviction** of the early believers, a conviction that would lead many through persecution. The point here is that the witness of the church to the resurrection was not relinquished in the face of persecution.

2) The resurrection of Jesus is not the most obvious teaching for a Jewish sect to promote. The doctrine of the general resurrection of the dead was common enough in Judaism, but the gospel accounts do not end with the vindication of Jesus in terms of his participation in that resurrection. He is not presented as a prophet who will be raised from the dead in "the last days". This would have been a natural end to the gospels, one that would have fitted the Jewish world view, but instead the gospels end with an

---

[1] Robinson, *Problem of History*, 38.

individual resurrection. This is an uncommon choice but would be explained if it was in fact what actually happened.[1]

3) The gospel stories do not make the strongest case for the resurrection in terms of the witnesses. Women had no legal status as witnesses, yet they ones who first see Jesus raised from the dead. Further, the response of the disciples is one of doubt in respect of the testimony of the women. If the stories in the gospels are a true reflection of events, these details are explained on that basis, but if the stories are self-serving in any way, then one would have expected them to be more robust.

These points, (1)-(3), are about the best historical explanation for the church and its story: is it true, or is the resurrection something that is capable of being explained away?

6. The Jesus of History and the Christ of Faith

This essay is not concerned with describing the Jesus of history; there have been many portraits. The task is valuable and necessary and, of course, it would take a book to do the subject matter any justice. We will conclude our remarks with a consideration of the relationship between faith and history.

It might be supposed that the job of the historian is to uncover the facts and strip away any faith-tradition or later interpretation of the facts. It might be said that the Gospel writers have included their faith in the narrative and it is the job of the historian to strip out this layer of faith. This is a common view and scholars routinely separate that layer in the text that they attribute to the author or an editor and which reflects a later point of view; the method of analysis they employ is known as Redaction Criticism. However, the existence in the gospels of the author's point of view is not inimical to the portrayal of the Jesus of History; rather, it is part of the history of the times that such points of view are included in a contemporary history. It is a cliché to observe that history writing involves perspective and interpretation; Jesus comes to the modern reader in a package. We may doubt the package, but it is substantially of its day.

We might ask: to what extent does historical investigation have a role to play in engendering Christian faith in a believer today? The question

---

[1] In fact, the resurrection might have been problematic to Jesus' followers as it interrupted what they had anticipated as the coming Kingdom of God.

concerns the relationship between history and faith. Some would argue that history has no relevance and argue that faith consists of a belief in a **story** regardless of any historical veracity. This view has been rejected by many on the grounds that the Christian faith has at its centre the belief that God has intervened in history in the person of Jesus of Nazareth. If he has so intervened, Christianity cannot disassociate itself from historical commitments and it is therefore vulnerable to any doubts put forward by historians. We cannot avoid engaging with such doubts and present the positive historical case for belief in Jesus. History has value for Christianity. It offers a basis for preaching the faith—a preacher can lay claim to facts; and such facts also form a basis for doctrine—they prevent doctrine from distorting the faith. This is our position but there is an important qualification. The apostle Paul declared that "So faith *comes* from hearing, and hearing by the word of Christ" (Rom 10:17, NASB). We can equally say that faith comes by reading the Word. An historical inquiry, of itself, cannot engender faith; a Christian faith will only be engendered by reading and/or hearing the Word.

Older (mainly German) critical scholarship on the question of the historical Jesus has largely been fruitless because it was founded on faulty Enlightenment philosophical assumptions. It presumed that the task of scholarship was to extract the Jesus of History from the Christ of Faith— that the early church had infused traditions about Jesus with their faith perspective. The dichotomy is false; it presumes that traditions were not preserved with regard to their historical veracity. Instead, Luke's method makes it plain that such veracity was fundamental to the existence of the written gospel(s). Furthermore, in the description and recording of Jesus' words and deeds, the perspective of faith is itself part of accurate historical writing and not a dispensable overlay. Faith is an understanding of the words and deeds and a way of seeing what actually happened. If we exclude a faith perspective we do not thereby gain a **neutral** description of what was said and done, we obtain another **competing** way of understanding. However, that faith is the *correct perspective* with which to describe Jesus' words and deeds is shown by the fact that they were directed to engendering faith.[1] If you try and represent a Jesus without the apparatus of faith in a modern "Life of Jesus", you falsify the intention of his words and deeds.

The faith with which the gospel writers record Jesus' words and deeds is however not the same as that which the Christian church developed in

---

[1] Dunn, *A New Perspective on Jesus*, chap. 1.

205

subsequent centuries. The average person starting out on a consideration of Jesus and the Christian faith probably believes that the Christian churches today preach the faith of the first century church. This is demonstrably not the case, and it was an advance of older critical scholarship to strip away the anachronistic superimposition of the later Christian faith upon the gospels. In rendering this service, they went too far, because they also took away the notion that the faith of the gospel writers was a valid historical perspective with which to present the words and deeds of Jesus.

7. Conclusion

A reader coming to the gospels for the first time will want to know if they are historically reliable. Our answer is that they are and that in order to establish this you should read conservative scholarship preferring its reasoning over and above that of critical scholars. While scholars of all persuasions have insights to offer, the historiographical approach of conservative scholarship is sounder and should be preferred where you come across scholarly conflict.

CHAPTER FIFTEEN
Finding God

1. Introduction[1]

The age that we live in is an "information age", the age of computers, satellite television, the information "superhighway" and the "internet". The past ages of man's history were very different. Historians categorize the history of man as a sequence of "ages", with each age being characterized by a main feature. For example, in English history the reigns of the various monarchs are often described as this or that "age". So you have the "Elizabethan Age" or the "Age of the Tudors". Historians divide up ages in various ways. The "Bronze Age" is that time in the development of a human culture, before the introduction of iron, when most tools and weapons were made of bronze. Similarly the "Iron Age" is that period in the development of any culture, when iron was commonly used for making tools and weapons.

As human history moves on, ages come and go. It is the same with religions - they come and go. For example, would anyone recognise these unusual Middle Eastern names?

> Ea, Apsu, Tiamat, Kingu, Mummu,
> Marduk

Some may know these names, but it would not be surprising if they were completely new to most people. In their day these names were the names of important figures. They commanded respect and loyalty across empires and peoples. They are the names of Babylonian gods. They are some of the gods involved, according to Babylonian texts, in the creation of the world. Nobody except scholars know of these names today, and they are mostly forgotten. Babylonian religion has come and gone. It survived as long as the people of Babylon survived.

Babylon was just one of the mighty empires that strutted across the world stage in Old Testament times. Other empires were the Egyptian empire, the Assyrian empire, and many others. Each of these empires came and

---

[1] This essay appeared in *Glad Tidings*.

went. And the gods of these empires, revered and honoured at the time, are no longer recognised.

We have here a test we can apply if we are trying to find God. The test is a simple one: *the true God stands the test of time.* There is one God worshipped today who was worshipped in the days of these bygone empires. This God is the God of Israel. The existence of a true God doesn't depend on man, but in the case of 'Tiamat' or 'Marduk', their "existence" *did* depend on man. They "existed" for as long as the culture that gave birth to them existed. Of all the gods of the Middle East, popular three thousand years ago, only one has survived, and this is strong evidence that *He* is God. However, there is *stronger* evidence.

2. Arguments for the Existence of God

We live in an age, it happens to be the modern age, but we might have born as Babylonians or Persians, or any other ancient people. Had we been born then, how would we have found out whether the gods of our nation were true or the cultural invention of our age? With hindsight, we can say that the gods of bygone peoples were the invention of their age, but we need to apply the question to ourselves. How do we know whether the gods of *our age* are true or false?

Philosophers have argued about the existence of God for millennia, and we might suppose that we could find God if we studied their arguments. There are two problems with such a proposal: the first difficulty is that philosophers disagree amongst themselves as to whether there are any valid *philosophical* arguments for God's existence. However, there is a more fundamental problem, even if we thought that philosophical arguments were valid. This problem concerns the identity of God. We can illustrate this problem with regard to the philosophical argument for God's existence which involves the concept of *design*.

Many people would say that there is design in nature and that this shows the existence of a creator. This is a powerful argument and it can be elaborated in great detail. However, the problem with the argument is that it is used by many different and conflicting religions. For example, had we been living in the days of the Babylonian Empire in Israel, the priests of the Babylonian religion would no doubt have claimed that *their* gods were the ones involved in the creation of the world, and they would have referred us to their epic tales (e.g. *The Gilgamesh Epic*) to substantiate their claim. We would also have heard the prophets of Israel make the same claim for the God of the Bible with great conviction and power using the account in Genesis.

As ordinary individuals living in those times, we might have agreed that the universe showed very intricate design, and that there was therefore a creator, but we might have been unsure as to *who* created the world. As individuals living today, we might find ourselves in the same position. We might see that there is a creator, but we might be unsure of who is that creator. Had we chosen to believe in the Babylonian gods of that era, we would have made the wrong choice, because those gods have come and gone. We need to avoid making a similar mistake today.[1]

We have said that the same philosophical arguments are claimed by all religions, and that they are not *specific* enough to find God. What we need in order to find God are arguments that *God himself uses* and which are unique to Him, and which can be evaluated and then received in faith. These arguments can only be found in words and sentences used by God, for arguments are tools of language.

3. Bible Arguments for God

The Bible supplies us with many arguments for the existence of the God of the Bible. If these arguments stand up, then we will have found the one true God. The strongest line of evidence proving that the God of Israel is the one true God is **prophecy**. Moreover, God himself uses this argument. The prophet Isaiah reports an occasion when the existence of God was in doubt. It was a time when Jerusalem was surrounded by the superpower of the day - Assyria, and it seemed to many that the city was about to fall. People were full of doubt. The Assyrians had proclaimed that their god was all-powerful, and by crushing the nations of the middle-east, they claimed that their god was showing that the gods of the other nations were nothing more than idols. The spokesman of the Assyrians at the time was a man called 'Rabshakeh', and the king of Jerusalem was called 'Hezekiah'. Rabshakeh says this to the inhabitants of Jerusalem:

---

[1] The God of the Bible has been worshipped throughout all ages, and this is strong evidence that He really exists. We can safely dismiss the gods that have come and gone, but there are other gods which have (so far) survived the vicissitudes of history. A few religions of the world are ancient religions, for example, Hinduism traces its beginnings back to approximately 1500 BC.

[Beware] lest Hezekiah persuade you, saying, The Lord will deliver us. Hath any of the gods of the nations delivered his land out of the hand of the king of Assyria? Where [are] the gods of Hamath and Arphad? where [are] the gods of Sepharvaim? and have they delivered Samaria out of my hand? Who [are they] among all the gods of these lands, that have delivered their land out of my hand, that the Lord should deliver Jerusalem out of my hand? Isa 36:18-20

And he says this to Hezekiah:

Let not thy God, in whom thou trustest, deceive thee, saying, Jerusalem shall not be given into the hand of the king of Assyria. Behold, thou hast heard what the kings of Assyria have done to all lands by destroying them utterly; and shalt thou be delivered? Have the gods of the nations delivered them which my fathers have destroyed, [as] Gozan, and Haran, and Rezeph, and the children of Eden which [were] in Telassar? Isa 37:10-12

The prophet Isaiah lived in Jerusalem at the time, and he countered the argument of Rabshakeh by arguing for his God's existence using the evidence of prophecy. The Assyrians had made claims about their prowess, but the prophet replies with God's words,

Hast thou not heard long ago, [how] I have done it; [and] of ancient times, that I have formed it? now have I brought it to pass, that thou shouldest be to lay waste defenced cities [into] ruinous heaps. Isa 37:26

In other words, Isaiah is reporting the fact that Assyria had been able to conquer the nations because the God of Israel had enabled them to do so, and not only this, God had predicted long ago that He would enable the Assyrians to conquer the Middle East.

In the earlier reign of Hezekiah's father - Ahaz - the prophet Isaiah had reported these predictions of God, which were made just after the birth of Hezekiah:

O Assyrian, the rod of mine anger, and the staff in their hand is mine indignation. I will send him against an

210

hypocritical nation, and against the people of my wrath will I give him a charge, to take the spoil, and to take the prey, and to tread them down like the mire of the streets. Howbeit he meaneth not so, neither doth his heart think so; but [it is] in his heart to destroy and cut off nations not a few. For he saith, [Are] not my princes altogether kings? [Is] not Calno as Carchemish? [is] not Hamath as Arpad? [is] not Samaria as Damascus? As my hand hath found the kingdoms of the idols, and whose graven images did excel them of Jerusalem and of Samaria; Shall I not, as I have done unto Samaria and her idols, so do to Jerusalem and her idols? Isa 10:5-11

The Assyrian kings used to be depicted with short rods in their hands on their bas-reliefs. So here Isaiah prophesies some 15-20 years before the event the fact that the Assyrian king would become a rod in God's hand against Judah and Jerusalem. The Assyrian king would not see himself as a tool in the hand of God. He had his own empire-building plan. Nevertheless, this was the reality of the situation. God was going to punish His people for their wickedness.

Isaiah had prophesied that by the time they came up against Judah and Jerusalem, Assyria would have cut off many nations, including Syria (Damascus) and Northern Israel (Samaria). Isaiah also records what would be said by Sennacherib - his bragging over his victories. This is what happened: when Sennacherib came against Jerusalem, he had conquered a number of nations, and there was a determined propaganda campaign centred on the fact that the Assyrian had vanquished the idols of the nations (Isa 36:18-19, 37:10). This then is rebuttal that Isaiah makes to the Sennacherib's propaganda: *God* had done this to punish Jerusalem for their unrighteousness. Moreover, and this the key point, the God had predicted this years before it happened.

Isaiah uses prophecy to establish the existence of the God of the Bible. And God challenges other gods to prove their existence with prophecy:

Produce your cause, saith the Lord; bring forth your strong [reasons], saith the King of Jacob. Let them bring [them] forth, and shew us what shall happen: let them shew the former things, what they [be], that we may consider them, and know the latter end of them; or declare us things for to come. Shew the things that are

211

to come hereafter, that we may know that ye [are] gods: yea, do good, or do evil, that we may be dismayed, and behold [it] together. Behold, ye [are] of nothing, and your work of nought: an abomination [is he that] chooseth you. Isa 41:21-24; cf. Deut 18:22

What is prophecy? A prophecy is a prediction, it may include much contemporary commentary, but it is essentially a prediction. Predictions are not unique to prophecy - they are an integral part of the scientific method. A scientific theory is both descriptive and predictive: it describes certain data and it predicts certain consequences given certain conditions. Predictions are very important to the practical business of science because they are used to test and verify a theory. If the predictions of a theory are realized in repeatable experiments, then this is taken as confirmation of the theory. The theory is only confirmed in a relative way, because the theory may be superseded by another that embraces its results and describes a greater field of data. Nevertheless, any subsequent theories will follow the same scientific method. Some scientific theories are short on experimental confirmation, for example, those theories that describe the past history of the universe. In these cases, the theories make predictions as to what further observational data will be found, and when this data is found, the theory is taken to be confirmed.

Prophecy is most closely akin to scientific prediction that requires confirmation by observational data, since experimentation is not possible for prophecy. Some may dismiss prophecy because it is "religious", but we ought to treat prophecy as a [social] science in which the history of nations is mapped out in advance in accordance with their behaviour. Broadly speaking, what we find in Bible prophecy are two forms of 'social' prediction and a manifesto: the first form of social prediction is this: the prophets declare that if Israel and the nations behave in certain ways, certain political consequences will follow, and these consequences are specified in detail; the second form of social prediction is this: the people have behaved in certain ways, and they must now bear the consequences of this behaviour, and these are detailed. The manifesto of the prophets is about the future age of the kingdom of God which will supersede the kingdoms of men.

A scientific theory can be falsified. A prophecy can be falsified if it fails to come true. With Bible prophecy we can tabulate a large number of prophecies that have come true. However, some prophecies have not yet come true. How do we tackle this fact? There are two logical responses:

212

the first is to reject the evidence of prophecy because some remain unfulfilled; the second is to have faith that these unfulfilled prophecies will come true, and base that faith on the success of fulfilled prophecy (cf. Heb 11:1). What response we take will depend on how we evaluate the cumulative evidence of Bible prophecy. Here it is the *quantity* of fulfilled prophecy that persuades the person who is seeking to find God.

The God of the Bible is the God of Israel, and he is an invisible God. He needs witnesses, and he has put forward one nation as his witnesses:

> "Ye [are] my witnesses, saith the Lord, and my servant whom I have chosen: that ye may know and believe me, and understand that I [am] he: before me there was no God formed, neither shall there be after me." Is 43:10, cf. v12, 44:8

The witness of Israel to God is found in the pages of her prophets. These prophecies are many and varied; there are both short term and long term prophecies. Many have been fulfilled and each points to the fact that the prophets spoke the words of the one true God. He can be found.

4. Conclusion

How do we find faith? How do we come to believe that the Bible is the Word of God? How do we come to have a conviction that its message is true and relevant for us today? If we are enquiring into these things, what should be our approach - our method?

One suggestion is that you must investigate all faiths and then decide which is the right one for you. This is a common academic view, and it smuggles in the idea that all faiths have some validity and that faith is all a matter of personal choice. It also suggests that you can't be certain of your own faith unless you have first considered all other options. This view is not often followed in practise because most people do not impartially investigate all faiths before making a commitment to a faith. It is a fact that people mostly adopt their 'national' or 'cultural' faith. So then, are all faiths equally valid in some way? Do we have to follow this method of impartial enquiry before making up our mind?

Religions are exclusive in their doctrines. They have articles of faith concerning God, concerning holy writings, concerning life after death and many other topics. These articles are in conflict. For example, it is obviously true that the gods differ from religion to religion. Or again, the holy writings are different and make competing claims. The moral codes

213

differ from religion to religion. The true Christian faith believes in one God, the God of Israel; it has one holy book, the Bible; and it has a definite moral code.

It is because religions are exclusive in their doctrines that they are not all equally valid. Contradictory doctrines can't all be true. Truth excludes falsehood. We might indeed investigate all faiths before choosing one, but we do not have to carry out such an enquiry. We might find the true faith and know it to be true straightaway. If we do find it, we will have no need of other faiths. If we investigate the faith of the Bible, this is what we will find - we will find the true faith.

BIBLIOGRAPHY

1. Primary Texts

1.1 Classical Texts

Dionysius: *Roman Antiquities*, (trans. E. Cary; Loeb Classical Library; Cambridge: Harvard Univ. Press, 1937).

Eusebius: *History of the Church*, (ed. A. Louth; trans. G. A. Williamson; rev. ed.; London: Penguin Books, 1989).

Herodotus, *The Histories* (ed. A. R. Burn; trans. A. De Sélincourt; London: Penguin Classics, 1972).

Josephus, (ed. W. Whiston; Grand Rapids: Kregel, 1980).

Polybius: *The Histories*, (trans. W. R. Paton; Loeb Classical Library; London: Heinemann, 1925).

Tatian, *Diatessaron* (ed., S. Hemphill; London: Hodder & Stoughton, 1888).

Thucydides, (trans., C. F. Smith; Loeb Classical Library; London: Heinemann, 1919).

1.2 ANE Texts

Ancient Near Eastern Texts (ed. J. B. Pritchard; Princeton: Princeton University Press, 1969).

The Annals of Sennacherib, (ed. D. Luckenbill; repr. Wipf & Stock, 2005; Chicago: Chicago University Press, 1924).

Near Eastern Religious Texts relating to the Old Testament (ed. W. Beyerlin; London: SCM Press, 1978).

The Gilgamesh Epic and Old Testament Parallels (ed. A. Heidel; 2nd ed.; Chicago: University of Chicago Press, 1949).

1.3 Second Temple Texts

The Old Testament Pseudepigrapha (ed., J. H. Charlesworth; 2 vols; New York: Doubleday, 1983, 1985).

1.4 Dead Sea Scrolls

The Dead Sea Scrolls: Study Edition (eds., Florentino García Martínez and Eibert J. C. Tigchelaar; 2 vols; Leiden: E. J. Brill, 1997).

The Dead Sea Scrolls Translated (ed., Florentino García Martínez, Leiden: E. J. Brill, 1996).

The Complete Dead Sea Scrolls in English (ed., G. Vermes; London: Penguin, 2004).

1.5 Scriptural Texts

Biblica Hebraica Stuttgartensia (eds., K. Elliger and W. Rudolph; 4th ed.; Deutsche Bibelgesellschaft, 1990).

Novum Testamentum Graece (ed., K. Aland *et al.*; 27th ed.; Stuttgart: Deutsche Bibelgesellschaft, 1993).

The Greek New Testament According to the Majority Text (eds. Z. C. Hodges and A. L. Farstad, Nashville: Thomas Nelson, second edition, 1985).

Septuaginta (ed., A. Rahlfs; 2 vols; Stuttgart: Deutsche Bibelgesellschaft, 1979).

1.6 Philosophical Texts

Frege, "The Thought: A Logical Enquiry" in *Philosophical Logic* (ed. P. F. Strawson; Oxford: Oxford University Press, 1967).

Hume, "On Miracles" in *Hume on Religion* (ed. R. Wollheim; London: Fontana, 1963), 205-229.

2. Encyclopaedias, Grammars and Dictionaries

ABD—Freedman, D. N., ed., *Anchor Bible Dictionary* (6 vols; New York: Doubleday, 1992).

Swan, M., *Practical English Usage* (Cambridge, University Press, 2005).

Swan, M., and B. Smith, *Learner English* (2nd ed.; Cambridge: Cambridge University Press, 2001).

Van der Merwe, C. H., J. J. A. Naudé, and J. H. Kroeze, *A Biblical Hebrew Reference Grammar* (Sheffield, Academic Press, 2002).

3. Secondary Literature

Allegro, J., *The Dead Sea Scrolls (A Reappraisal)* (London: Penguin, 1964).

Alter, R., *The Art of Biblical Narrative* (New York: Basic Books, 1981).

Attridge, H. W., "Jewish Historiography" in *Early Judaism and Its Modern Interpreters* (eds. R. A. Kraft and G. W. Nickelsburg; Philadelphia: Fortress Press, 1986), 311-43.

Aune, D. E., *The New Testament in its Literary Environment* (Philadelphia: The Westminster Press, 1987).

Baigent M., and R. Leigh, *The Dead Sea Scrolls Deception* (London: Jonathan Cape, 1991).

Bailey, L. R., *Noah: The Person and the Story in History and Tradition* (Columbia: University of South Carolina Press, 1989).

Becking, R., "Chronology: A Skeleton without Flesh? Sennacherib's Campaign as a Case-Study" in *Like a Bird in a Cage* (ed., L. L. Grabbe; Sheffield: Sheffield Academic Press, 2003), 46-72.

Bimson, J. J., *Redating the Exodus and Conquest* (Sheffield: Almond Press, 1981).

Biran, A., "An Aramaic Stele Fragment from Tel Dan" *IEJ* 43/2-3 (1993): 1-18.

Black, M., *An Aramaic Approach to the Gospels and Acts* (3rd. ed.; Oxford: Oxford University Press, 1967).

Bock, D. L., "Proclamation from Prophecy and Pattern" in *The Gospels and the Scriptures of Israel*, (eds. C. A. Evans and W. R. Stegner; Sheffield: Sheffield Academic Press, 1994), 280-307.

Bovon, F., *Luke 1* (Hermeneia; Minneapolis: Fortress Press, 2002).

Bright, J., *A History of Israel* (London: SCM Press, 1972).

Brindle, W., "The Census and Quirinius: Luke 2:2" *JETS* 27/1 (1984): 43-52.

Brodie, T. L., "Luke 7:11-17 as an imitation of 1 Kings 17:17-24" *NTS* (1986): 247-267.

Bruce, F. F., *The Acts of the Apostles* (London: Tyndale Press, 1952).

Burkert, W., *Greek Religion* (Oxford: Basil Blackwell, 1985).

Burridge, R., *What are the Gospels?* (Cambridge: Cambridge University Press, 1992).

Cadbury, H. J., *The Making of Luke-Acts* (London: SPCK, 1968).

— "The Greek and Jewish Traditions of Writing History" in *The Beginnings of Christianity: Part 1: The Acts of the Apostles: Vol. II: Prolegomena II: Criticism*, (eds., F. J. Foakes-Jackson & K. Lake; London: Macmillan, 1922), 7-29.

Childs, B. S., *Introduction to the Old Testament as Scripture* (Philadelphia: Fortress Press, 1979).

Clarke, W. K. L., "The Use of the Septuagint in Acts" in *The Beginnings of Christianity: Part 1* (eds. F. J. Foakes-Jackson and Kirsopp Lake; 5 vols; London: Macmillan, 1920-33), 66-105.

Clements, R. E., *Isaiah and the Deliverance of Jerusalem* (Sheffield: JSOT Press, 1980).

Cook, E. M., *Solving the Mysteries of the Dead Sea Scrolls* (Carlisle: Paternoster Press, 1994).

Crossley, J. G., *The Date of Mark's Gospel* (London: T & T Clark, 2004).

Culler, J., *Literary Theory: A Very Short Introduction* (Oxford: Oxford University Press, 1997).

Daube, D., "Typology in Josephus" *JJS* 31 (1980): 18-36.

Dumbrell, W. J., *The End of the Beginning* (Eugene, Oregon: Wipf & Stock, 2001).

Dummett, M. A. E., *Frege: Philosophy of Language* (London: Duckworth, 1973).

Dunn, J. D. G., *A New Perspective on Jesus* (London: SPCK, 2005).

Du Toit, D. S., "Redefining Jesus: Current Trends in Jesus Research" in *Jesus, Mark and Q: The Teaching of Jesus and its Earliest Records* (eds., M. Labahn and A. Schmidt; Sheffield, Sheffield Academic Press, 2001), 82-124.

Eddy P. R. and J. K. Beilby, "The Quest for the Historical Jesus" in *The Historical Jesus: Five Views* (eds. P. R. Eddy and J. K. Beilby; London: SPCK, 2010), 9-54.

Ellis, E. E., *Paul's Use of the Old Testament* (Edinburgh, Oliver & Boyd, 1957).

Evans, C. A., and W. R. Stegner, eds., *The Gospels and the Scriptures of Israel* (Sheffield: Sheffield Academic Press, 1994).

Evans, C. D., W. Hallo, and J. B. White, eds., *Scripture in Context: Essays on the Comparative Method* (Pittsburgh: Pickwick Press, 1980).

Evans, C. F., *Saint Luke* (London: SCM Press, 1990).

Firmage, E., "Zoology" in *ABD*, 6:1145.

Fleming, D. E., "Genesis in History and Tradition: The Syrian background of Israel's Ancestors, Reprise" in *The Future of Biblical Archaeology: Reassessing Methodologies and Assumptions* (eds. J. K. Hoffmeier and A. Millard; Grand Rapids: Eerdmans, 2004), 193-232.

Foakes-Jackson, F. J. and Kirsopp Lake, eds., *The Beginnings of Christianity: Part 1* (5 vols; London: Macmillan, 1920-33).

Fowler, A., *Kinds of Literature: An Introduction to the Theory of Genres and Modes* (Oxford: Oxford University Press, 1982).

Gaus, A., *The Unvarnished New Testament* (London: Phanes Press, 1991).

Gitin, S. and W. G. Dever, eds., *Recent Excavations in Israel: Studies in Iron Age Archaeology* (AASOR 49; Winona Lake: Eisenbrauns, 1989).

Grabbe, L. L., ed., *Like a Bird in a Cage* (Sheffield: Sheffield Academic Press, 2003).

Grintz, J. M., "Ai which is beside Beth-Aven" *Biblica* 42 (1961): 201-216.

Goppelt, L., *Typos: The Typological Interpretation of the Old Testament in the New* (trans. D. H. Madvig; Grand Rapids: Eerdmans, 1982).

Gowler, D. B., *The Historical Jesus?* (New York: Paulist Press, 2007).

Guthrie, D., *New Testament Introduction* (Leicester: Apollos, 1990).

Haas, W., "The Theory of Translation" in *The Theory of Meaning* (ed. G.H.R. Parkinson; Oxford: Oxford University Press, 1968).

Hallo, W., "Biblical History in its Near Eastern Setting: The Contextual Approach" in *Scripture in Context: Essays on the Comparative Method* (ed., C. D. Evans, W. Hallo, and J. B. White; Pittsburgh: Pickwick Press, 1980), 1-26.

Harrison, R. K., "From Adam to Noah: A Reconsideration of the Antediluvian Patriarchs' Ages" *JETS* 37/2 (1994): 161-168.

Hendel, R., "When the Sons of God cavorted with the Daughters of Men" in *Understanding the Dead Sea Scrolls* (ed. H. Shanks; London: SPCK, 1992), 167-177.

Hill, A. E., "Quantitative Hydrology of Noah's Flood" in *Perspectives on Science and the Christian Faith* 58/2 (2006): 130-141.

Hill, C. A., "The Noachian Flood: Universal or Local" Perspectives on Science and the Christian Faith 54/3 (2002): 170-183.

Hills, E. F., *The King James Version Defended* (Des Moines, The Christian Research Press, fourth edition, 1984).

Hoffmeier, J. K., and A. Millard, eds., *The Future of Biblical Archaeology: Reassessing Methodologies and Assumptions* (Grand Rapids: Eerdmans, 2004).

— *Israel in Egypt: The Evidence for the Authenticity of the Exodus Tradition* (Oxford: Oxford University Press, 1997).

Kaiser, W. C., *The Old Testament Documents: Are they Reliable and Relevant?* (Downers Grove: InterVarsity Press, 2001).

Käsemann, E., *Essays on New Testament Themes* (London: SCM Press, 1964).

Kermode, F., *The Genesis of Secrecy* (Cambridge, Massachusetts: Harvard University Press, 1979).

Kitchen, K. A., *On the Reliability of the Old Testament* (Grand Rapids: Eerdmans, 2003).

Klauck, H., *Apocryphal Gospels* (London: T & T Clark, 2003).

Kraft R. A. and G. W. Nickelsburg, eds., *Early Judaism and Its Modern Interpreters* (Philadelphia: Fortress Press, 1986).

Kurz, W. S., "Luke-Acts and Historiography in the Greek Bible" *SBLSP* 19 (1980): 283-300.

Labahn, M. and A. Schmidt, eds., *Jesus, Mark and Q: The Teaching of Jesus and its Earliest Records* (Sheffield, Sheffield Academic Press, 2001).

Lapp, P. W., "The Conquest of Palestine in the Light of Archaeology" *CThm* 38 (1967): 283-300.

Leick, G., *Mesopotamia* (London: Penguin Books, 2002).

Lemaire, A., "'House of David' Restored Moabite Inscription" *BAR* 20/3 (1994): 30-37.

Lewis, J. P., *A Study of the Interpretation of Noah and the Flood in Jewish and Christian Literature* (Leiden: E. J. Brill, 1968).

Livingston, D., "The location of Biblical Bethel and Ai reconsidered" *WTJ* 33, (1970): 20-44.

Long, L., *Translating the Bible* (Aldershot, Ashgate, 2001).

Maddox, R., *The Purpose of Luke-Acts* (Edinburgh: T & T Clark, 1982),

Malina, B. J. and J. H. Neyrey, "First Century Personality: Dyadic, not Individualistic" in *The Social World of Luke-Acts* (ed. J. H. Neyrey; Peabody: Hendrickson, 1991).

Marshall, I. H., "Acts and the Former Treatise" in *The Book of Acts in its Ancient Literary Setting* (eds., B. W. Winter and A. D. Clarke; Grand Rapids: Eerdmans, 1993, 163-182 (178).

Martin, R., *Accuracy of Translation and the New International Version* (Edinburgh: Banner of Truth, 1989).

Macdonald, D. R. "Introduction" in *Mimesis and Intertextuality* (ed., D. R. Macdonald; Harrisburg: Trinity Press International, 2001), 1-9.

Macdonald, A. H., "Herodotus on the Miraculous" in *Miracles* (ed. C. F. D. Moule; London: Mowbray, 1965).

McKnight, S., *A Light among the Gentiles in the Ancient World* (Minneapolis: Fortress Press, 1991).

Metzger, B. M., *The Text of the New Testament* (Oxford, Clarendon Press, second edition, 1968).

— ed., *The Oxford Companion to the Bible* (Oxford: Oxford University Press, 1993).

Millard A. R., and W. G. Lambert, *Atra-Hasis: The Babylonian Story of the Flood* (Oxford: Clarendon Press, 1969).

Moessner, D. P., "The 'script' of the Scriptures in Acts: suffering as God's plan (βουλῆ) for the world for the 'release of sins'" in *History, Literature, and Society in the Book of Acts* (ed. B. Witherington III; Cambridge: Cambridge University Press, 1996), 218-250.

Moule, C. F. D., ed., *Miracles* (London: Mowbray, 1965).

Mullen, N., "Beyond Babel" in *Which Translation?* (ed. T. Benson; Norwich: The Testimony, 2000), 27-36.

Niehaus, J. J., "Joshua and Ancient Near Eastern Warfare" *JETS* 31 (1988): 45-50.

Odorico, M. De, The *Use of Numbers and Quantifications in the Assyrian Royal Inscriptions* (SAAS II; The Neo Assyrian Text Corpus Project; Helsinki: Helsinki University Press, 1995).

Parkinson, G.H.R., ed., *The Theory of Meaning* (Oxford: Oxford University Press, 1968).

Partridge, A. C., *English Biblical Translation* (London, André Deutsch, 1973).

Patzia, A. G., *The Making of the New Testament* (Downers Grove: InterVarsity Press, 1994).

Penner, T., *In Praise of Christian Origins* (Edinburgh: T & T Clark, 2004).

Perry, A., *Beginnings and Endings* (3rd ed.; Sunderland: Willow Publications, 2011).

— *Demons and Politics* (2nd ed.; Sunderland: Willow Publications, 2010).

Pervo, R. I., "The Ancient Novel becomes Christian" in *The Novel in the Ancient World* (ed., G. Schmeling; Leiden: E. J. Brill, 1996), 685-711.

Pollock, S., *Ancient Mesopotamia* (Cambridge: Cambridge University Press, 1999).

Porter, S. E., *The Criteria for Authenticity in Historical-Jesus Research* (JSNTS 191; London: T & T Clark, 2000).

Potter, D. S., "Quirinius" *ABD*, 5:588-589.

Robinson, J., *The Problem of History in Mark* (London: SCM Press, 1957).

Robinson, J. A. T., *Redating the New Testament* (London: SCM Press, 1976).

Rothschild, C. K., *Luke-Acts and the Rhetoric of History* (WUNT; Tubingen: Mohr Siebeck, 2004).

Rowley, H. H., ed., *The Old Testament and Modern Study* (Oxford: Oxford University Press, 1951).

Scanlin, H., *The Dead Sea Scrolls and Modern Translations of the Old Testament* (Cambridge: Tyndale Press, 1993).

Shanks, H., "Of Caves and Scholars, An Overview" in *Understanding the Dead Sea Scrolls* (ed. H. Shanks; London: SPCK, 1992).

Sheeley, S. M., *Narrative Asides in Luke-Acts* (JSNTSup 72; Sheffield: JSOT Press, 1992).

Shepherd, W. H., *The Narrative Function of the holy Spirit as a Character in Luke-Acts* (Atlanta: Scholars Press, 1994).

Sherwin-White, A. N., *Roman Law and Roman Society in the New Testament* (Oxford: Oxford University Press, 1963).

Shiloh, Y., "Judah and Jerusalem in the Eighth-Sixth Centuries B.C.E." in *Recent Excavations in Israel: Studies in Iron Age Archaeology* (eds., S. Gitin and W. G. Dever; AASOR 49; Winona Lake: Eisenbrauns, 1989), 97-106.

Schweitzer, A., *The Quest of the Historical Jesus* (ed. J. Bowden; London: SCM Press 2000).

Tannehill, R. C., "Israel in Luke-Acts: A Tragic Story" *JBL* 104 (1985): 69-85.

Theissen, G. and A. Merz, *The Historical Jesus: A Comprehensive Guide* (London: SCM Press, 1998).

Thomas, D. W., "The Textual Criticism of the Old Testament" in *The Old Testament and Modern Study* (ed. H. H. Rowley; Oxford: Oxford University Press, 1951).

Uehlinger, C., "Clio in a World of Pictures—Another Look at the Lachish Reliefs from Sennacherib's Southwest Palace at Nineveh" in *Like a Bird in a Cage* (ed., L. L. Grabbe; Sheffield: Sheffield Academic Press, 2003), 221-305.

VanderKam, J. C., *The Dead Sea Scrolls Today* (London: SPCK, 1994).

Vermes, G., *The Dead Sea Scrolls, (Qumran in Perspective)* (London: SCM, 1994).

— "The Jesus Notice of Josephus Re-examined" *JJS* 38/1 (1987): 1-10.

Von Rad, G., *Genesis* (London: SCM Press, 1961).

Walton, J. H., *Ancient Israelite Literature in its Cultural Context* (Grand Rapids: Zondervan, 1989).

Weippert, M., *The Settlement of the Israelite Tribes in Palestine* (London: SCM Press, 1971).

Weissbort, D., and A. Eysteinsson, eds., *Translation: Theory and Practice - A Historical Reader* (Oxford: Oxford University Press, 2006).

Westermann, C., *Genesis 1-11* (Minneapolis: Fortress Press, 1994).

White, J. R., *The King James Only Controversy* (Minneapolis, Bethany House Publishers, 1995).

Winter, B. W. and A. D. Clarke, eds., *The Book of Acts in its Ancient Literary Setting* (Grand Rapids: Eerdmans, 1993).

Wiseman, P. J., *New Discoveries in Babylonia about Genesis* (4th ed.; London: Marshall, Morgan & Scott, 1946).

Witherington III, B., ed., *History, Literature, and Society in the Book of Acts* (Cambridge: Cambridge University Press, 1996).

Wolterstorff, N., *Divine Discourse* (Cambridge: Cambridge University Press, 1995).

Wood, B. G., "Did the Israelites Conquer Jericho: A New Look at the Archaeological Evidence" *BAR* 16/2 (1990): 44-59.

Wright, N. T., "Towards a Third 'Quest'? Jesus Then and Now" *ARC* (Montreal, McGill In-house Journal) 10 (1982): 20-27

Würthwein, E., *The Text of the Old Testament* (Oxford, Basil Blackwell, 1957).

Young, D. A., *The Biblical Flood: A Case Study of the Church's Response to Extrabiblical Evidence* (Grand Rapids: Eerdmans, 1995).

Younger, K. L., *Ancient Conquest Accounts: A Study in Ancient Near Eastern and Biblical History Writing* (Sheffield: JSOT Press, 1990).

Zvi, E. Ben, "Malleability and its Limits: Sennacherib's Campaign against Judah as a Case-Study" in *Like a Bird in a Cage* (ed., L. L. Grabbe; Sheffield: Sheffield Academic Press, 2003), 73-105.